Perspectives
of Power

Advanced Curriculum From Vanderbilt University's Programs for Talented Youth

Perspectives of Power

ELA Lessons for Gifted and Advanced Learners in Grades 6–8

Emily Mofield, Ed.D.,
& Tamra Stambaugh, Ph.D.

Routledge
Taylor & Francis Group

NEW YORK AND LONDON

First published in 2016 by Prufrock Press Inc.

Published in 2021 by Routledge
605 Third Avenue, New York, NY 10017
2 Park Square, Milton Park, Abingdon, Oxon OX14 4RN

Routledge is an imprint of the Taylor & Francis Group, an informa business

Copyright © 2016 Taylor & Francis Group

Cover design by Raquel Trevino and layout design by Allegra Denbo

Cover image: Souza-Cardoso, Amadeo de (1887-1918). Untitled, 1913. CAM - Modern Art Centre ©The Calouste Gulbenkian Foundation / Scala / Art Resource, NY

All rights reserved. No part of this book may be reprinted or reproduced or utilised in any form or by any electronic, mechanical, or other means, now known or hereafter invented, including photocopying and recording, or in any information storage or retrieval system, without permission in writing from the publishers.

Notice:
Product or corporate names may be trademarks or registered trademarks, and are used only for identification and explanation without intent to infringe.

ISBN: 9781032143859 (hbk)
ISBN: 9781618214935 (pbk)

DOI: 10.4324/9781003237143

Table of Contents

Acknowledgements ix
Introduction 1
Pretest 14
Pretest Rubric 16

INTRODUCTION
Lesson 1 "I like to see it lap the Miles": The Power of Change/Technology 19
by Emily Dickinson

POWER OF OPPRESSION
Lesson 2 "The Dutchman": The Power of Cultural Heritage 33
by Moyo Okediji

Lesson 3 "Blue Beard": Unjust Rules 41
by Charles Perrault

Lesson 4 "On Women's Right to Vote": The Power of Persuasion 57
by Susan B. Anthony

Lesson 5 Dystopian Literature: The Abuse of Power 69

POWER OF PAST, PRESENT, AND FUTURE
Lesson 6 "A Sound of Thunder": The Power of Choice 83
by Ray Bradbury

Lesson 7 "The Persistence of Memory": The Power of Memory 95
by Salvador Dali

Lesson 8 "The Wild Swans at Coole": The Power of Nostalgia 107
by W. B. Yeats

POWER OF PERSONAL RESPONSE
Lesson 9 "The Pursuit of Disarmament": The Power
of Cooperation Versus Competition 119
by John F. Kennedy

Lesson 10 "The Perils of Indifference": The Power of Response 135
by Elie Wiesel

Lesson 11 "We never know how high we are": The Power of Risk 153
by Emily Dickinson

CONCLUSION
Lesson 12 Final Reflection and Culminating Project 165

VI	
Posttest	170
Posttest Rubric	172
References	173
Appendix A: Instructions for Using the Models	175
Appendix B: Blank Models and Guides	201
Appendix C: Rubrics	213
About the Authors	217
Common Core State Standards Alignment	219

Dedication

To my former students. Your joyful love of learning continues to inspire me.
—Emily

To my nieces and nephews and other gifted students I have worked with who need an accelerated curriculum to stay engaged and to grow in their learning.
—Tamra

Acknowledgements

We would like express heartfelt gratitude to those dedicated administrators and teachers who implemented the lessons and provided valuable feedback for revisions. You know who you are and we are most grateful! We especially want to recognize Emilie Hall for organizing data and fine-tuning lessons during the editing process. Dr. Elizabeth Covington is appreciated for her professional insight into the development of the literary and rhetorical analysis models to verify the scholarly validity of their use. We also appreciate the work of our editor, Katy McDowall, for her steadfast work and patience as we continued to fine-tune lessons and ask questions well into the editing process. Finally, we are honored to build these lessons on a solid foundation of knowledge, theory, and best practices in gifted education and curriculum development established from the inspiring work of Dr. Joyce VanTassel-Baska.

Introduction

Perspectives of Power is designed specifically with gifted and high-achieving middle and early high school learners in mind. The concept-based lessons are accelerated beyond typical grade-level standards and include advanced models and organizers to help students analyze a variety of texts. This unit emphasizes the theme of power in literature, historical documents, poetry, and art. Lessons include a major focus on rigorous evidence-based discourse through the study of common themes and content-rich, challenging nonfiction and fictional texts. Aligned to Common Core State Standards for ELA, this unit guides students to explore the power of oppression; the power of the past, present, and future; and the power of personal response by engaging in simulations, skits, creative projects, literary analyses, Socratic seminars, and debates. Texts illuminate content extensions that interest many high-ability students including the bystander effect, social class structure, game theory, the use and abuse of technology, cultural conflict, the butterfly effect, women's suffrage, and surrealism as each relates to power. Lessons include close readings with text-dependent questions, choice-based differentiated products, rubrics, formative assessments, and ELA writing tasks that require students to analyze texts for rhetorical features, literary elements, and themes through argument, explanatory, and/or prose-constructed writing. The unit features texts from Emily Dickinson, W. B. Yeats, and Charles Perrault; art from Moyo Okediji and Salvador Dali; and speeches by Elie Wiesel, Susan B. Anthony, and John F. Kennedy. As a result from the learning in the unit, students will be able to examine powerful influences in their own lives and identify their own power in personal responsibility.

CONCEPTUAL FRAMEWORK

Perspectives of Power is one of four units designed to support the acquisition of textual analysis skills, including identifying relationships between literary elements to support a text, evaluating arguments, enhancing thinking and communication skills, and connecting conceptual generalizations from cross-curricular themes through a variety of media including literary texts, art, and primary source documents. The Integrated Curriculum Model (ICM; VanTassel-Baska, 1986) is the conceptual framework used for the unit design. Components of the framework are embedded in each lesson: accelerated content, advanced literacy processes of the discipline (e.g., rhetorical analysis and literary analysis), and conceptual understandings. For example, the accelerated content includes ELA (English language arts) standards, aligned to the Common Core State Standards (CCSS). The CCSS selected for each unit are above the grade level(s) for which the unit was intended. Each unit also includes process skills and specific models to help students evaluate the development of effective arguments; analyze a variety of texts, art, and primary sources; and connect literature to real-word applications (see Appendices A and B for more information on the models). The content of each lesson is connected by an overarching theme and key generalizations that span a variety of disciplines. These concepts vary by unit and include power, truth versus perception, individuality versus conformity, and freedom. Table 1 shows how each unit in this series aligns with the ICM features. The ICM model was selected based on its evidence-supported success in increasing gifted student achievement (see VanTassel-Baska & Stambaugh, 2008).

INTENDED GRADE LEVEL(S)

It is well known in gifted education that accelerated content is essential for increasing the academic achievement and social-emotional growth of gifted students (Assouline, Colangelo, VanTassel-Baska, & Lupkowski-Shoplik, 2015; Colangelo, Assouline, & Gross, 2004; Steenbergen-Hu & Moon, 2011). This unit is intended for and has been piloted with gifted students in grades 6–8. The unit is aligned to CCSS standards primarily focused on grades 9–10 with some lower grade standards included as needed. The accelerated content is necessary so that gifted students have the opportunity to gain new language arts content knowledge at a pace and level that is appropriate for their learning needs. Gifted students' readiness and experience levels vary, as do their abilities. Because school contexts and content emphases are different, it is up to each teacher to determine which unit is best suited for their particular students and at which grade levels. Some gifted students may find this unit engaging as a sixth grader while others may need to wait until grade 7 or 8 to fully participate and understand the unit concepts. Teachers of 9th and 10th graders may find that these units are on target for many of their general education students.

Table 1
The Integrated Curriculum Model Alignment by Unit

Unit	Accelerated Content	Advanced Processes Models/Organizers	Concept/Generalizations
Finding Freedom	Aligned to grade 9 and 10 CCSS standards	Advanced Models: - Social Studies Connections - Rhetorical Analysis Organizers: - Reasoning About a Situation or Event - Big Idea Reflection: Primary Sources	- Freedom requires sacrifice. - Freedom requires responsibility. - Freedom is threatened by internal and external forces.
Perspectives of Power	Aligned to grade 9 and 10 CCSS standards	Advanced Models: - Literary Analysis - Visual Analysis - Rhetorical Analysis Organizers: - Big Idea Reflection - Reasoning About a Situation or Event	- Power is the ability to influence. - Power is connected to a source. - Power may be used or abused.
I, Me, You, We: Individuality Versus Conformity	Aligned to grade 9 and 10 CCSS standards	Advanced Models: - Literary Analysis - Visual Analysis - Rhetorical Analysis Organizers: - Big Idea Reflection - Reasoning About a Situation or Event	- Both conformity and individuality are agents of change. - Both conformity and individuality involve sacrifice. - There are positives and negatives to both conformity and individuality.
In the Mind's Eye: Truth Versus Perception	Aligned to grade 9 and 10 CCSS standards	Advanced Models: - Literary Analysis - Visual Analysis - Rhetorical Analysis Organizers: - Big Idea Reflection - Reasoning About a Situation or Event	- Although truth is constant, one's perception of truth varies. - There are negatives and positives in realizing the truth. - There are consequences to believing perception rather than the truth.

LESSON FORMAT AND GUIDELINES

Each lesson in this unit follows a similar format for ease of use. Teachers select from a variety of questions, activities, and differentiated products to best meet their students' needs.

Alignment to Standards

The unit incorporates the key pedagogical shifts highlighted as part of the CCSS. For example, students read both literary and informational texts from a variety of sources and perspectives. Through the use of primary sources, they learn domain-specific content from their readings and are required to provide text-based evidence to support their answers or ideas. Each lesson also supports opportunities for students to make or analyze an argument, defend a position, or interpret a text. Of course, part of close reading and understanding of a text includes the use of domain-specific vocabulary. The readings selected throughout the unit build upon specific concepts and highlight multiple perspectives. Many readings use vocabulary of the time period or a specific discipline, for which students must understand and define.

The beginning of each lesson includes a list of the overarching goals and objectives as well as CCSS specific to each lesson. The end of the unit includes a CCSS alignment chart (p. 219). This unit was not designed to meet every CCSS ELA standard for a particular grade level.

Materials

When differentiating for the gifted, it is important for the materials and readings to be at a level commensurate with the student's ability. The readings and resources in this unit have been carefully selected and include either sophisticated concepts or reading selections above most middle school grade levels. The materials section includes a list of resources needed for the lesson. Some of the listed materials are optional and many of the selected texts, visuals, or videos are readily available online as a free download. When possible, reliable sites and specific links, available at the time of this unit's printing, are provided. *A word of caution*: It is important to note that some of the readings may be controversial or contain advanced or sensitive concepts and content. A cautionary note is provided in lessons with the most controversial issues. Still, it is up to the teacher and school administration to understand the context of his or her district and to determine whether or not a reading or discussion is appropriate or whether a different text or discussion-based question should be used. As the lessons follow a specific format and the analysis models can be used with any text, teachers may easily substitute a more appropriate source and then apply questions and activities for that source using a selected analysis model as a guide (see Appendix A for specific descriptions of each model).

Introductory Activities

The introductory activities provide a real-world connection or "hook" that sets the tone for the remainder of the lesson and enhances student engagement. Sample options include quick debates about an issue or dilemma, symbol designs to illustrate a key concept or idea, or key discussion questions that help students better understand the relevance of a lesson's text, art, or primary source.

Text-Dependent Questions

This section provides questions that ensure students understand the text. These close reading questions are varied and the majority focus on comprehension and inference making. Students are to answer these questions using textual evidence. Note that prediction or speculation questions that cannot be supported with evidence from the text are not appropriate for this section. A variety of questions are listed, but not all questions should be asked in a given lesson. Instead, teachers select four to six questions from the list for students to discuss in small groups, Socratic seminars, or as an entire class. Of course, if students are struggling to understand the text, additional questions or background information may be required. The questions in this section are *not* intended as homework or to be responded to in writing on a consistent basis. These questions are designed for discussion purposes so that teachers can check for understanding and help students support new ideas or clarify misunderstandings.

Analysis Section

This is the most comprehensive and complex section of each lesson and includes a variety of advanced processes and specific models so that students make real-world connections to big ideas and better analyze literature, rhetorical arguments, and visual prompts. These models were created after extensive research and consultation with an ELA expert to ensure content validity. See Appendix A for a detailed explanation, instructions, and an example lesson using each model.

When implementing the unit, it is recommended that each model be presented in its entirety at least three times, with emphasis given to the literary analysis and rhetorical analysis models. Teachers are encouraged to use the complex features of the models, as these add depth and complexity to the unit content and encourage gifted students to think about the relationships between key ideas in more sophisticated ways. It is at the teacher's discretion to determine which model(s) are to be used for each lesson based upon students' interest, level of understanding, and engagement.

In-Class Activities to Deepen Learning

The activities included here provide hands-on or thought-provoking ideas that support or solidify student learning. Tasks incorporate real-world connections and include issue-based questions linked to a big idea, quick debates about a controversial issue, or technology extensions. These activities also include opportunities for self-reflection on how the lesson content impacted their learning. One or all of the activities in this section may be taught.

Concept Connections

The concept connections section focuses on the third component of the ICM. The purpose of this section is to help students see the relationships between different texts and perspectives as these relate to key generalizations about power. A graphic organizer comprised of the conceptual generalizations and key unit readings is provided in the unit to help students organize their ideas and determine patterns among the various readings. It is important to refer to the concept generalizations in each lesson, even if the concept chart is not completed for every reading.

Choice-Based Differentiated Products

Several choice-based differentiated products are also part of each lesson. Students may select one of the choice products to showcase their strengths and individual understanding or, if pressed for time, teachers may require two or three choice-based products for students to complete during the course of the unit. The options listed allow students an opportunity to pursue their interests and to gain a deeper understanding of a learning objective as they present their understanding in a creative way. Differentiated products vary by lesson and may include investigating a real-world problem, designing visuals, applying an advanced model to other related sources, writing essays, and developing products or presentations for an audience. Rubrics are provided in Appendix C to guide product creation and teacher feedback. The rubrics may also be used for peer and self-evaluations.

ELA Practice Tasks

Designed with the CCSS assessments in mind, the ELA practice tasks support the writing and argument analysis items typically assessed as part of a state assessment. The ELA tasks incorporate multiple standards and require complex thinking.

Students are asked to respond to a prompt by creating a well-developed essay in which they create or analyze arguments, critique texts, explain an issue from multiple perspectives, or determine key concepts presented in a text. It is at the teacher's discretion to determine how many ELA practice tasks students should write throughout the course of the unit. Although not explicitly stated in the unit, teachers are encouraged to model the writing process, help students analyze exemplars and inappropriate responses, and provide individual feedback.

Formative Assessment

The formative assessment section focuses on assessing a student's understanding of a single-faceted objective such as making inferences or determining how an author used a literary element to convey an idea or theme. A rubric is included with each prompt so that teachers can quickly assess responses, provide feedback, and determine next steps in their students' learning. Questions require a written response of no more than a paragraph. The formative assessments may be used to determine the extent to which students understand the meaning of a text and can provide supporting evidence and target instruction based on individual needs. Teachers may require students to complete an ELA practice task in one lesson and a formative assessment task in another so that students' thinking and understanding can be measured in a variety of ways.

Handouts

Following each lesson, all necessary handouts for lesson completion are included (e.g., readings, visuals, organizers, blank analysis models, and other sources not readily available online). As previously stated in the materials section, sometimes teachers are led to specific web-based links or it is recommended that popular sources be found online. This is especially important for featured art (which doesn't copy well) and popularized primary sources and texts. Any source that is essential to the lesson or is difficult to access is included as a handout.

Other Unit Features

This unit includes a culminating lesson that synthesizes many of the learning objectives into a comprehensive project so that students may showcase their learning in a creative way. These options may include the application of the advanced content learned throughout the unit, real-world problem solving, and the development of authentic products. Additionally, the culminating lesson includes in-depth self-reflections that guide students to relate their own lives to concept-themes. Rubrics are provided so that students understand the expectations of a task and teachers can easily analyze student products given set criteria. The rubrics are also useful for peer and self-evaluations.

Teacher background information is another feature of many lessons, especially those with more complicated texts. Although some background information is provided, teachers are encouraged to study specific literary analysis critiques for a particular reading, research the history of a specific primary source (if not already known), and seek varied interpretations of the text or visual. Online links to literary critiques are provided for some lessons, when appropriate.

Sample responses are also included for many complex questions and analysis models. It is important to understand that the answers provided are a guide and should not be construed as the only correct response. Student answers will vary and many unanticipated responses may be correct. Teachers are encouraged to use the provided answers to better understand the intent of the question, to model how to arrive at an appropriate response, to demonstrate how to use a specific analysis model, or to familiarize themselves with the intent of a particular passage.

Finally, this unit features instructions for using models, sample lessons, blank model handouts, and guides to support students' thinking about each element of a given analysis model. Rubrics are also provided to assess student products and responses. Specifically, Appendix A highlights instructions, handouts, and examples for each analysis model. Appendix B includes blank models and guides for thinking about each element of a particular model, and Appendix C includes rubrics for assessing student progress.

Time Allotment

Most lessons can be taught within 90–120 minutes, although some lessons may take longer. The length of the lesson also depends upon how many models and activities are employed, how interested students are in a particular issue or text, and how many times a text needs to be read or analyzed for students to gain understanding. In general, it is anticipated that this unit can be taught with approximately 45 hours of instruction time if teachers follow the recommended guidelines as reported in this section.

Differentiation

Gifted students are a heterogeneous group and their ability levels, pace of learning, interests, and depth of understanding vary. Although this unit was written with gifted middle school students in mind, differentiation is still necessary. A variety of differentiated opportunities are embedded in the unit, such as choice-based product options, open-ended questions, and more simple and complex ways to adapt the analysis models and adjust instruction based on students' readiness and interest levels.

The "choice-based differentiated products" section in each lesson allows students to select a task of interest and to showcase their learning in a way that best meets their individual preferences and learning styles. In addition, the final lesson synthesizes unit goals and provides opportunities for students to select a project of their own choosing to explore in depth. The close reading questions can also be differentiated. Teachers may assign specific questions to individual students or groups of students based on their responses from formative assessments or ELA tasks.

The ELA process models (e.g., literary analysis, rhetorical analysis, and big idea reflection) are easily differentiated as well. For example, the literary and rhetorical analysis wheels automatically provide a framework for teachers to ask simple questions using only one element, or more complex questions by emphasizing relationships among various elements (e.g., how setting influences conflict, how figurative language contributes to characterization). Examples of simple and complex questions are included in selected lessons and also in Appendix A. Likewise, students who need more practice understanding a text may use the simpler text-based model (also in Appendix A) instead of the rhetorical analysis model. The teacher may also differentiate the in-class activities by assigning different groups of students to specific tasks. These can be designed as differentiated stations. Of course not all students would complete work at every station but would be assigned a station based on their readiness. After the complexity of the task is established, then activities, questions, or product choices may also be included to accommodate various learning styles or interests.

The positive academic effects of grouping gifted students and accelerating the content they are taught are well documented (see the meta analyses of Kulik & Kulik, 1992, and Rogers, 2007). However, not all middle schools are designed to support accelerated courses for their high-achieving students. Experienced teachers of general classrooms may use this unit with their gifted and high-achieving students as part of a deliberate differentiated approach that includes in-class flexible groupings and tiered questions, stations, and assignments.

Assessment and Grading

Formative, diagnostic-prescriptive, and summative performance-based assessments are an essential part of the unit. Assessment data come from a variety of sources and are used to monitor student growth, provide student feedback, allow for student self-reflection, or to differentiate content or instruction. Descriptions of the assessments used in this unit are as follows:

- **Diagnostic-prescriptive assessment:** The unit pretest provides a first glimpse of a student's current level of performance. Each question focuses on a different key understanding. For example, Question 1 focuses on the relationship between different literary elements, Question 2 focuses on making inferences and providing evidence, and Question 3 focuses on concepts or themes. Reponses for each question can be used to differentiate questions for different groups of students and to assign specific tasks that support student learning in a key area. Prior to Lesson 1, administer the pretest (p. 14) and use the rubric (p. 16) to score responses.

- **Formative assessment:** There are many opportunities throughout the unit for teachers to check for student understanding. Teachers may occasionally ask students to expand, in writing, upon their answer to an assigned question from the text-dependent questions of a particular lesson so that comprehension can be assessed. A rubric is provided as part of the Formative Assessment section in each lesson to check for understanding. This rubric can also be used to monitor student growth and to provide feedback. The ELA Practice Tasks and Formative Assessment sections may also be assigned and graded to determine the level of student understanding as well as misconceptions about specific sources or texts that may need reteaching or further exploration. It is not recommended that every lesson's formative assessment or ELA task be assigned or graded, although teachers may select two or three of each throughout the course of the unit to use for this purpose. Informally, teachers may gather formative assessment data by listening to student discussions to ensure that students understand the text. Differentiated choice products may also be used as a formative assessment and graded using the provided rubric. Teachers should encourage students to engage in self-reflection as they receive feedback from a variety of assessments.
- **Summative assessment:** There are two different summative assessments in the unit. The final lesson (Lesson 12) includes culminating choice-based products for students to showcase their understanding of key unit content, processes, and concepts through selected product-creations. In addition, the postassessment of the unit can also be used as a summative assessment and also to measure student growth, when compared with the preassessment.

Appendix C includes rubrics for the various product-based assessments, which can also be used for peer and self-evaluations. Rubrics for the pre- and postassessments are included with the appropriate assessment at the beginning or end of the unit.

EVIDENCE SUPPORT FOR THE UNIT

Besides the use of an evidence-supported Conceptual Framework (ICM), this unit was piloted in a variety of classrooms middle school classrooms with either cluster grouped or homogeneous groups of gifted students. Teaching training was provided and teacher feedback was solicited regarding lesson clarity, student engagement, and the impact on student achievement and engagement. Lessons were modified as a result of teacher feedback and student responses. Pre- and postachievement data were also collected for this unit.

Students who were exposed to at least five lessons (almost half the unit) showed significant growth as evidenced by their pre-post-performance on the provided assessments. The unit preassessment was administered to students prior to teaching and the postassessment was administered upon conclusion of the unit. Trained individuals who had no association with writing or teaching the units scored the assessments. Students ($N = 46$) made statistically significant pretest ($M = 1.08$, $SD =. 278$) to posttest ($M = 1.6$, $SD = .399$) gains [$t(-8.55)$ $p = .000$] with important academic effects ($d = 1.3$) after correcting for dependence (see Morris & DeShon, 2002). These descriptive data suggest that after exposure to five or more lessons students increase significantly in their ability to provide evidence or reasoning, justify a specific concept or idea, make inferences, and analyze specific literary elements.

Anecdotally, teachers reported that their students were more likely to notice connections among key ideas, concepts, literary and rhetorical elements, and multiple texts than before the unit was taught. In addition, their students discussed topics at a deeper level and offered more insights. They also liked that "teaching complexity was made easy" when using the unit's analysis models (e.g., literary analysis, rhetorical analysis) and as a result they were more confident that they were meeting the needs of their gifted learners than before unit implementation.

MAKING THE MOST OUT OF THE UNIT

The following ideas are important to consider before teaching the unit:
- Provide professional development about the units that includes both content and pedagogy. Some of the unit content is complex and background knowledge may be needed. Read Appendix A instructions and examples for using the analysis models before teaching the unit. Practice completing the models on your own using specific texts before asking the students to do so until you understand how the models are used.

- For those students who need more scaffolding, consider teaching the models separately first with easier texts to get students accustomed to different ways of thinking before adding complex resources, issues, and concepts.
- You may need to teach the individual elements of each analysis model before combining them. Still, it isn't necessary to teach an entire unit on mood or tone, for example, before using the literary analysis model, although students may need explanations and practice applying the individual elements first if they haven't been exposed prior. Because gifted students learn at a faster pace, teaching individual elements can be done more quickly so that you can focus on depth and complexity through the relationships between the different elements. (This concept applies to each of the models.)
- Ensure that each individual lesson incorporates advanced content, an analysis model (e.g., literary, visual, or rhetorical), and links to the concept generalizations, as these are critical components of the ICM framework.
- Read the texts and prompts ahead of time to make sure the selections are appropriate for your district context. Substitute readings and visuals as appropriate.
- Make sure the online resources and YouTube videos are still available before teaching a particular lesson.
- Follow your students. Sometimes a lesson or reading may prompt important discussions that continue beyond the allotted time period.
- Know the intent of the models and the lesson outcomes so that you can best guide students toward important process, content, and concept goals. Otherwise, the issues discussed may supersede the objectives, especially with passionate gifted students.
- Don't assign text-dependent questions as in-depth writing activities or homework as the norm. Discussion and teacher feedback are important and most of the questions in the unit are intended to be part of a small- or whole-group discussion. By engaging students through group discussions, you can correct misconceptions right away and solicit multiple perspectives and ideas that can enhance student learning.
- Be sure to emphasize the use of supporting evidence and the complex relationships among various elements of a model when facilitating student discussions.
- Have fun! We have enjoyed teaching these units and listening to teacher feedback. We hope these units not only show academic gains in your students but also encourage them to become citizens who can critically analyze situations and enact positive change.

UNIT GOALS AND OBJECTIVES

Content

Goal 1: To analyze and interpret texts and art. Students will be able to:
- explain with evidence how literary or visual elements contribute to the overall meaning of a work;
- respond to interpretations of texts through a variety of contexts by justifying ideas and providing new information;
- compare and contrast the impact of various texts, art, experiences, and real-world events on themes and generalizations,
- explain verbally and in writing how a writer develops and supports his claim; and
- identify rhetorical devices that influence effective argumentation within primary source documents and justify why they are effective.

Process

Goal 2: To develop thinking, writing, and communication skills in the language arts. Students will be able to:
- reason through an issue by combining a variety of reasoning strategies (determine implications and consequences, consider multiple points of view, examine assumptions behind multiple points of view, inferring from data);
- use evidence to develop appropriate inferences;
- evaluate the use of effective argumentation;
- analyze purposes, assumptions, and consequences of primary sources within a historical context; and
- analyze societal or individual conflicts resulting from the struggle for power.

Concept

Goal 3: To understand the theme of power and related generalizations within the language arts. Students will be able to:
- defend "power may be used or abused" with evidence from text, media, or experiences;
- explain how the generalizations "power is the ability to influence" and "power is connected to a source" manifest within various fictional, historical, and personal contexts;
- explain how the omnipresence of power is shown through various art and literary forms within multiple contexts; and
- explain the relationship of power to other universal themes.

Name: _____ Date: _____

Pretest
"The Fox Without a Tail" by Aesop

Directions: Read the text and write your responses to the questions below citing evidence from the text. After reading, complete the questions within 30 minutes.

It happened that a Fox caught its tail in a trap, and in struggling to release himself lost all of it but the stump. At first he was ashamed to show himself among his fellow foxes. But at last he determined to put a bolder face upon his misfortune, and summoned all the foxes to a general meeting to consider a proposal which he had to place before them. When they had assembled together the Fox proposed that they should all do away with their tails. He pointed out how inconvenient a tail was when they were pursued by their enemies, the dogs; how much it was in the way when they desired to sit down and hold a friendly conversation with one another. He failed to see any advantage in carrying about such a useless encumbrance. "That is all very well," said one of the older foxes; "but I do not think you would have recommended us to dispense with our chief ornament if you had not happened to lose it yourself."

Name: _____ Date: _____

Pretest, Continued

QUESTIONS

1. How does the author's use of literary techniques (e.g., point of view, conflict, plot, language, symbolism, characterization, setting, etc.) contribute to the overall meaning of the passage?

2. "He pointed out how inconvenient a tail was when they were pursued by their enemies, the dogs." What inferences can be made about the Fox's motivation and conflict?

3. What does this story suggest about power? Use evidence from the passage to support your answer.

Name: _____ Date: _____

Pretest Rubric
"The Fox Without a Tail" *by Aesop*

	0	1	2	3	4
Question 1: Content: Literary Analysis	Provides no response.	Response is limited and vague. There is no connection to how literary elements contribute to the meaning, main idea, or theme. A literary element is merely named.	Response is accurate with 1–2 literary techniques described with vague or no connection to a main idea or theme. Response includes limited or no evidence from text.	Response is appropriate and accurate describing at least 2 literary elements and a main idea or theme. Response is literal and includes some evidence from the text.	Response is insightful and well-supported describing at least 2 literary elements and the theme. Response includes abstract connections and substantial evidence from the text.
Question 2: Inference From Evidence	Provides no response.	Response is limited, vague, and/or inaccurate. There is no justification for answers given.	Response is accurate, but lacks adequate explanation. Response includes some justification for either the character's motivation or conflict.	Response is accurate and makes sense. Response includes some justification about the character's motivation and conflict.	Response is accurate, insightful, interpretive, and well-written. Response includes thoughtful justification about the character's motivation and conflict.
Question 3: Concept/Theme	Provides no response.	Response is limited, vague, and/or inaccurate.	Response lacks adequate explanation. Response does not relate or create a generalization about power. Little or no evidence from text.	Response is accurate and makes sense. Response relates to or creates an idea about power with some relation to the text.	Response is accurate, insightful, and well-written. Response relates to or creates a generalization about power with evidence from the text.

Note: Adapted from *Jacob's Ladder Reading Comprehension Program: Level 4* (p. 148) by T. Stambaugh & J. VanTassel-Baska, 2001, New York, NY: Taylor & Francis. Copyright 2001 by Taylor & Francis. Adapted with permission.

INTRODUCTION

Lesson

"I like to see it lap the Miles" by Emily Dickinson
The Power of Change/Technology

Goals/Objectives

Content: To analyze and interpret texts and art, students will be able to:
- explain with evidence how literary or visual elements contribute to the overall meaning of a work,
- respond to interpretations of texts through a variety of contexts by justifying ideas and providing new information, and
- compare and contrast the impact of various texts, art, experiences, and real-world events on themes and generalizations.

Process: To develop thinking, writing, and communication skills, students will be able to:
- use evidence to develop appropriate inferences, and
- analyze societal or individual conflicts resulting from the struggle for power.

Concept: To understand the theme of power and related generalizations, students will be able to:
- defend "power may be used or abused" with evidence from text, media, or experience;
- explain how the generalizations "power is the ability to influence" and "power is connected to a source" are manifest within various fictional, historical, and personal contexts;
- explain how the omnipresence of power is shown through various art and literary forms within multiple contexts; and
- explain the relationship of power to other universal themes.

Accelerated CCSS ELA Standards

- RL.9-10.1
- RL.9-10.2
- RL.9-10.3
- RL.9-10.4
- RL.9-10.5
- W.9-10.4
- SL.9-10.1c
- SL.9-10.1d
- SL.9-10.4

Perspectives of Power

- SL.9-10.1

Materials

- Butcher paper for groups of 3–4 and markers for each group
- Handout 1.1: "I like to see it lap the Miles" by Emily Dickinson (*Note:* This poem is also titled "Railway Train;" do not disclose this title to students.)
- Handout 1.2: Blank Literary Analysis Wheel
- Handout 1.3: Big Idea Reflection
- Handout 1.4: Concept Organizer
- Rubric 1: Product Rubric (Appendix C)

Introductory Activities

1. Introduce the unit by explaining that this unit will explore the concept of power. Distribute butcher paper to groups of three to four students. Assign students to draw the concept of *power* on their paper. Students may include symbols to represent power but no words. Encourage students to be creative and symbolic. Have students then share their drawings, explaining any symbols.
2. At the end of discussion, ask the class to come to a consensus agreement on a definition for power. Ask: *What is power? What other words are related to power (e.g., control, authority, etc.)? How are these words different?* Share examples and similarities of actual definitions of these terms. Explain that this unit is about the nature of power. Students will be examining various works of art, literature, and nonfiction text to gain more insight into this concept.
3. Show the following concepts on the board. Ask students to sort these words into three categories (one category cannot be "other"). Students should justify their answers. Discuss how these concepts are related to power. Explain that these concepts will also be explored in the unit and that students should consider how they are related over the next several lessons. Students may also generate broad statements that include a few concepts together (e.g., the past is a powerful force on the present and future).
    - Conflict
    - Freedom
    - Oppression
    - Persuasion
    - Expression
    - Change
    - Past

- Empowerment
- Pride
- Memory

Read Text

1. Distribute Handout 1.1: "I like to see it lap the Miles" by Emily Dickinson. Do not mention that the poem is also known as "Railway Train." Explain that Emily Dickinson often wrote poems as riddles.
2. Ask a student to read the poem aloud first. As it is read, students should underline words they do not know.
3. Ask: *What words did you not know?* Guide students in understanding these terms through morphological analysis and context clues. Make sure students know these terms:
    - **Prodigious:** Large, enormous
    - **Supercilious:** Proud, condescending, arrogant
    - **Boangeres:** "Sons of thunder;" name Jesus gave his two vociferous disciples, James and John; a loud preacher
    - **Omnipotent:** All powerful
    - **Quarry:** Open excavation where minerals are extracted
    - **Pare:** To cut

Text-Dependent Questions

Select from the following questions for leading a Socratic seminar or class discussion (*Note:* Do not give away that the poem is about a train; students should continue to hypothesize and discuss with textual evidence):
- According to the poem, does the author enjoy watching this object? How do you know? (Sample response: Yes, "I like to see it . . . ")
- According to the poem, does the author like the object itself? How do you know? (Sample response: No, negative connotations about the object—supercilious, complaining, horrid, hooting—are combined with its omnipotence. It carves out the quarry to fit its own needs, to "fit its sides"—which is not welcomed in Dickinson's world.)
- What feelings can we associate with some of the words in this poem? What emotions do some of the words/lines evoke in us (e.g., horrid, hooting, omnipotent, supercilious, complaining, docile, punctual)? Are the connotations positive or negative?
- How do these connotations change and what effect does it have on the poem? (Sample response: They change from negative to positive.)

Perspectives of Power

- After the second reading, students should respond to a partner: What is this poem about? (Most may say a horse, but help students understand that it is being compared to a horse, continue to guide them as they "discover" it is a railway train.) What evidence is there to support your idea? Ask students to highlight or underline all comparisons of the train symbolized through a horse. Note that a train was referred to as an "iron horse" during the time period.
- What are the consequences of the train's actions? What message is Dickinson relating to her audience regarding a train's role in nature?
- How does the rhythm affect the poem's meaning? (Sample response: It has the "feel" of a train moving.)
- What evidence supports that the train is more powerful than nature/humans? (Sample response: It peers down at shanties, it's omnipotent, it pares a quarry.) What evidence supports that humans have more power than the train? (Sample response: The train is docile.)
- What does this poem teach us about the power of change? What does this poem teach us about the power of technology? (Sample response: We are in awe of it, but annoyed by it.)

Literary Analysis

Note: You may wish to consult analyses of the poem online before guiding student discussion, such as: http://www.gradesaver.com/emily-dickinsons-collected-poems/study-guide/section22.

1. Guide students through a literary analysis using Handout 1.2: Blank Literary Analysis Wheel. Lead students through a basic discussion of each literary element; then, emphasize the interaction of the elements with more complex questions. Refer to Appendix A for detailed instructions about the Literary Analysis Wheel and how to make a hands-on model. The Literary Analysis Wheel Guide (Appendix B) shows specific ideas for each element of the wheel. Encourage students to cite textual evidence throughout discussion. They may take notes on the Blank Literary Analysis Wheel using arrows to show how elements relate. Consider making a poster of the Literary Analysis Wheel Guide to post in the classroom and refer to throughout the unit.
2. Focus on the following complex questions (see p. 179 in Appendix A for detailed questions and sample responses for this text):
    - How does the character (train) interact with the setting to develop the theme?
    - How does Dickinson's tone help shape the theme of the poem?

- How does figurative language enhance the use of symbolism on the poem?

3. The following notes may be helpful in guiding students through the analysis:
   - **Themes:** Themes relate to the intrusion of technology on nature, the power of change, and the power of technology.
   - **Character:** The train can be considered the main character, the "iron horse," who is proud and powerful, changing the landscape to fit its own needs. The train's values are to be efficient and strong, with a motivation to arrive punctually at its destination.
   - **Setting:** The use of "shanties" in the setting implies how the train condescendingly looks down upon human things. The train "pares" a quarry, indicative of invading the landscape.
   - **Conflict:** Consider the conflict of technology versus nature and how symbols support that theme.
   - **Symbols:** Symbols such as the horse imagery (lick, stop, neigh, stable door) and Boangeres, an allusion to a vociferous Biblical disciple, should be explored.
   - **Tone:** Dickinson's tone toward the object is ambiguous—both positive and negative (she hates it, but she is in awe of its power). At times, her tone may be described as unwelcoming or disapproving. The tone shifts to be more positive toward the end.
   - **Language:** Dickinson uses alliteration with *l*'s and *st*. The *st-* helps create the sound a train might make. The rhythm of the poem almost sounds like a train. The entire poem is a metaphor (horse compared to train) and supported through similes (e.g., "neigh like Boangeres") and personification ("lick the valleys," "feed itself," "step").
   - **Context:** Dickinson lived 1830–1886 and this poem was first published in 1955. Dickinson lived in Amherst, MA. Her works were published posthumously. There was an enormous railway boom in America in 1830–1860. Her purpose may be to express her feelings toward the new technology.

Big Idea Reflection

Use Handout 1.3: Big Idea Reflection to help students transfer knowledge of the poem to real life.
- **Concepts:** Conflict, technology, change, nature.
- **Generalizations:** Technology is a powerful force on the environment. Human invention can have positive and negative influence.
- **Issue/Problem:** Technology versus nature.

- **Insight:** We can be both in awe and annoyed by the power of technology in our lives.
- **World/Community/Individual:** Individual—I may enjoy technologies in my life, but they are also imposing on my life. Technology is too powerful to let go of; it is here to stay, though it may be imposing on my life.
- **Implications:** I can reflect upon the extent I use or abuse technology to enhance my life or hurt it. I may consider, "how does technology impose on *human* nature?"

In-Class Activity to Deepen Learning

Engage students in a quick debate. Ask: *Does technology help or hurt individuals' lives today?* Students can stand on opposite sides of the room to agree or disagree. Students may discuss their opinions.

Concept Connections

1. Ask: *What general statements can we say about power? We will call these general statements "generalizations" because we can take an idea from a specific work and generalize it to the broader world. We will look at ideas from the lesson and think about how they fit together to make a broad idea.*
2. Explain that in this unit, they will focus on three major generalizations related to the concept/theme of power. They are:
    - Power is the ability to influence.
    - Power is connected to a source.
    - Power may be used or abused.

Consider writing these on butcher paper or on the board for the duration of the entire unit. Throughout the unit, other generalizations can be added as students gain more insight into the concept of power. Remember that a generalization is a statement that can be applied universally, so they should remain broad.

3. Use Handout 1.4: Concept Organizer to relate power generalizations to the text. Students can record thoughts on this handout in future lessons to compare and contrast texts and art across the unit. For this lesson, they will write responses in the first column.
4. Provide guidance as needed. Students should list examples about how the work demonstrates some of these generalizations. Ask: *How are these generalizations exemplified in the poem?* Ask students to develop a generalization of their own noting the relationship between power and another concept (e.g., conflict, change). The sentence should be relevant to the poem. Some sample responses are show in Figure 1.1.

Power is the ability to influence.
The train had a negative impact on environment; it is not welcome. Technology has a tremendous influence on our own lives. We must live examined lives to control it.
Power is connected to a source.
The train's source of power is derived by man's invention, yet it invades man's environment.
Power may be used or abused.
The train uses its power to do what it's supposed to do (arrive punctually); however, its impact on the environment is abusive in nature.
Examine the relationship between power and another concept.
The power of technology can be imposing and change the way we view the world.

Figure 1.1. *How are these generalizations exemplified in the poem?* Sample responses.

Choice-Based Differentiated Products

Students may choose one of the following independent products to complete (*Note*: Use Rubric 1: Product Rubric in Appendix C to assess student products):

- Create a picture that illustrates the "power" of technology in the poem. Use as many details from the poem as possible to develop your illustration.
- Create your own poem by comparing a piece of technology in our world to a familiar object/figure. Just as Dickinson compared a train to a horse, develop your own metaphor using at least three types of figurative language throughout your poem. Also include how technology carves into the landscape of our daily lives.
- Read another poem by Emily Dickinson such as "The Brain is Wider than the Sky." In a paragraph, explain three ways literary elements contribute to developing an idea related to power. Cite specific evidence from the poem.
- Write an editorial about the imposing nature of technology in our daily lives. In your editorial, provide suggestions for individuals to take control over technology rather than allowing technology to control lives.

ELA Practice Tasks

Assign one of the following tasks as a performance-based assessment for this lesson:

- How does Dickinson's use of metaphor contribute to the main message of the poem? In an essay, answer the question by providing sufficient relevant textual evidence to support your response.

	Concept/Theme
0	Provides no response.
1	Response is limited, vague, and/or inaccurate.
2	Response lacks adequate explanation. Response does not relate or create a generalization about power.
3	Response is accurate and makes sense. Response relates to or creates an idea about power with some relation to the text.
4	Response is accurate, insightful, and well-written. Response relates to or creates a generalization about power with evidence from the text.

Figure 1.2. Scoring guidelines for Lesson 1 formative assessment.

- Write a review that evaluates Dickinson's use of literary elements. Was she effective in developing her idea with these elements? Support your response with textual evidence from the poem.
- Is the poem relevant to today? In an argumentative essay, support your claim by referring to specific evidence in the poem and to contemporary life.

Formative Assessment

1. Ask students to respond to the following prompt in a single paragraph: *What does "I like to see it lap the Miles" reveal about the nature of power? Explain in a well-developed paragraph with support from the text. Be sure to relate to a power generalization.*
2. Use the scoring guidelines in Figure 1.2 to evaluate students' responses.

Name: _____ Date: _____

Handout 1.1
"I like to see it lap the Miles" *by Emily Dickinson*

I like to see it lap the miles,
And lick the valleys up,
And stop to feed itself at tanks;
And then, prodigious, step

Around a pile of mountains,
And, supercilious, peer
In shanties by the sides of roads;
And then a quarry pare

To fit its sides, and crawl between,
Complaining all the while
In horrid, hooting stanza;
Then chase itself down hill

And neigh like Boanerges;
Then, punctual as a star,
Stop—docile and omnipotent—
At its own stable door.

Name: _____ Date: _____

Handout 1.2
Blank Literary Analysis Wheel

Directions: Draw arrows across elements to show connections.

Text: _____

Purpose/Context

- Setting
- Mood
- Language Structure Style
- Symbols
- Plot/Conflict
- Characters
- Theme
- Point of View
- Tone

Interpretation

Created by Tamra Stambaugh, Ph.D., & Emily Mofield, Ed.D., 2015.

Name: _____ Date: _____

Handout 1.3
Big Idea Reflection

What?	**Concepts:** What concepts/ideas are in the text?	
	Generalizations: What broad statement can you make about one or more of these concepts? Make it generalizable beyond the text.	
	Issue: What is the main issue, problem, or conflict?	
So What?	**Insight:** What insight on life is provided from this text?	
	World/Community/Individual: How does this text relate to you, your community, or your world? What question does the author want you to ask yourself?	
Now What?	**Implications:** How should you respond to the ideas in the text? What action should you take? What are the implications of the text? What can you do with this information?	

Created by Emily Mofield, Ed.D., & Tamra Stambaugh, Ph.D., 2015.

Name: _____ Date: _____

Handout 1.4
Concept Organizer

Directions: How does each work exemplify each generalization? What new generalization can you make?

Literature, Art, or Media: _____	Literature, Art, or Media: _____	Literature, Art, or Media: _____
Power is the ability to influence.		
Power is connected to a source.		
Power may be used or abused.		
Examine the relationship between power and another concept.		

POWER OF OPPRESSION

Lesson

"The Dutchman"
by Moyo Okediji
The Power of Cultural Heritage

Goals/Objectives

Content: To analyze and interpret texts and art, students will be able to:
- explain with evidence how literary or visual elements contribute to the overall meaning of a work,
- respond to interpretations of texts through a variety of contexts by justifying ideas and providing new information, and
- compare and contrast the impact of various texts, art, experiences, and real-world events on themes and generalizations.

Process: To develop thinking, writing, and communication skills, students will be able to:
- use evidence to develop appropriate inferences, and
- analyze societal or individual conflicts resulting from the struggle for power.

Concept: To understand the theme of power and related generalizations, students will be able to:
- defend "power may be used or abused" with evidence from text, media, or experience;
- explain how the generalizations "power is the ability to influence" and "power is connected to a source" are manifest within various fictional, historical, and personal contexts;
- explain how the omnipresence of power is shown through various art and literary forms within multiple contexts; and
- explain the relationship of power to other universal themes.

Accelerated CCSS ELA Standards

- SL.8.2
- SL.9-10.1
- SL.9-10.1c
- SL.9-10.1d
- SL.9-10.4
- W.9-10.4
- W.9-10.5
- RI.9-10.7

Materials

- Copy of Moyo Okediji's "The Dutchman" retrieved online
- Handout 2.1: Blank Visual Analysis Wheel
- Rubric 1: Product Rubric (Appendix C)

Introductory Activities

1. Show a picture of Moyo Okediji's print, "The Dutchman." Do not share the title with the students yet or disclose any background information. Ask every student to respond in round robin (no discussion yet) to the following statements. This round-robin response will allow students to see various aspects of the painting before analyzing it.
   - Say: *I see something you don't see.* Ask students to say one thing they see in the painting that they think others have difficulty seeing (e.g., *I see a ship that says, "Dutch" on it*; *I see a man holding a baton*).
   - Ask: *What is one word you associate with this painting?*

2. Lead a discussion about the art.
   - What event is represented in this painting? (Sample response: Trans-Atlantic slave trade.) What evidence supports this?
   - How many slaves do you see? (Sample response: This is debatable; Eight—mostly at the top.)
   - How many slave traders do you see? What are they holding? (Sample response: Two—baton and gun.)
   - What title would you give this painting? Why? (Students may share with partner and then with whole group.)

3. Provide context and background of the painting: Moyo Okediji is from Nigeria. He received his college degree in Nigeria, his master's in Benin, and a Ph.D. at the University of Wisconsin in art history. He lectures, paints, and writes about art history through the lens of colonialism's destruction of ancient African art and the rediscovery of ancient art forms. Okediji painted "The Dutchman" in 1995 after spending time in the United States and seeing the daily realities of African American life in the U.S. He noticed that many African Americans were distant from their heritage and culture. This influenced him to paint this picture.

Visual Analysis

Using Handout 2.1: Blank Visual Analysis Wheel, guide students in taking notes on the painting during class discussion. Students may take notes on the wheel and draw arrows to illustrate connections between elements. See Appendix A for detailed instructions. Sample questions and responses to lead the analysis are included. Ideas in this analysis are adapted from Smith (1999).

- **Context/Purpose:**
  - *What is the context?* It was painted in 1995. Refer to background knowledge previously discussed.
  - *What is the purpose?* It shows the shattering of a culture as a result of conflict.

- **Main Idea:**
  - *What is the main idea?* Power can be abused; people suffer when power is abused; African culture is stripped and robbed. Main themes include conflict, oppression, and reflecting on cultural heritage.

- **Point of View/Assumptions:**
  - *What assumptions does the artist have regarding his work?* He assumes an African American perspective of history; power was imposed upon them and shattered their culture.

- **Images/Technique/Structure:**
  - **Images:** *What important images or symbols do you see? Are any of them repeated? What do you think these could symbolize?*
    - **Blue:** Atlantic Ocean, African American blues, blue associated with sadness.
    - **Shattering effect:** African American culture was shattered by the slave trade.
    - **Wavy lines:** Water; something was shattered and water was poured over the painting, just as African culture was shattered and other cultures spilled upon it. There is a half black/white individual in the bottom right corner, representing dual identity.

  - **Technique:** *What techniques does the artist use to enhance visual effects? What makes this an interesting painting?* Tints of blue and orange—opposites on the color wheel—symbolize the conflict of slaves versus traders; the collage organization portrays a shattering effect.
  - **Structure:** *What is interesting about Okediji's placement of objects and people within the painting?* Most works of art are created with a triangular structuring of visual elements—the bottom of the triangle at

the bottom and top vertex at the top; however, the visual placement of elements in this painting give it an upside-down triangle effect. This creates a chaotic upside-down feel. The slave trade turned the Africans' lives upside down.

- **Emotions/Technique/Structure:**
  - *What emotions does this evoke in you? What emotions are portrayed? What techniques were used to evoke or portray emotion?* Deep sadness; tears of slaves.
  - *How did the artist organize his art to portray or evoke emotion?* The shattering effect and upside-down triangle organization portray chaos.

- **Artist Background/Technique/Structure:**
  - *How does the artist's background influence his techniques and structure?* His background and views on African culture influence his use of shattering effects and collage-like structure in his art.

- **Implications:**
  - *What are the implications/consequences of viewing this art?* It evokes emotional reactions to the history of the slave trade. It helps viewers gain more personal historical perspective to the topic.

- **Evaluation:**
  - *Do you like this art? Why? Does it make you think? Was the artist successful in presenting his ideas? Justify your answers with evidence.*

In-Class Activities to Deepen Learning

Engage students in a quick debate. Discuss the following questions. Students may stand on opposite sides of the room to defend their points of view.
- Do you think Okediji intended his audience to think more about the past or the present when viewing his painting? Why or why not?
- Do you think Okediji's work has more positive or negative effects on its viewers? Explain.
- Does this art tell more about the oppressor or the victim? Why?

Concept Connections

Discuss connections to power by asking the following questions. Students may reflect on concept connections using Handout 1.4: Concept Organizer, continued from Lesson 1. Figure 2.1 provides some sample responses.

Power is the ability to influence.
The "shattered" effects on the painting reveal the shattering of the African culture. The dominating power of the White culture negatively shattered the African culture.
Power is connected to a source.
Power is connected to the dominating culture in conflict. Evidence: Conflicting complementary colors (purple and orange).
Power may be used or abused.
Upside-down triangle effect shows that the lives of Africans were turned upside down by the dominating culture.
Examine the relationship between power and another concept.
Abuse of power causes conflict for many involved.

Figure 2.1. Sample student responses to power generalizations.

- How does Okediji show abuse of power through artistic techniques?
- What does this art reveal about the power of cultural heritage?

Choice-Based Differentiated Products

Students may choose one of the following independent products to complete (*Note*: Use Rubric 1: Product Rubric in Appendix C to assess student products.):

- Learn more about Okediji's life and works through online research. Use the Blank Visual Analysis Wheel (Appendix B) to analyze another work such as "The New Seed" terrachroma or "Fela in Mamiwataland." In a couple of paragraphs, explain how Okediji's works show similarities about the power of cultural heritage.
- Think of a song that matches the mood of the painting "The Dutchman." Explain why the song complements the painting with at least four supporting features of the music (specific lyrics, use of elements in music, etc.).
- Draw a picture conveying conflict and a dominating power. Apply at least three techniques Okediji uses (complementary colors, upside down structure, shattering effect, hidden images) in your own drawing or painting.
- View various pieces of art from an art museum or virtual museum. As you view art, consider how the artist depicts conflict or ideas of power. Write a journal response about a piece of art by considering the following questions: How does the artist depict a conflict? What visual techniques are used? How does the artist depict culture? What are the main ideas of the art? What are the main symbols depicted and what could they mean? How has this experience impacted your understanding of power, culture, or conflict?

	Content: Claim/Message and Evidence
0	Provides no response.
1	Response is limited, vague, and/or inaccurate. Only the central idea is mentioned with little support.
2	Response lacks adequate explanation. Some parts of the response are correct, but the response only vaguely addresses the artist's central idea and evidence. Response lacks support.
3	Response is accurate and makes sense. Response includes 1–2 examples of support for the central idea.
4	Response is accurate, insightful, and well written. Response includes 2–3 examples of support for the central idea with evidence.

Figure 2.2. Scoring guidelines for Lesson 2 formative assessment.

ELA Practice Task

Assign one of the following tasks as a performance-based assessment for this lesson:

- Research more about Okediji's background and examine other pieces of his art. Use multiple sources to develop a short research paper that describes motivations behind his art. Cite evidence from your background research and evidence from his artistic techniques used in specific pieces of art.
- Write a narrative from the perspective of a person in the painting. Use evidence from the art to shape a vivid story that alludes to the message of the work.

Formative Assessment

1. Ask students to respond to the following prompt in a single paragraph: *What is the central idea of Okediji's "The Dutchman" and how is it supported?*
2. Use the scoring guidelines in Figure 2.2 to evaluate students' assessments.

Looking Ahead

Students are asked to read a novel in Lesson 5. A short story option is also suggested. Depending on time you may want to assign the novel and prereading now so students are prepared to discuss this novel by Lesson 5.

Name: _____ Date: _____

Handout 2.1
Blank Visual Analysis Wheel

Directions: Draw arrows across elements to show connections.

Art Piece: _____

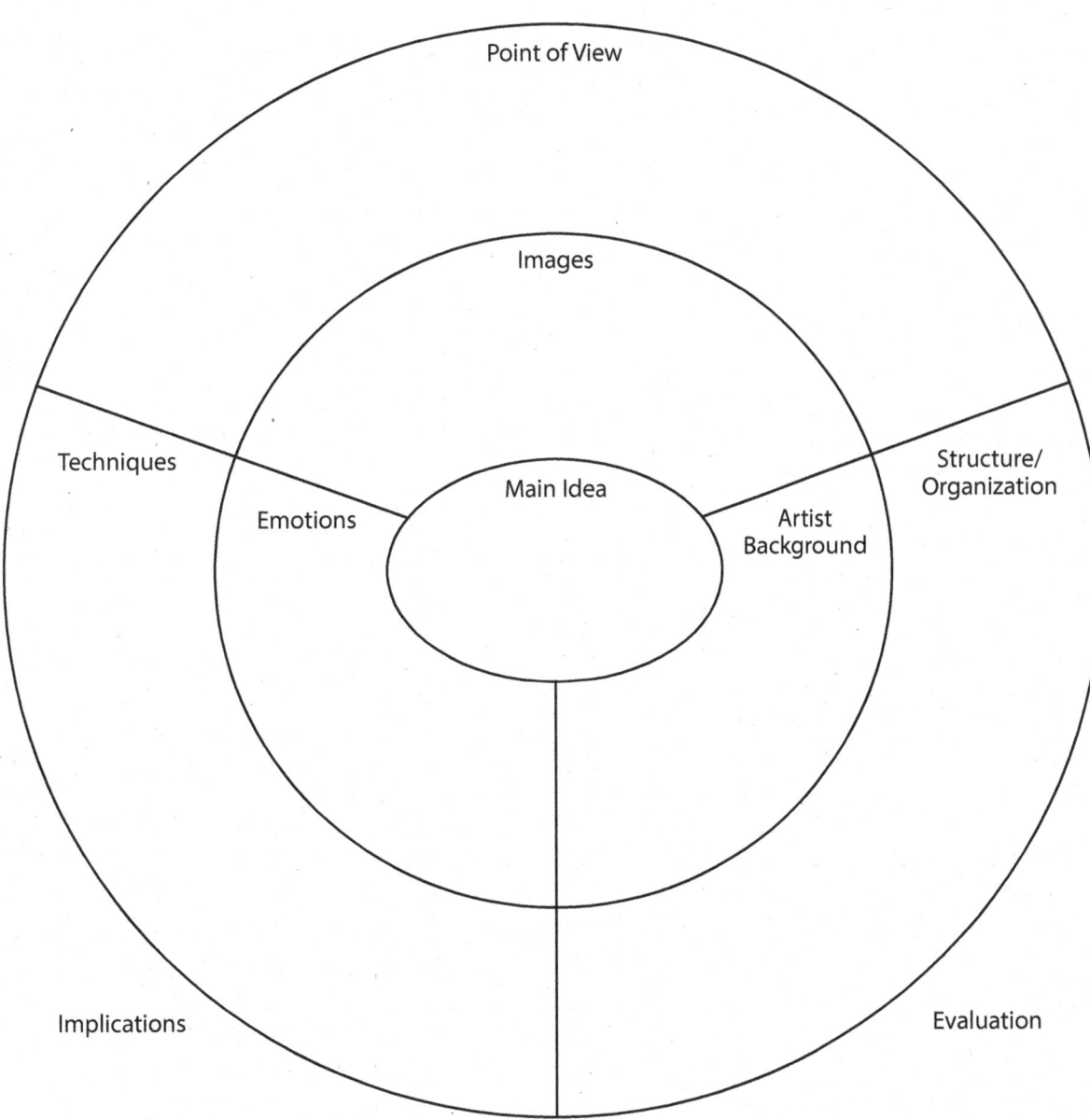

Created by Tamra Stambaugh, Ph.D., & Emily Mofield, Ed.D., 2015.

Lesson 3

"Blue Beard"
by Charles Perrault
Unjust Rules

Goals/Objectives

Content: To analyze and interpret texts and art, students will be able to:
- explain with evidence how literary or visual elements contribute to the overall meaning of a work,
- respond to interpretations of texts through a variety of contexts by justifying ideas and providing new information, and
- compare and contrast the impact of various texts, art, experiences, and real-world events on themes and generalizations.

Process: To develop thinking, writing, and communication skills, students will be able to:
- reason through an issue by using multiple points of view, assumptions, and implications to defend a statement or idea;
- use evidence to develop appropriate inferences; and
- analyze societal or individual conflicts resulting from the struggle for power.

Concept: To understand the theme of power and related generalizations, students will be able to:
- defend "power may be used or abused" with evidence from text, media, or experience;
- explain how the generalizations "power is the ability to influence" and "power is connected to a source" are manifest within various fictional, historical, and personal contexts;
- explain how the omnipresence of power is shown through various art and literary forms within multiple contexts; and
- explain the relationship of power to other universal themes.

Accelerated CCSS ELA Standards

- W.9-10.4
- SL.9-10.1
- SL.9-10.1c

Perspectives of Power

- SL.9-10.1d
- SL.9-10.4
- RL.9-10.1
- RL.9-10.2
- RL.9-10.3
- RL.9-10.4
- RL.9-10.6
- RL.9-10.9

Materials

- Handout 3.1: "Blue Beard" by Charles Perrault (*Note:* This famous fairy tale often found in children's anthologies involves Blue Beard's wife discovering dead bodies in a closet. Please be aware of this content and handle with discretion.)
- Handout 3.2: Blank Literary Analysis Wheel
- Handout 3.3 Big Idea Reflection
- Handout 3.4: Reasoning About a Situation or Event
- Rubric 1: Product Rubric (Appendix C)

Introductory Activity

Engage students in a quick debate: Ask students the following agree/disagree statements. Challenge students to choose either agree or disagree (no in between). Students may stand on opposite sides of the room to defend their answers. Call on a few students to justify their answers from their own experiences or from situations they know of in real life.

- Is it right to be punished for breaking a rule?
- What if it is an unfair rule? Is it right to be punished for breaking it?

Read Text

1. Distribute Handout 3.1: "Blue Beard" by Charles Perrault. Explain that this was written in 1696 by Charles Perrault as a children's story during the rise of Protestantism in France.
2. Assign students to read the text silently or you may conduct a scaled-down version of reader's theater. Students are assigned parts and read at the appropriate time. Students can be savvy to know when to speak and when not to speak. The narrator reads everything not in quotes. Assign the following parts:
   - Narrator
   - Blue Beard
   - The wife
   - The sister

Text-Dependent Questions

Select from the following text-dependent questions for leading a Socratic seminar or class discussion:

- What can you infer about Blue Beard's past?
- What can you infer about Blue Beard's motivation to murder his wife (and previous wives)?
- What is Blue Beard testing of his wife by forbidding her to view one wardrobe? Is this a true test of obedience? Is this a true test of love?
- Why does the author emphasize the blood on the key?
- Based on evidence in the text, what might the key, blood, and door each symbolize? (Sample response: Blood = guilt; key = power to know; door = hides what is unknown; hiding secrets = all Biblical allusions to Tree of Knowledge in Genesis.)
- Would it have been better for the wife to have never known about the wardrobe with the dead wives? Would it have been better for her to stay *innocent* of the *knowledge* that her husband is a murderer? Why or why not?
- How does Perrault develop the reader's sympathy for the wife?
- In what ways is this story an allegory for "The Fall" in Genesis?
- What message does Perrault give the reader about mercy? (Sample response: She deserved punishment for giving into temptation, but was rescued/redeemed.) What specific textual evidence supports this?
- Is this story appropriate for children? Refer to evidence in the text to support your answer. Why is this a children's story and what message can children take from this?
- Are the wife's brothers necessary in telling the story? Why or why not? If so, how do they help enhance the themes? (Sample response: Without the brothers, the story would not have any redemption.)
- Why are we drawn to tales of horror such as this story? What does this story reveal about our deepest fears? (Sample response: We fear trusting someone and then being deceived.)
- What social/political/movements may have influenced his writing, and what evidence in the text supports this? What additional background knowledge would you like to know? (Sample response: The rise of Protestantism influenced this story; it is an allusion of "The Fall" in Genesis 3; the temptation to "bite" the fruit is symbolized by the temptation to open the closet; the brother "saves" the wife from her guilty actions, similar to Protestant beliefs. She did not get death that she "deserved.")

Literary Analysis

1. Guide students in analyzing the story using Handout 3.2: Blank Literary Analysis Wheel. Lead students through a basic discussion of each literary element, then emphasize the interaction of the elements with more complex questions. Refer to Appendix A for detailed instructions about the Literary Analysis Wheel. Encourage students to cite textual evidence throughout discussion. Students can take notes on the wheel and draw arrows to illustrate connections between elements.
2. Focus on the following complex questions:
   - What do conflicts reveal about the characters' values and motives, and how does this help shape the theme?
   - How do symbols (including allusions) help develop the theme?
   - How does the ending (brothers rescuing wife) influence the theme?
   - How does the narrator's point of view affect the mood of the story?
3. The following notes may be helpful in guiding students through the analysis:
   - **Themes:** Themes include jealousy, control, power, curiosity, and temptation.
   - **Symbols:** "blue" beard = uniqueness, sadness, or cold-heartedness; blood = guilt that could not be erased; key = ability to unlock the unknown, ability to see the "knowledge" of good and evil (like the fruit in Genesis 3); door = hides the unknown; allusion = the story is a symbol for "The Fall" in Genesis.
   - **Tone:** Tone is matter-of-fact, child-like, and simple.
   - **Point of View:** Because the story is written in third person objective, we do not know the thoughts of the characters and the story is more suspenseful.
4. Help students understand the pattern—rule given, rule broken, receives or almost receives punishment, rescued from punishment. This is a "redemption" pattern that is in several pieces of literature. Ask students to list other stories that have this same pattern (e.g., most fairy tales and many Disney movies).

Big Idea Reflection

Use Handout 3.3: Big Idea Reflection to connect the story to real life:
- **Concepts:** Temptation, fear, knowledge, disobedience, trust, masculine superiority.

- **Generalizations:** What generalization about power do you see as most evident in the story? What other generalizations can be made?
- **Issue:** Should someone be punished for breaking an unjust rule?
- **Insight:** Human nature is to be curious and to want what we can't have.
- **World/Community/Individual:** World—are there unjust rules in the world for which people are punished?
- **Implications:** In what ways might we address unjust rules in the world today?

In-Class Activities to Deepen Learning

1. **Engage students in a quick debate.** Revisit the question, *Is it right to be punished for an unfair rule?* Ask students if they changed their mind, why or why not? Students may discuss their opinions and relate to evidence within the story.
2. Guide students through considering multiple perspectives of the story by applying Handout 3.4: Reasoning About a Situation or Event. Figure 3.1 provides some sample responses.
   - **Point of View:** The perspective taken by the stakeholder(s) and how they feel toward the issue
   - **Assumptions:** What each stakeholder takes for granted in the situation
   - **Implications:** The possible consequences of what could happen if the stakeholder's point of view is fulfilled

Concept Connections

Discuss connections to power by asking the following questions. Students may reflect on concept connections using Handout 1.4: Concept Organizer, continued from previous lessons. The connections in Figure 3.2 may be helpful in guiding discussion.
- How does an "unfair rule" relate to a generalization about power?
- How is curiosity related to a generalization about power?
- What new generalization about power can you make?

Choice-Based Differentiated Products

Students may choose one of the following independent products to complete (*Note*: Use Rubric 1: Product Rubric in Appendix C to assess student products):
- Some researchers contend that Blue Beard was based on a real person. Consult at least three others sources to investigate this. What additional information will you need in order make a conclusion about your find-

Perspectives of Power

Stakeholders	Blue Beard	Wife	Brother	Reader
Point of View	Yes, she broke a rule.	No, the rule is unfair.	No, she does not deserve the harsh punishment.	Varies
Assumptions (What stakeholders take for granted and presuppose)	He assumes superiority of power, distrust toward wife.	She should be trusted as his loving wife.	Assumes his role to take care of his sister.	Assumes point of view from 21st-century culture—this punishment is too cruel.
Implications (Consequences of what could happen)	Wife will justly die as he has power over her.	She will escape, but must depend on someone to rescue her.	He will have honor for rescuing her.	Pulled into the story from the suspense of the scenario.

Figure 3.1. *Should the wife be punished?* Sample responses.

Power is the ability to influence.
Curiosity is the power to influence one into tempting situations.
Power is connected to a source.
Power is connected to dominance of the ruling person (Blue Beard or men, in this story).
Power may be used or abused.
Power is abused by creating an unfair rule.
Examine the relationship between power and another concept.
Temptation is a powerful force. Curiosity is a powerful influence.

Figure 3.2. Sample student responses to power generalizations.

ings? Present your findings to the class with a visual to accompany your presentation.

- Read another version of "Blue Beard" by another author, such as the Brothers Grimm. In what ways does the author's use of literary elements differ and how does it contribute to a different effect? Be sure to comment on the author's word choice. Present your findings in a Venn diagram or chart. In a couple of paragraphs, be sure to include at least four thoughtful contrasts and comparisons.

- Read another story by Charles Perrault. Examine at least *four* ways the stories are similar in terms of literary elements. You may wish to develop a chart (*Note:* Figure 3.3 is an example). Include textual evidence within your chart. One aspect has been completed for an example.
- Rewrite the story from a different point of view that maintains the same plot sequence. Reveal insight into a character's thoughts, feelings, and motives related to ideas of power.

ELA Practice Tasks

Assign one of the following tasks as a performance-based assessment for this lesson:

- Identify one of the themes in "Blue Beard" and write a multiparagraph essay in which you analyze in detail how the theme is developed in the short story.
- Did Blue Beard's wife deserve to be punished? In an argument essay, use evidence from the story and your own ideas to support your claim.
- Examine how women are portrayed in "Blue Beard." In an explanatory essay, explain how Perrault portrays women and how this affects themes in the story. Note specific examples from the text in your essay.

Formative Assessment

1. Ask students to respond to the following prompt in a single paragraph: *What can you infer about Blue Beard's character from the following: "Blue Beard having very attentively considered it, said to his wife, 'Why is there blood on the key?'" Additionally, how does this relate to the central conflict in the story?*
2. Use the scoring guidelines in Figure 3.4 to evaluate students' assessments.

	"Blue Beard"	Similarity	"Sleeping Beauty in the Wood"
Setting			
Characterization			
Point of View			
Plot	Brother saves wife at the end, though she "deserved" her punishment.	Both show the need for a woman to be "rescued" from a man. Both include Biblical allusions.	Woman saved by a servant. Servant sacrificed animals as a substitute sacrifice instead of Sleeping Beauty.
Theme			
Symbols			

Figure 3.3. Comparing stories sample chart.

	Inference from Evidence
0	Provides no response.
1	Response is limited, vague, and/or inaccurate. There is no justification for answers given.
2	Response is accurate, but lacks adequate explanation. Response includes some justification about the conflict.
3	Response is accurate and makes sense. Response includes some justification about the conflict.
4	Response is accurate, insightful, interpretive, and well-written. Response includes thoughtful justification about the conflict.

Figure 3.4. Scoring guidelines for Lesson 3 formative assessment.

Name: _____ Date: _____

Handout 3.1
"Blue Beard" *by Charles Perrault*

There was a man who had fine houses, both in town and country, a deal of silver and gold plate, embroidered furniture, and coaches gilded all over with gold. But this man had the misfortune to have a blue beard, which made him so frightfully ugly, that all the women and girls ran away from him.

One of his neighbours, a lady of quality, had two daughters who were perfect beauties. He desired of her one of them in marriage, leaving to her the choice which of the two she would bestow upon him. They would neither of them have him, and each made the other welcome of him, being not able to bear the thought of marrying a man who had a blue beard. And what besides gave them disgust and aversion, was his having already been married to several wives, and nobody ever knew what became of them.

Blue Beard, to engage their affection, took them, with the lady their mother, and three or four ladies of their acquaintance, with other young people of the neighbourhood, to one of his country seats, where they stayed a whole week. There was nothing then to be seen but parties of pleasure, hunting, fishing, dancing, mirth and feasting. Nobody went to bed, but all passed the night in playing tricks upon each other. In short, every thing succeeded so well, that the youngest daughter began to think the master of the house not to have a beard so very blue, and that he was a mighty civil gentleman. As soon as they returned home, the marriage was concluded.

About a month afterwards Blue Beard told his wife that he was obliged to take a country journey for six weeks at least, about affairs of very great consequence, desiring her to divert herself in his absence, to send for her friends and acquaintances, to carry them into the country, if she pleased, and to make good cheer wherever she was.

"Here," said he, "are the keys of the two great wardrobes, wherein I have my best furniture; these are of my silver and gold plate, which is not every day in use; these open my strong boxes, which hold my money, both gold and silver; these my caskets of jewels; and this is the master-key to all my apartments. But for this little one here, it is the key of the closet at the end of the great gallery on the ground floor. Open them all; go into all and every one of them; except that little closet which I forbid you, and forbid it in such a manner that, if you happen to open it, there will be no bounds to my just anger and resentment."

She promised to observe, very exactly, whatever he had ordered; when he, after having embraced her, got into his coach and proceeded on his journey.

Her neighbours and good friends did not stay to be sent for by the new married lady, so great was their impatience to see all the rich furniture of her house, not daring to come while her husband was there, because of his blue beard which frightened them. They ran thro' all the rooms, closets, and wardrobes, which were all so rich and fine, that they seemed to surpass one another.

After that, they went up into the two great rooms, where were the best and richest furniture; they could not sufficiently admire the number and beauty of the tapestry, beds,

Name: _____ Date: _____

Handout 3.1, Continued

couches, cabinets, stands, tables, and looking-glasses in which you might see yourself from head to foot; some of them were framed with glass, others with silver, plain and gilded, the finest and most magnificent which were ever seen. They ceased not to extol and envy the happiness of their friend, who in the meantime no way diverted herself in looking upon all these rich things, because of the impatience she had to go and open the closet of the ground floor. She was so much pressed by her curiosity, that, without considering that it was very uncivil to leave her company, she went down a little back-stair-case, and with such excessive haste, that she had twice or thrice like to have broken her neck.

Being come to the closet door, she made a stop for some time, thinking upon her husband's orders, and considering what unhappiness might attend her if she was disobedient; but the temptation was so strong she could not overcome it. She took then the little key, and opened it trembling; but could not at first see anything plainly, because the windows were shut. After some moments she began to perceive that the floor was all covered over with clotted blood, in which were reflected the bodies of several dead women ranged against the walls: these were all the wives whom Blue Beard had married and murdered one after another. She was like to have died for fear, and the key, which she pulled out of the lock, fell out of her hand.

After having somewhat recovered her senses, she took up the key, locked the door, and went upstairs into her chamber to recover herself; but she could not, so much was she frightened. Having observed that the key of the closet was stained with blood, she tried two or three times to wipe it off, but the blood would not come off; in vain did she wash it, and even rub it with soap and sand, the blood still remained, for the key was a Fairy, and she could never make it quite clean; when the blood was gone off from one side, it came again on the other.

Blue Beard returned from his journey the same evening, and said, he had received letters upon the road, informing him that the affair he went about was ended to his advantage. His wife did all she could to convince him she was extremely glad of his speedy return. Next morning he asked her for the keys, which she gave him, but with such a trembling hand, that he easily guessed what had happened.

"What," said he, "is not the key of my closet among the rest?"

"I must certainly," answered she, "have left it above upon the table."

"Fail not," said Blue Beard, "to bring it me presently."

After putting him off several times, she was forced to bring him the key. Blue Beard, having very attentively considered it, said to his wife:

"How comes this blood upon the key?"

"I do not know," cried the poor woman, paler than death.

"You do not know," replied Blue Beard; "I very well know, you were resolved to go into the closet, were you not? Mighty well, Madam; you shall go in, and take your place among the ladies you saw there."

Upon this she threw herself at her husband's feet, and begged his pardon with all the signs of a true repentance for her disobedience. She would have melted a rock, so beautiful and sorrowful was she; but Blue Beard had a heart harder than any rock.

"You must die, Madam," said he, "and that presently."

Name: _____ Date: _____

Handout 3.1, Continued

"Since I must die," answered she, looking upon him with her eyes all bathed in tears, "give me some little time to say my prayers."

"I give you," replied Blue Beard, "half a quarter of an hour, but not one moment more."

When she was alone, she called out to her sister, and said to her:

"Sister Anne" (for that was her name), "go up I beg you, upon the top of the tower, and look if my brothers are not coming; they promised me that they would come to-day, and if you see them, give them a sign to make haste."

Her sister Anne went up upon the top of the tower, and the poor afflicted wife cried out from time to time, "Anne, sister Anne, do you see any one coming?"

And sister Anne said:

"I see nothing but the sun, which makes a dust, and the grass growing green."

In the mean while Blue Beard, holding a great scimitar in his hand, cried out as loud as he could bawl to his wife:

"Come down instantly, or I shall come up to you."

"One moment longer, if you please," said his wife, and then she cried out very softly:

"Anne, sister Anne, dost thou see any body coming?"

And sister Anne answered:

"I see nothing but the sun, which makes a dust, and the grass growing green."

"Come down quickly," cried Blue Beard, "or I will come up to you."

"I am coming," answered his wife; and then she cried:

"Anne, sister Anne, dost thou see any one coming?"

"I see," replied sister Anne, "a great dust that comes this way."

"Are they my brothers?"

"Alas! no, my dear sister, I see a flock of sheep."

"Will you not come down?" cried Blue Beard.

"One moment longer," said his wife, and then she cried out:

"Anne, sister Anne, dost thou see nobody coming?"

"I see," said she, "two horsemen coming, but they are yet a great way off."

"God be praised," she cried presently, "they are my brothers; I am beckoning to them, as well as I can, for them to make haste."

Then Blue Beard bawled out so loud, that he made the whole house tremble. The distressed wife came down, and threw herself at his feet, all in tears, with her hair about her shoulders.

"Nought will avail," said Blue Beard, "you must die"; then, taking hold of her hair with one hand, and lifting up his scimitar with the other, he was going to take off her head.

The poor lady turning about to him, and looking at him with dying eyes, desired him to afford her one little moment to recollect herself.

"No, no," said he, "recommend thyself to God," and was just ready to strike.

At this very instant there was such a loud knocking at the gate, that Blue Beard made a sudden stop. The gate was opened, and presently entered two horsemen, who drawing their swords, ran directly to Blue Beard. He knew them to be his wife's brothers, one a dragoon, the other a musqueteer; so that he ran away immediately to save himself; but the two brothers pursued so close, that they overtook him before he could get to the steps of the porch,

Name: _____ Date: _____

Handout 3.1, Continued

when they ran their swords thro' his body and left him dead. The poor wife was almost as dead as her husband, and had not strength enough to rise and welcome her brothers.

    Blue Beard had no heirs, and so his wife became mistress of all his estate. She made use of one part of it to marry her sister Anne to a young gentleman who had loved her a long while; another part to buy captains' commissions for her brothers; and the rest to marry herself to a very worthy gentleman, who made her forget the ill time she had passed with Blue Beard.

Name: _____   Date: _____

Handout 3.2
Blank Literary Analysis Wheel

Directions: Draw arrows across elements to show connections.

Text: _____

Purpose/Context

- Setting
- Language Structure Style
- Mood
- Symbols
- Plot/Conflict
- Characters
- Theme
- Point of View
- Tone

Interpretation

Created by Tamra Stambaugh, Ph.D., & Emily Mofield, Ed.D., 2015.

Name: _____ Date: _____

Handout 3.3
Big Idea Reflection

What?	**Concepts:** What concepts/ideas are in the text?	
	Generalizations: What broad statement can you make about one or more of these concepts? Make it generalizable beyond the text.	
	Issue: What is the main issue, problem, or conflict?	
So What?	**Insight:** What insight on life is provided from this text?	
	World/Community/Individual: How does this text relate to you, your community, or your world? What question does the author want you to ask yourself?	
Now What?	**Implications:** How should you respond to the ideas in the text? What action should you take? What are the implications of the text? What can you do with this information?	

Created by Emily Mofield, Ed.D., & Tamra Stambaugh, Ph.D., 2015.

Name: _____   Date: _____

Handout 3.4
Reasoning About a Situation or Event

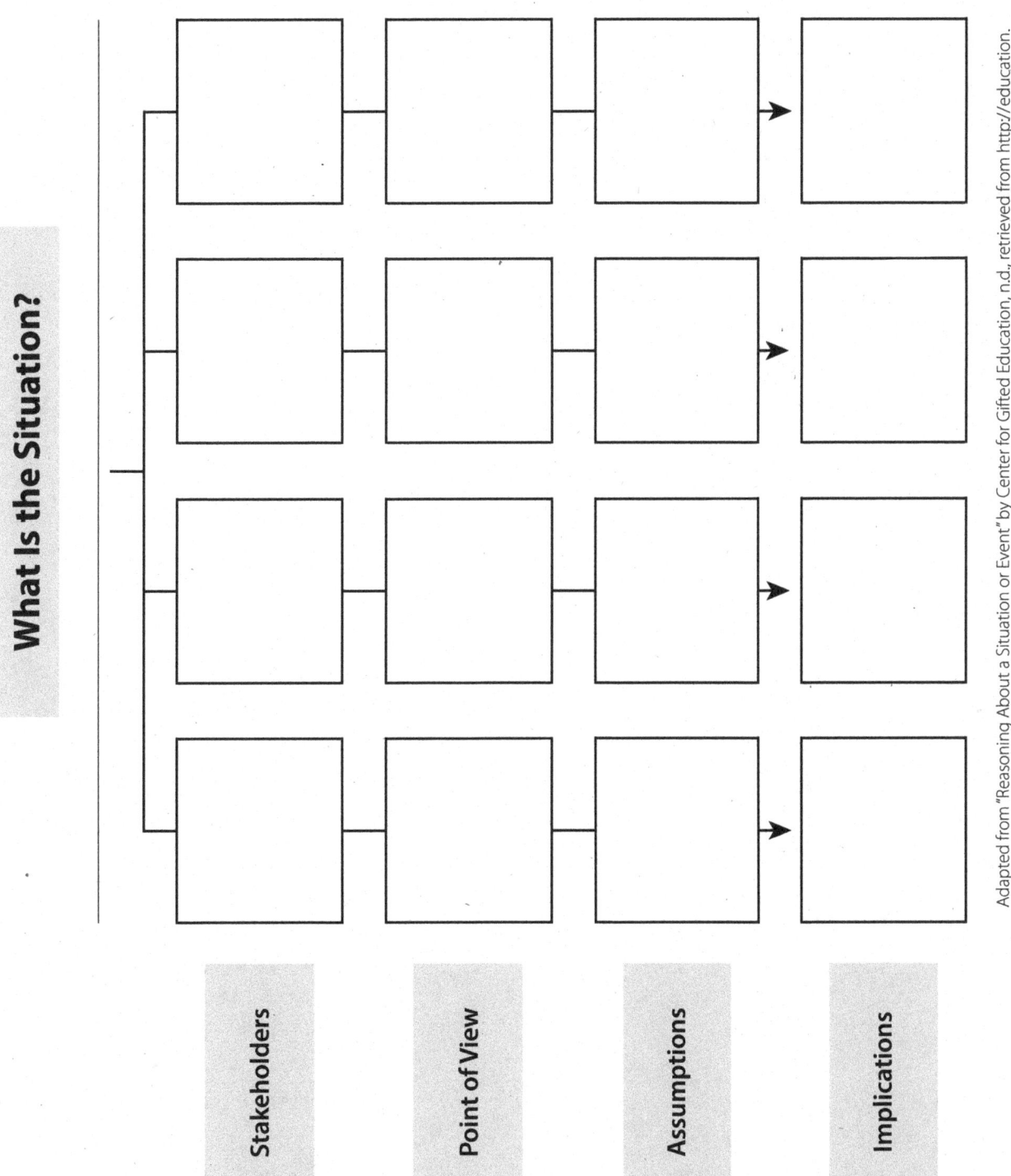

Lesson 4

"On Women's Right to Vote" by Susan B. Anthony
The Power of Persuasion

Goals/Objectives

Content: To analyze and interpret texts and art, students will be able to:
- respond to interpretations of texts through a variety of contexts by justifying ideas and providing new information;
- compare and contrast the impact of various texts, art, experiences, and real-world events on themes and generalizations; and
- identify rhetorical devices that influence effective argumentation within primary source documents and justify why they are effective.

Process: To develop thinking, writing, and communication skills, students will be able to:
- evaluate the use of effective argumentation;
- analyze purposes, assumptions, and consequences of primary sources within a historical context; and
- analyze societal or individual conflicts resulting from the struggle for power.

Concept: To understand the theme of power and related generalizations, students will be able to:
- defend "power may be used or abused" with evidence from text, media, or experience;
- explain how the generalizations "power is the ability to influence" and "power is connected to a source" are manifest within various fictional, historical, and personal contexts;
- explain how the omnipresence of power is shown through various art and literary forms within multiple contexts; and
- explain the relationship of power to other universal themes.

Accelerated CCSS ELA Standards

- RI.9-10.1
- RI.9-10.2
- RI.9-10.3

Perspectives of Power

- RI.9-10.4
- RI.9-10.5
- RI.9-10.6
- RI.9-10.9
- SL.9-10.1
- SL.9-10.1c
- SL.9-10.1d
- SL.9-10.4
- RH.9-10.1
- RH.9-10.2
- RH.9-10.4
- RH.9-10.5
- RH.9-10.6
- RH.9-10.8
- RH.9-10.9
- W.9-10.5
- W.9-10.4

Materials

- Primary sources arguing against women's suffrage retrieved online. Recommended sources:
  - "Some Reasons Why We Oppose Votes for Women" from Library of Congress, available at http://hdl.loc.gov/loc.rbc/rbpe.1300130c
  - "Arguments Against Women's Suffrage" by J. B. Sanford, available at http://sfpl.org/pdf/libraries/main/sfhistory/suffrageagainst.pdf

- Handout 1.4: Concept Organizer
- Handout 4.1: "On Women's Right to Vote" by Susan B. Anthony
- Handout 4.2: Blank Rhetorical Analysis Wheel
- Rubric 1: Product Rubric (Appendix C)

Introductory Activities

1. Remind students of the issue explored in "Blue Beard": *Is it fair to be punished for an unjust rule?* Guide them to make connections to this issue as they explore the content of this lesson.
2. Guide students through the following simulation:
   - Tell the class that at the end of the lesson, there will be 5 minutes of free time. Ask students for ideas of what they can do for their free time (e.g., go outside, shoot paper wads into the trashcan, paint fingernails, watch a movie, etc.).
   - Discuss options. After thorough discussion, tell the students there will be a class vote. However, only the girls are allowed to vote. If the teacher would like to push the discussion further, tell students that if the boys voted, then they would have a severe punishment (e.g., extra homework, detention, etc.). Elicit reactions from the boys.
   - Ask: *Was this fair? Why not? Is there any evidence in American documents that this is not fair?* (Assess students' knowledge about Constitutional freedoms.)

- Ask: *Can you make connections to our unit so far?* ("Blue Beard": woman punished for an unfair rule). Ask boys: *Is it fair for you to be punished for a rule you had no say in establishing?*

3. Divide the class into two groups. Ask students to imagine themselves as 19th-century American citizens. One group will write reasons why women should have the right to vote. The other group will write reasons why women should not have the right to vote. Ask students to share ideas with the class. Examine the types of appeals they bring up (e.g., allusion to Bill of Rights, ethics, justice, etc.). Encourage multiple perspectives and cultural contextualization among those writing for opposition to women's suffrage. Explain that not only men, but also some women were opposed to women's suffrage.

4. Give some brief background knowledge on the women's suffrage movement. Ask students what they know already about the movement. Students may be assigned the following individuals or events to research or the teacher may briefly discuss. (Recommended source: http://www.historynet.com/womens-suffrage-movement)
   - Seneca Falls Convention 1848
   - Lucretia Mott
   - Elizabeth Cady Stanton
   - Susan B. Anthony
   - 15th Amendment and its exclusion of women
   - Frederick Douglass, first a supporter of women's suffrage, later an opponent
   - 19th Amendment
   - Women's Suffrage Movement in New Zealand and Europe

5. You may want to show a short YouTube clip about Susan B. Anthony's life, such as: http://www.youtube.com/watch?v=9Pa4VS5-YLM

Read Text

1. Briefly describe the historical context of Susan B. Anthony's speech presented in 1873. Explain that the speech was given after her arrest for voting in the 1872 Presidential election. She was tried in court and required to pay a fine of $100, but refused. She gave this speech in 29 towns after her arrest and before her trial.
2. Ask: *Did she deserve to be punished for breaking the law?*
3. Distribute Handout 4.1: "On Women's Right to Vote" by Susan B. Anthony. You may ask a student to deliver this speech dramatically.

Perspectives of Power

Text-Dependent Questions

Select from the following text-dependent questions for leading a Socratic seminar or class discussion:
- What is Anthony's main purpose in giving this speech? What four words from the speech most capture her purpose?
- What is her main claim and how does she justify her claim? What is her primary evidence?
- How does Anthony use deductive logic to develop her argument in the paragraph beginning "It was we, the people . . . "?
- What pattern does Anthony establish in the paragraph "For any State . . . "? How does this help establish reasoning?
- What effect does the repetition of "oligarchy" have on the speech's purpose? Based on the context of the text, do you think oligarchy has a positive or negative connotation? What evidence supports this? What is the denotation (definition) of the word "oligarchy?"
- How does Anthony bring the argument to a more personal level? (Sample response: She discusses that this can cause discord in every home.)
- What value does the phrase "Webster, Worcester and Bouvier all . . . "bring to the speech? (Sample response: She is establishing credibility to her premise and argument.)
- How does Anthony arrive at her final conclusions about discrimination against women and Negroes?
- What phrases are most powerful for audience listeners? Why?
- Does Anthony rely more on logic (logos) or emotion (pathos)?

Introduce Elements Of Rhetorical Analysis

1. Go over a few elements students may see in historical speeches and documents. You may choose to focus on a few rather than all. The ones in bold are especially important in Anthony's speech.
    - **Language**: Consider how word choice affects the tone.
    - *Positive and negative connotations of words:* Consider how word choice evokes feelings.
    - *Simile:* A figure of speech that compares two unlike things using like or as.
    - *Metaphor:* A direct comparison between two unlike things.
    - *Hyperbole:* An extreme exaggeration.
    - *Allusion:* A reference to a historical or Biblical work, person, or event; the writer assumes the reader can make connections between the allusion and text being read.

- *Imagery:* Formation of mental images that appeal to the senses.
- *Parallelism:* Using similar grammatical structures in order to emphasize related ideas.
- **Repetition:** Repeating the same wording for emphasis, clarity, or emotional impact.
- *Contrast:* Showing a stark difference in ideas.
- **Rhetorical question**: A question asked by the writer that is not expected to be answered aloud. It evokes reflection.
- **Liberty rhetoric**: Using patriotic appeals for freedom (*Note:* "Liberty rhetoric" [arguments for liberty] was a common way for feminists of the 19th century to voice their arguments. They used the same language that was used to break away from Britain to break away from male authority).
- *War rhetoric:* Reasoning to convince war is necessary.
- **Syllogism:** A form of deductive logic; a conclusion drawn from two premises (e.g., if x = y, y = z, then x = z. If citizens can vote and if women are citizens, then women should be allowed to vote).

2. Briefly explain Aristotle's Elements of Rhetoric. Aristotle's rhetoric includes logos, ethos, and pathos appeals. They enhance a writer's ability to persuade an audience.
   - **Logos:** How the author establishes good reasoning to make the document/speech make sense; this includes major points, use of evidence, syllogisms, examples, evidence, facts, statistics, etc.; text-focused.
   - **Pathos:** How the author appeals to the audience's emotion; audience-focused.
   - **Ethos:** How the author develops credibility and trust; author-focused.

3. Tell students: *We will now look at how Susan B. Anthony uses these appeals in her speech. We will see how her point of view, techniques, and organization of the speech are used to develop logos, ethos, and pathos appeals. All of these elements together develop the main claim.*

Rhetorical Analysis

Guide students through evaluating Anthony's argument by using Handout 4.2: Blank Rhetorical Analysis Wheel. Refer to Appendix A for detailed instructions about the Rhetorical Analysis Wheel and how to make a hands-on model. Sample questions and responses to lead the analysis include:

- **Context/Purpose:**
  - *What is the historical context?* The speech was given after her arrest for voting in the 1872 presidential election. She was tried in court and

required to pay a fine of $100, but refused. She gave this speech in 29 towns after her arrest and before her trial.
- *What is Anthony's purpose?* She aims to persuade/convince the audience that she is not a criminal.

- **Message/Claim:**
  - *What is Anthony's main claim?* Because women are citizens, they should be able to vote.

- **Point of View/Assumptions:**
  - *What are Anthony's assumptions?* She assumes the audience accepts the premise that all individuals are citizens.

- **Logos/Techniques/Structure:**
  - *What are her main points?* The Constitution has given the blessing of liberty and liberty has been denied. The government is not a true democracy. Women are persons, persons are citizens, citizens can vote, thus women should vote.
  - *What techniques were used to develop her reasoning?* She develops the last point as a syllogism (women = persons, persons = citizens, citizens = can vote, women = can vote).
  - *How does she structure her argument to make sense?* She structures her argument with deductive reasoning. Her main thesis is at the beginning and then it is supported.

- **Pathos/Techniques/Structure:**
  - *How does Anthony develop emotional appeals? What techniques are used and where are they placed?* She evokes a negative feeling toward the government through the technique of loaded words (mockery, odious, repetition of oligarchy). Feelings of shame are evoked by repetition of "oligarchy" contrasted with democracy. Feelings of patriotism are developed by liberty rhetoric. She ends with a powerful rhetorical question, "Are women people?" evoking emotional reflection.

- **Ethos/Techniques/Structure:**
  - *Is Anthony credible and trustworthy?* She develops credibility by citing the preamble at the beginning of the speech and referring to it throughout. She does acknowledge the other side, but ridicules it in a biased way. Some may argue this bias lessens her credibility.

- **Implications:**
  - *What are the implications/consequences of this document?* Eventually her voice, along with the women's suffrage movement, led to the 19th Amendment.

- **Evaluation:**
  - *How effective is she in supporting her claim? Is there a balance of pathos, ethos, and logos appeals? Is there too much bias or emotional manipulation? Is the claim fully supported?* Anthony accomplishes her purpose with a balance of appeals. Her deductive reasoning through the use of syllogisms develops strong logos appeals. Her pathos appeals are not manipulative; rather, they evoke patriotism. She establishes credibility by appealing to the Constitution, though some may say her language about the U.S. oligarchy is overly negative and biased.

In-Class Activities to Deepen Learning

1. With partners, have students create a dialogue between Susan B. Anthony and the wife of Blue Beard. These individuals should discuss how they had similar experiences related to oppression and power (e.g., punished for an unjust rule). They should include evidence from the texts.
2. Have students examine primary source documents pertaining to arguments against women's suffrage. Ask students to identify the major claim/argument in the texts. *What persuasive techniques are being used? What are the assumptions? What are the economic, political, and social factors that are being addressed within the source? What are the implications/consequences of the text?*

Concept Connections

Use Handout 1.4: Concept Organizer to relate power generalizations to the text. Ask: *How are these generalizations exemplified in the speech?* Students should also develop their own generalization about power and another concept. Figure 4.1 provides possible responses for this lesson, though various interpretations are encouraged.

Choice-Based Differentiated Products

Students may choose one of the following independent products to complete (*Note*: Use Rubric 1: Product Rubric in Appendix C to assess student products):

Perspectives of Power

Power is the ability to influence.
Through the use of liberty rhetoric, she was able to make a powerful logical case for women's suffrage.
Power is connected to a source.
She appealed to the source of the Constitution.
Power may be used or abused.
Power was not representative of the people.
Examine the relationship between power and another concept.
Students may examine the relationship between power, persuasion, democracy, and equality.

Figure 4.1. Sample student responses to power generalizations.

- Compare The Declaration of Independence (Introduction and Preamble) to the Declaration of Sentiments (written at the Seneca Falls Convention). Create a diagram or chart that shows how arguments for breaking away from British authority are similar to breaking away from male authority.
- In what ways have you seen the use of liberty rhetoric in election campaigns, current events, or controversies? Provide at least five examples. Which example is the most powerful and why?
- Imagine that you were an audience member listening to Susan B. Anthony's speech. Write a newspaper editorial that explains your reaction to the speech and includes your opinion about women's suffrage. (It is acceptable to write from the perspective of an anti-suffrage woman or man and draw from other primary source ideas within this lesson.)
- Using primary and secondary sources, identify ways in which women across the world face inequity in contemporary society. This may include a disparity of girls attending school versus boys or disparity in pay distributions. After determining a specific problem, address the following: In what ways might equality for women be improved? Brainstorm at least five possibilities and write a detailed action plan to address your problem. Include who, what, when, where, how, who will assist your efforts, and how you will accomplish the goal of creating equity for women. Your action plan may be explained in a mock UN resolution, state law, newspaper editorial or column, letter to a person in power, or any other authentic product of your choice.

ELA Practice Tasks

Assign one of the following tasks as a performance-based assessment for this lesson:

	Effective Rhetoric
0	Provides no response.
1	Response is limited and vague. Response only partially answers the question. A rhetorical element is not mentioned.
2	Response is accurate with 1–2 rhetorical elements named. Response includes limited or no evidence from text. OR Response includes evidence from text, but does not relate to a rhetorical element.
3	Response is appropriate and accurate, describing 1–2 rhetorical elements to support effective argumentation. Response includes some evidence from the text.
4	Response is insightful and well supported, describing 2–3 rhetorical elements. Response includes evidence from the text.

Figure 4.2. Scoring guidelines for Lesson 4 formative assessment.

- Was America a democracy in 1873? Write an argument essay in which you respond to the question from Susan B. Anthony's perspective. Cite relevant evidence from the speech to support your claim.
- Does Susan B. Anthony rely more on logos, pathos, or ethos appeals? Write an argument essay articulating your point of view with relevant evidence from the speech.

Formative Assessment

1. Ask students to respond to the following prompt in a single paragraph: *How effective is Anthony in developing her argument? Support your answer by referring to elements of effective argumentation.*
2. Use the scoring guidelines in Figure 4.2 to evaluate students' assessments.

Name: _____ Date: _____

Handout 4.1
"On Women's Right to Vote" *by Susan B. Anthony*

Friends and fellow citizens: I stand before you tonight under indictment for the alleged crime of having voted at the last presidential election, without having a lawful right to vote. It shall be my work this evening to prove to you that in thus voting, I not only committed no crime, but, instead, simply exercised my citizen's rights, guaranteed to me and all United States citizens by the National Constitution, beyond the power of any state to deny.

The preamble of the Federal Constitution says:

"We, the people of the United States, in order to form a more perfect union, establish justice, insure domestic tranquillity, provide for the common defense, promote the general welfare, and secure the blessings of liberty to ourselves and our posterity, do ordain and establish this Constitution for the United States of America."

It was we, the people; not we, the white male citizens; nor yet we, the male citizens; but we, the whole people, who formed the Union. And we formed it, not to give the blessings of liberty, but to secure them; not to the half of ourselves and the half of our posterity, but to the whole people—women as well as men. And it is a downright mockery to talk to women of their enjoyment of the blessings of liberty while they are denied the use of the only means of securing them provided by this democratic-republican government—the ballot.

For any state to make sex a qualification that must ever result in the disfranchisement of one entire half of the people, is to pass a bill of attainder, or, an ex post facto law, and is therefore a violation of the supreme law of the land. By it the blessings of liberty are forever withheld from women and their female posterity.

To them this government has no just powers derived from the consent of the governed. To them this government is not a democracy. It is not a republic. It is an odious aristocracy; a hateful oligarchy of sex; the most hateful aristocracy ever established on the face of the globe; an oligarchy of wealth, where the rich govern the poor. An oligarchy of learning, where the educated govern the ignorant, or even an oligarchy of race, where the Saxon rules the African, might be endured; but this oligarchy of sex, which makes father, brothers, husband, sons, the oligarchs over the mother and sisters, the wife and daughters, of every household—which ordains all men sovereigns, all women subjects, carries dissension, discord, and rebellion into every home of the nation.

Webster, Worcester, and Bouvier all define a citizen to be a person in the United States, entitled to vote and hold office.

The only question left to be settled now is: Are women persons? And I hardly believe any of our opponents will have the hardihood to say they are not. Being persons, then, women are citizens; and no state has a right to make any law, or to enforce any old law, that shall abridge their privileges or immunities. Hence, every discrimination against women in the constitutions and laws of the several states is today null and void, precisely as is every one against Negroes.

Name: _____ Date: _____

Handout 4.2
Blank Rhetorical Analysis Wheel

Directions: Draw arrows across elements to show connections.

Text: _____

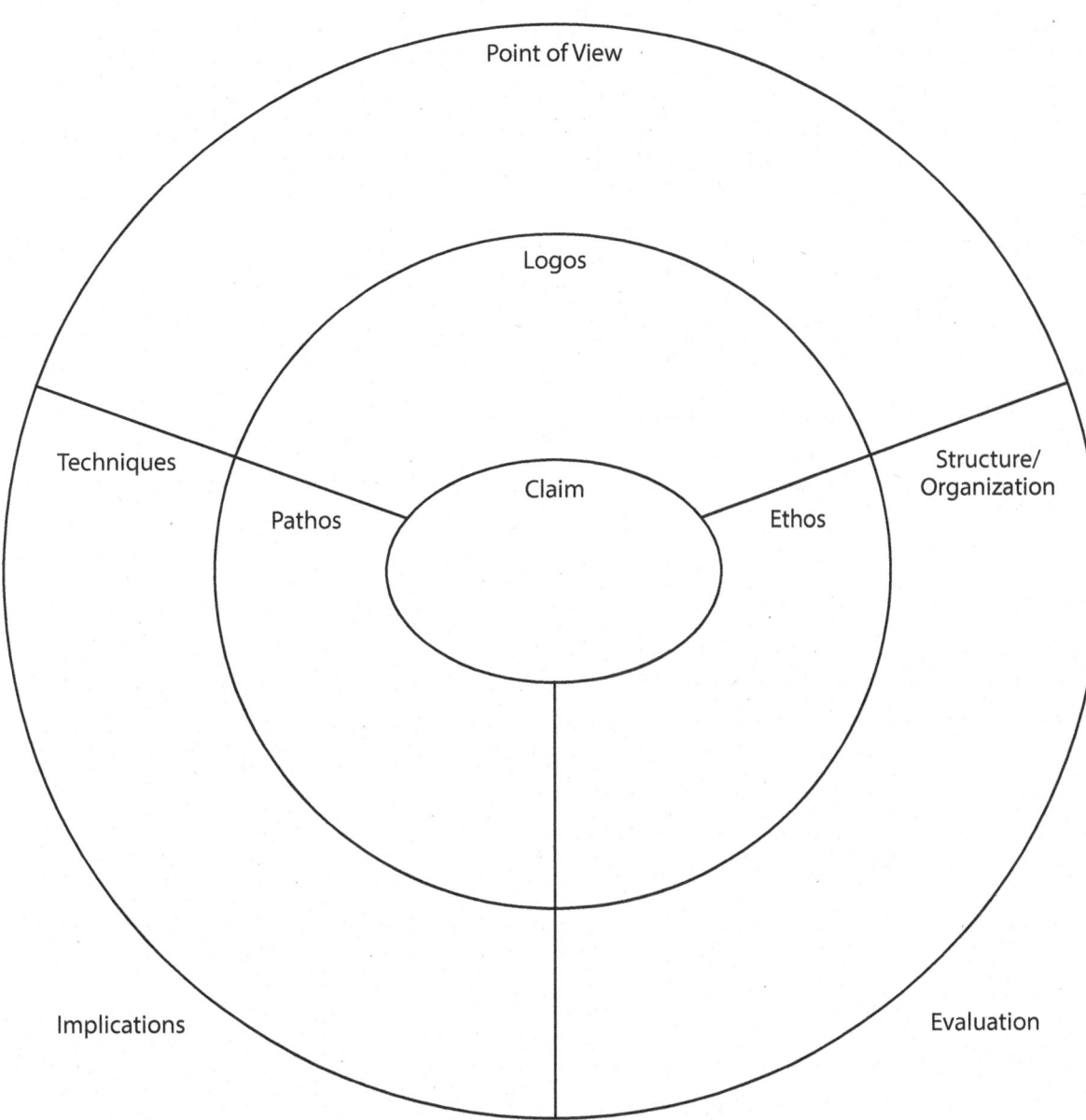

Created by Emily Mofield, Ed.D., & Tamra Stambaugh, Ph.D., 2015.

Lesson 5

Dystopian Literature: The Abuse of Power

Goals/Objectives

Content: To analyze and interpret texts and art, students will be able to:
- explain with evidence how literary or visual elements contribute to the overall meaning of a work,
- respond to interpretations of texts through a variety of contexts by justifying ideas and providing new information, and
- compare and contrast the impact of various texts, art, experiences, and real-world events on themes and generalizations.

Process: To develop thinking, writing, and communication skills, students will be able to:
- reason through an issue by using multiple points of view, assumptions, and implications to defend a statement or idea;
- use evidence to develop appropriate inferences; and
- analyze societal or individual conflicts resulting from the struggle for power.

Concept: To understand the theme of power and related generalizations, students will be able to:
- defend "power may be used or abused" with evidence from text, media, or experience;
- explain how the generalizations "power is the ability to influence" and "power is connected to a source" are manifest within various fictional, historical, and personal contexts;
- explain how the omnipresence of power is shown through various art and literary forms within multiple contexts; and
- explain the relationship of power to other universal themes.

Accelerated CCSS ELA Standards

- SL.9-10.1
- SL.9-10.1c
- SL.9-10.4

Perspectives of Power

- SL.9-10.1d
- W.9-10.4
- W.9-10.5
- RL.9-10.1
- RL.9-10.2
- RL.9-10.3
- RL.9-10.4

Materials

- Student copies of any dystopian novel (e.g., *The Hunger Games, The Giver, House of the Scorpion, Animal Farm, Divergent*, etc.) This lesson may also work with a children's story such as Dr. Seuss's "Yurtle the Turtle" or a short story such as Kurt Vonnegut's "Harrison Bergeron" if there is not enough time to incorporate a novel, though some specific aspects of "dystopia" may not apply. The teacher may also consider assigning independent reading on a dystopian novel and assigning Handout 5.1.
- Materials for Star Power Simulation:
  - Instructions, available at https://www.msu.edu/~eheilman/iss/simluation/simulations.html
  - Different color chips (5 per student, such as: poker chips), solid cups, and a nametag with a symbol (square, circle, or triangle) for each student
  - Star Power Teacher background reading "Why Would Anyone Want to Play Star Power" by Donella Meadows (available at http://www.donellameadows.org/archives/why-would-anyone-want-to-play-starpower). *Note:* The Star Power simulation is extremely powerful for students in making connections about entitlement, corruption of power, and social status. It is often cited as students' favorite activity in the unit. Strongly consider making time for the simulation.

- Handout 5.1: Dystopian Literature Reading Guide
- Handout 5.2: Blank Literary Analysis Wheel
- Handout 5.3: Big Idea Reflection
- Handout 5.4: Reasoning About a Situation or Event
- Handout 1.4: Concept Organizer (continued from previous lessons)
- Rubric 1: Product Rubric (Appendix C)

Introductory Activities

1. **Engage students in a quick debate.** Ask students to agree or disagree with the following quote (from *The Hunger Games*): "The only thing stronger than hope is fear." Discuss different points of view.
2. Play a version of "Star Power Simulation." (Retrieve specific instructions as noted in Materials section). This game was developed by Garri Shirts in 1969 and should be played with a minimum of 12 students. This simulation can

take 1–2 class periods, but can greatly enhance discussion and reflection of power concepts. Through the simulation, teacher/authority figure purposely favors the upper class. Throughout the simulation, students are led to believe there is a strategy used to get a high amount of points. Toward the end of the game, the upper class is given the opportunity to change the rules of the game, and they almost always change the rules to benefit themselves. The upper class begins acting arrogantly, inevitably illustrating that power corrupts. When students reflect on this experience, they are able to see how behaviors vary across groups. The lower class may rebel, think negatively about the upper class and authority figure, form camaraderie among themselves, give up on the game, and feel that the game is completely unfair. The upper class usually feels that the game is fair and that they have "earned" their status. Typically, the upper class does not feel sympathy for the lower class because they believe they are functioning within a fair system. The middle class's main prerogative is to maintain their status or move up to the upper class.

3. After the simulation, students should reflect upon their feelings toward other groups and/or the authority figure. Students can also make a chart (see Figure 5.1) to record behaviors and feelings experienced by each group and relate this to life in school and the real world.

4. Ask students to reflect on the following questions:
   - What is it about power that can influence people to become corrupt?
   - Was the government (authority) legitimate?
   - To what extent does this reflect our society?
   - Is this game fair? What makes this game unfair? Are any parts fair?
   - What would make this game fair? (Students are likely to want to start out with an even amount of tokens, but point out that this is an idea central to communism or governments portrayed in many dystopian novels.) Solutions to fair distribution of power/wealth have been explored for centuries, but they all have flaws to some extent. Explain that this demonstration is intended to help participants reflect on current systems of social status/power and this simulation sheds insight into the reasons behind social behaviors within a system.

5. Ask students to develop their own generalizations about power as it relates to the simulation. Then, share the following from Simulation Training Systems (n.d.):
   - Each of us may be more vulnerable to the temptation to abuse power than we realize.
   - Few people are likely to participate in an endeavor if they feel powerless.

Perspectives of Power

Status	Behaviors Observed	Connections to Real Life
Upper Class		
Middle Class		
Lower Class		

Figure 5.1. Simulation reflection chart.

- What seems fair to those in power is not likely to seem fair to those who are out of power.
- Persons who are promoted rarely remember those they leave behind.
- Power is like fire, it can be used to help make the world a better place to live or it can be terribly destructive.
- In any system, there needs to be checks on power. If there are no checks, power will almost certainly be abused. (para. 9)

As students read a dystopian novel, they may make several connections to these generalizations.

Read Text

Assign students to read a dystopian novel or a short story as suggested. Students may choose from a variety of novels, as available. Pre-, during-, and after-reading reflections are provided on Handout 5.1: Dystopian Literature Reading Guide.

Literary Analysis

Guide students in analyzing the story/novel using Handout 5.2: Blank Literary Analysis Wheel. Working in pairs or small groups, students may take notes on the wheel. Emphasize the interaction of literary elements throughout discussion.

Big Idea Reflection (Optional)

Use Handout 5.3: Big Idea Reflection to help translate knowledge from the text to real life (in whole group, small groups, or pairs).

In-Class Activities to Deepen Learning

1. Students can discuss reflections and patterns from Handout 5.1: Dystopian Literature Reading Guide in small groups or as a whole group.
2. Then, use Handout 5.4: Reasoning About a Situation or Event to explore multiple points of view on an issue posed by the dystopian fiction (e.g., Should the protagonist reveal the truth? Should the protagonist take action against the status quo?).

Concept Connections

Use Handout 1.4: Concept Organizer to relate power generalizations (see Figure 5.2) to the novel or short story. Also refer to the Star Power generalizations mentioned earlier in the lesson to discuss connections (even if students did not participate in the simulation, the generalizations may still be relevant to their readings). Ask: *How did the text exemplify these generalizations?*

Choice-Based Differentiated Products

Students may choose one of the following independent products to complete (*Note*: Use Rubric 1: Product Rubric in Appendix C to assess student products):

- Write a persuasive speech or essay from the perspective of the protagonist in your novel/short story that convinces others to realize the ill qualities of the dystopian society. Consider relating your techniques to the methods Susan B. Anthony used to develop her argument against the status quo. Develop a sound argument by developing a claim and supporting it with evidence from instances in the novel. Appeal to logos, ethos, and pathos in your argument.
- Write a corresponding chapter from the point of view of the government or highest hierarchy in the book (e.g., write Chapter X from a new perspective). Shed insight into the motives of the power source within your chapter. Explain why the government or head hierarchy acts as they do.
- Consider how a contemporary issue relates to a facet of a dystopian society. Find a newspaper or magazine article that addresses the issue. Develop a chart with four quotes/evidence from the article and how it relates to features of dystopian societies.

Perspectives of Power

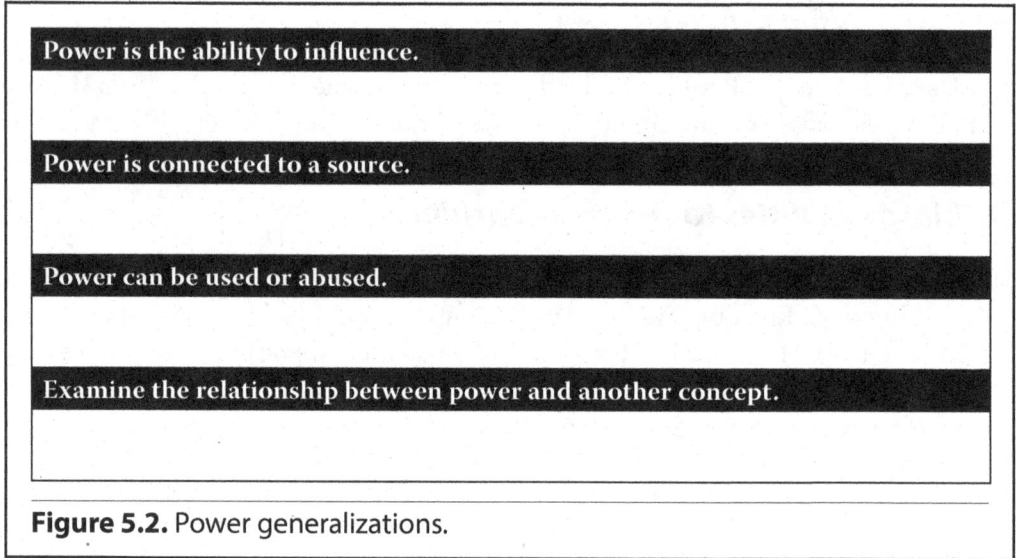

Figure 5.2. Power generalizations.

ELA Practice Tasks

Assign one of the following tasks as a performance-based assessment for this lesson:

- How does the power force maintain control over its citizens (in the novel/short story)? In an expository essay, explain your answer and note the arguments used by the power force. Cite textual evidence from the novel to support your answer.
- In a comparison essay, compare the protagonist to another character or individual from this unit. Explain how they are similar in at least three ways, citing textual evidence from both texts.

Formative Assessment

1. Ask students to respond to the following prompt in a single paragraph: *What does the novel/story reveal about one of the generalizations of power we have been studying? Explain in a well-developed paragraph with support from the work. Be sure to relate to a power generalization.*
2. Use the scoring guidelines in Figure 5.3 to evaluate students' assessments.

	Concept/Theme
0	Provides no response.
1	Response is limited, vague, and/or inaccurate.
2	Response lacks adequate explanation. Response does not relate or create a generalization about power.
3	Response is accurate and makes sense. Response relates to or creates an idea about power with some relation to the text.
4	Response is accurate, insightful, and well-written. Response relates to or creates a generalization about power with evidence from the text.

Figure 5.3. Scoring guidelines for Lesson 5 formative assessment.

Name: _____ Date: _____

Handout 5.1
Dystopian Literature Reading Guide

Reflections for First Half of Reading

- How does the government maintain its power?
- Examine the treatment of humanity in the novel. Give examples from the text about inhumane treatments.
- Examine the role of the individual within society versus the group. Which is more valued, the individual or society? What evidence supports this?

Pattern Chart

Find examples from the text of the following patterns often seen in dystopian literature. Cite textual evidence.

Pattern	Textual Evidence (Page Number, Direct Quote, or Summary of Situation)
Lies: ■ Lies, deception, and propaganda are used to control individuals. ■ Euphemisms are used.	
Distractions: ■ Order, regulation, or tradition is used to prevent individuals from making choices. ■ An absence of nature distracts characters from feelings and reflection. ■ Personal reflection, spirituality, emotion, creativity, and thinking are repressed. ■ The government keeps society busily distracted through order, abundant pleasure, or constant want.	

Name: _____ Date: _____

Handout 5.1, Continued
_____

Humanity Treatment: ■ There is a presence of dehumanization (numbers assigned, the devaluation of human life, remarkable evil disguised as acceptable). ■ Government creates an individual's reality, creating a predictable human being.	
Society vs. Individual: ■ The individual is safe as long as the status quo is maintained. ■ The individual is only important because he or she is part of the whole. ■ Familial names are used for leaders to develop loyalty. ■ The society is an illusion of an ideal world.	

Reflection Questions: After Reading

1. At what point does the protagonist realize that something is wrong in society and something must change?
2. How does the protagonist come to this realization?
3. What is the result of this realization (e.g., usually an awareness of human rights, lies must be brought to light, and society should be corrected)?
4. In what ways does the novel reflect contemporary issues?

Adapted from "Decoding *The Matrix* Exploring Dystopian Characters through Film" by Junius Wright, 2006, retrieved from http://readwritethink.org/classroom-resources/lesson-plans/decoding-matrix-exploring-dystopian-926.html.

Name: _____ Date: _____

Handout 5.2
Blank Literary Analysis Wheel

Directions: Draw arrows across elements to show connections.

Text: _____

Purpose/Context

- Setting
- Symbols
- Characters
- Point of View
- Tone
- Interpretation
- Plot/Conflict
- Language Structure Style
- Mood
- Theme

Interpretation

Created by Tamra Stambaugh, Ph.D., & Emily Mofield, Ed.D., 2015.

Perspectives of Power © Taylor & Francis Group

Name: _____ Date: _____

Handout 5.3
Big Idea Reflection

What?	**Concepts:** What concepts/ideas are in the text?	
	Generalizations: What broad statement can you make about one or more of these concepts? Make it generalizable beyond the text.	
	Issue: What is the main issue, problem, or conflict?	
So What?	**Insight:** What insight on life is provided from this text?	
	World/Community/Individual: How does this text relate to you, your community, or your world? What question does the author want you to ask yourself?	
Now What?	**Implications:** How should you respond to the ideas in the text? What action should you take? What are the implications of the text? What can you do with this information?	

Created by Emily Mofield, Ed.D., & Tamra Stambaugh, Ph.D., 2015.

Name: _____ Date: _____

Handout 5.4
Reasoning About a Situation or Event

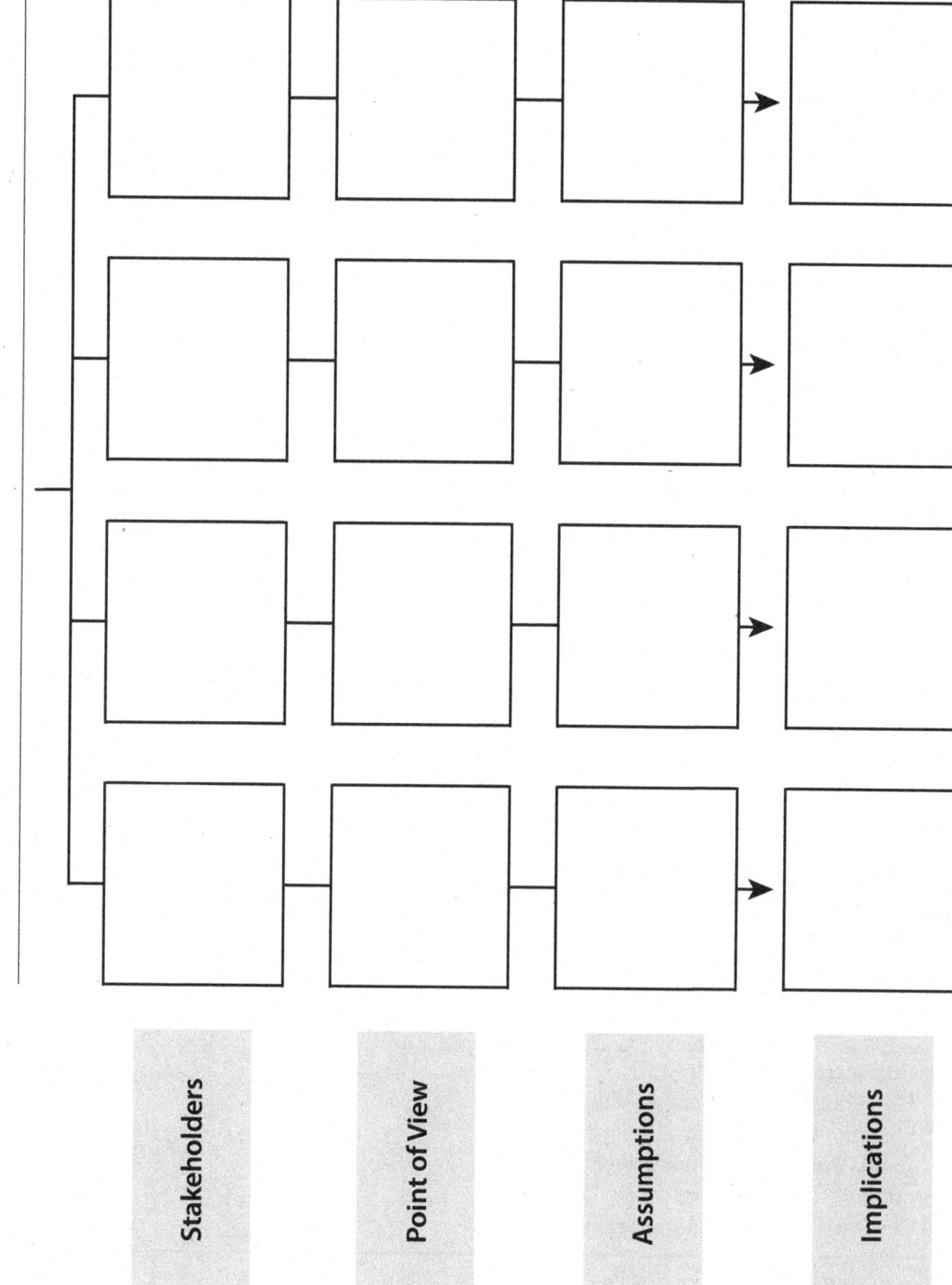

POWER OF PAST, PRESENT, AND FUTURE

Lesson 6

"A Sound of Thunder"
by Ray Bradbury
The Power of Choice

Goals/Objectives

Content: To analyze and interpret texts and art, students will be able to:
- explain with evidence how a work's literary or visual elements contribute to the overall meaning of a work,
- respond to interpretations of texts through a variety of contexts by justifying ideas and providing new information, and
- compare and contrast the impact of various texts, art, experiences, and real-world events on themes and generalizations.

Process: To develop thinking, writing, and communication skills, students will be able to:
- use evidence to develop appropriate inferences, and
- analyze societal or individual conflicts resulting from the struggle for power.

Concept: To understand the theme of power and related generalizations, students will be able to:
- defend "power may be used or abused" with evidence from text, media, or experience;
- explain how the generalizations "power is the ability to influence" and "power is connected to a source" are manifest within various fictional, historical, and personal contexts;
- explain how the omnipresence of power is shown through various art and literary forms within multiple contexts; and
- explain the relationship of power to other universal themes.

Accelerated CCSS ELA Standards

- SL.9-10.1
- SL.9-10.1c
- SL.9-10.1d
- SL.9-10.4
- W.9-10.4
- W.9-10.5
- RL.9-10.1
- RL.9-10.2
- RL.9-10.3

Perspectives of Power

- RL.9-10.4

Materials

- Student copies of "A Sound of Thunder" by Ray Bradbury (*Note:* Some may interpret the ending of the story as a character committing suicide. Please handle this issue with discretion.)
- 7–8 dominoes per group of 3–4 students (optional)
- Audio from Holst's *Planets* (optional)
- Handout 6.1: Blank Literary Analysis Wheel
- Handout 6.2: Big Idea Reflection (optional)
- Handout 6.3: Reasoning About a Situation or Event
- Rubric 1: Product Rubric (Appendix C)

Introductory Activities

1. **Engage students in a quick debate.** *Are our lives controlled by choices or fate?* Students may stand on either side of the room (choices versus fate) to argue their point of view.
2. Ask students: *Have you ever thought of how one choice has a profound effect on history? Small choices can have lasting effects. For example, Rosa Parks's choosing not to give up her bus seat to a White passenger had profound historical implications. What other examples can you think of where consequences for one small action resulted in significant differences in the future?* Optional: Students may discuss domino effects in small groups using 7–8 dominoes to explain the multiple effects.
3. Preteach the following vocabulary. Students may sort vocabulary words into words they know, think they know, or don't know. Students can also note the connotations of these words.
    - **Annihilate:** To destroy completely
    - **Paradox:** A statement that seems impossible, but is true
    - **Resilient:** Rebounding readily
    - **Remit:** Send money in a hurry
    - **Undulate:** Wavelike motion
    - **Expendable:** Not worth keeping
    - **Primeval:** Resembling the early stages of the history of the world
    - **Subliminal:** Below the level of consciousness

Read Text

1. Assign students to read Bradbury's short story "A Sound of Thunder" (available online). Students may read silently or you may conduct a scaled-down version of reader's theater. Students are assigned parts and read at the appropriate time. Students can be savvy to know when to speak and when not to speak. The narrator reads everything not in quotes. Assign the following parts:
   - Narrator (can change every page)
   - Eckels
   - Travis
   - Lesperance
   - Other people with small lines (the official, man behind the desk).
   - Playing music in the background (e.g., selections from *Planets* by Holst) will add to the effect of the story (optional).

2. As students read, ask them to note Bradbury's use of language. Ask them to underline or sticky note at least four instances of creative figurative language (use of similes, personification, metaphors) and consider their purpose within the story.

Text-Dependent Questions

Select from the following text-dependent questions for leading a Socratic seminar or class discussion:
- Citing examples from the text, what specific phrases does Bradbury use to create a mood of uneasiness?
- How does Bradbury establish the idea of time travel through imagery?
- Citing examples from the text, what can you infer about Eckel's motivation to go on the Time-Travel Safari?
- Identify some of the imagery and figurative language Bradbury uses to describe the dinosaur. How does this language affect the tension in the story?
- Indirect characterization is when an author develops the character through dialogues, actions, appearances, thoughts, and other character reactions. How does Bradbury use indirect characterization to develop Eckel's character? Cite evidence from the text.
- Trace the times the word "thunder" is used in the story. To what is it referring each time? Why is this word choice important to the development of the story?
- What do Travis's actions toward Eckels reveal about Travis's character?

- What is significant about the butterfly being the cause of long-term consequences? Why not a worm or ant? (Sample response: Butterflies represent change, which is a major idea in the story. The term "butterfly effect" was established from this story. It is defined as the sensitive dependence on initial conditions. This theory notes that even the flap of a butterfly wing could create conditions in the atmosphere to accelerate a tornado in one area and prevent a tornado in another area.)
- Upon returning to the present, the narrator states, "The room was there as they had left it, but not the same as they had left it. The same man sat behind the desk. But the same man did not quite sit behind the same desk." What effect does this word choice and style have on the mood? Why is this important to the development of the plot?
- Why was it important that the story took place in prehistory rather than medieval days? What effect does it have on the story?
- What is Bradbury's view of fate? Support your answer with textual evidence.
- What was the "sound of thunder?" (This should elicit considerable debate. Some may argue that it is Travis committing suicide, Travis killing Eckels, or Travis killing a dinosaur.) During discussion, students must justify their opinions with evidence from the text.

Literary Analysis

1. In pairs, small groups, or whole group, guide students in analyzing the story using Handout 6.1: Blank Literary Analysis Wheel. Lead students through a basic discussion of each literary element, then emphasize the interaction of the elements with more complex questions. Students can take notes on the wheel and draw arrows to illustrate connections between the various elements.
2. Focus on the following complex questions:
    - How does the setting contribute to the conflict of the story?
    - How does the point of view (e.g., third person limited) influence the mood of the story? How does this influence the reader's interpretation of the ending? If written in a different point of view, what information might we know or not know?
    - How does Bradbury's use of figurative language contribute to the tone of the story?

The following notes may be helpful in guiding students through the analysis:
- **Themes:** The power of choices, cause-effect, time, and regret.
- **Symbols:** The butterfly (a foreshadowing of change). The term "butterfly-effect" was established from this story. It is defined as the sensitive depen-

dence on initial conditions. This theory notes that even the flap of a butterfly wing could create conditions in the atmosphere to accelerate a tornado in one area and prevent a tornado in another area.
- **Tone:** Foreboding, ominous, serious.
- **Point of View:** Third person limited—the reader is mostly connected to Eckels as we know some of his thoughts/feelings. Experiencing from his perspective rather than Travis's brings ambiguity to the ending.

Big Idea Reflection

(Optional) Distribute Handout 6.2: Big Idea Reflection for relating the text to real life (in whole group, small groups, or pairs).
- **Concepts:** Conflict, change, fate, choice.
- **Generalizations:** What generalization about power do you see as most evident in the story? What other generalizations can be made?
- **Problem:** Fate versus choice. Key learning concept: Bradbury's message is that personal *choices* have more *power* than *fate*.
- **Insight:** Small changes have large effects.
- **World/Community/Individual:** Individual—the choices I make today have the power to affect my future in profound ways.
- **Implications:** What are the implications of knowing that choice is more powerful than fate on my life?

In-Class Activities to Deepen Learning

1. Use Handout 6.3: Reasoning About a Situation or Event to explore various interpretations of the ending, "What is the sound of thunder?" Figure 6.1 provides some sample responses.
2. Divide students into groups of 4–5. Assign groups to create a skit of 1–2 particular scenes in the story.
   - **Group 1:** Change the point of view
   - **Group 2:** Change the setting
   - **Group 3:** Change a character's motivation and values

   If there are more than three groups, create your own changes, or repeat the suggested ones. This activity will help students understand the effects of literary elements on a story. Students should perform the skits in front of the class.

3. Assign specific excerpts from the text and have students paint/draw the scene based on the literary details Bradbury provides.

Perspectives of Power

Stakeholders	Those who think Travis committed suicide	Those who think Travis killed Eckels	Those who think Travis killed a dinosaur	Other interpretations
Point of View	Textual evidence to support this point of view.	Textual evidence to support this point of view.	Textual evidence to support this point of view.	Textual evidence to support this point of view.
Assumptions	Travis is deeply upset and cannot live in this world with the mistakes that were made.	Travis is angry at Eckels for his mistake and wants to seek revenge.	One small choice affected the world so greatly, dinosaurs continue to exist in the present.	Varies.
Implications*	Bradbury leaves the reader with a sense of regret.	Bradbury leaves the reader thinking about the power of revenge.	Bradbury leaves the reader contemplating the ideas of the butterfly effect.	The reader is pulled into the story from the suspense of the scenario.

*Regarding each point of view, what are the implications or consequences of the how we interpreted the ending?

Figure 6.1. *What is the "Sound of Thunder"?* Sample responses.

Concept Connections

Discuss connections to power by asking the following questions. Students may reflect on concept connections using Handout 1.4: Concept Organizer, continued from previous lessons. Figure 6.2 may be helpful in guiding discussion.
- How does choice relate to power?
- In what ways was the "power of choice" abused?

Choice-Based Differentiated Products

Students may choose one of the following independent products to complete (*Note*: Use Rubric 1: Product Rubric in Appendix C to assess student products):
- Imagine how stepping on a butterfly actually caused the effects described in the story. Create a sequence that shows the change that takes place from

Power is the ability to influence.
Choices are a powerful force. (Butterfly affected history.) Small choices will have large effects on influencing history.
Power is connected to a source.
Power to change the future was connected to the source of choice. Eckel's choosing to go off the path affected history.
Power can be used or abused.
Students may argue the power of choice was abused by the characters.
Examine the relationship between power and another concept.
Power is present in the choices made. In relationships, someone always dominates. The presence of power will change the future.

Figure 6.2. Sample student responses to power generalizations.

- a dying butterfly to the election of Deutscher as president. These can be sequenced in at least 20 steps as a flowchart, list, or diagram.
- Using the principles of the butterfly effect, develop a sequence of how the oil spill of 2010 (or any other environmental catastrophe) will affect the future 200 years from now. Create a flowchart that shows the powerful long-term implications for multiple groups of people.
- Research more about the butterfly effect. Are these reasonable theories? In what ways are they applied to fields and disciplines? Develop a presentation and teach the class about the contributions of this theory on fields of study.
- Imagine how your life would be different if a single choice you (or someone else) made had the power to alter your present life. Write in third person limited a 1–2 page creative scenario describing this alternate world.

ELA Practice Tasks

Assign one of the following tasks as a performance-based assessment for this lesson:

- How does the narrator's point of view affect the reader's response to "Sound of Thunder?" In an explanatory essay, describe how the point of view influences suspense for the reader. Provide textual evidence to support your answer.
- In an argumentative essay, describe Bradbury's position on the role of fate versus choice. Cite textual evidence to support your claim.

	Inference From Evidence
0	Provides no response.
1	Response is limited, vague, and/or inaccurate. There is no justification for answers given.
2	Response is accurate, but lacks adequate explanation. Response includes some justification about the conflict and character.
3	Response is accurate and makes sense. Response includes some justification about the conflict and character.
4	Response is accurate, insightful, interpretive, and well written. Response includes thoughtful justification about the conflict and character.

Figure 6.3. Scoring guidelines for Lesson 6 formative assessment.

Formative Assessment

1. Ask students to respond to the following prompt in a single paragraph: *What can you infer about Eckels's character from the following: "Get me out of here," said Eckels. "It was never like this before. I was always sure I'd come through alive. I had good guides, good safaris, and safety. This time, I figured wrong. I've met my match and admit it. This is too much for me to get hold of...." How does this relate to the conflict?*
2. Use the scoring guidelines in Figure 6.3 to evaluate students' assessments.

Name: _____ Date: _____

Handout 6.1
Blank Literary Analysis Wheel

Directions: Draw arrows across elements to show connections.

Text: _____

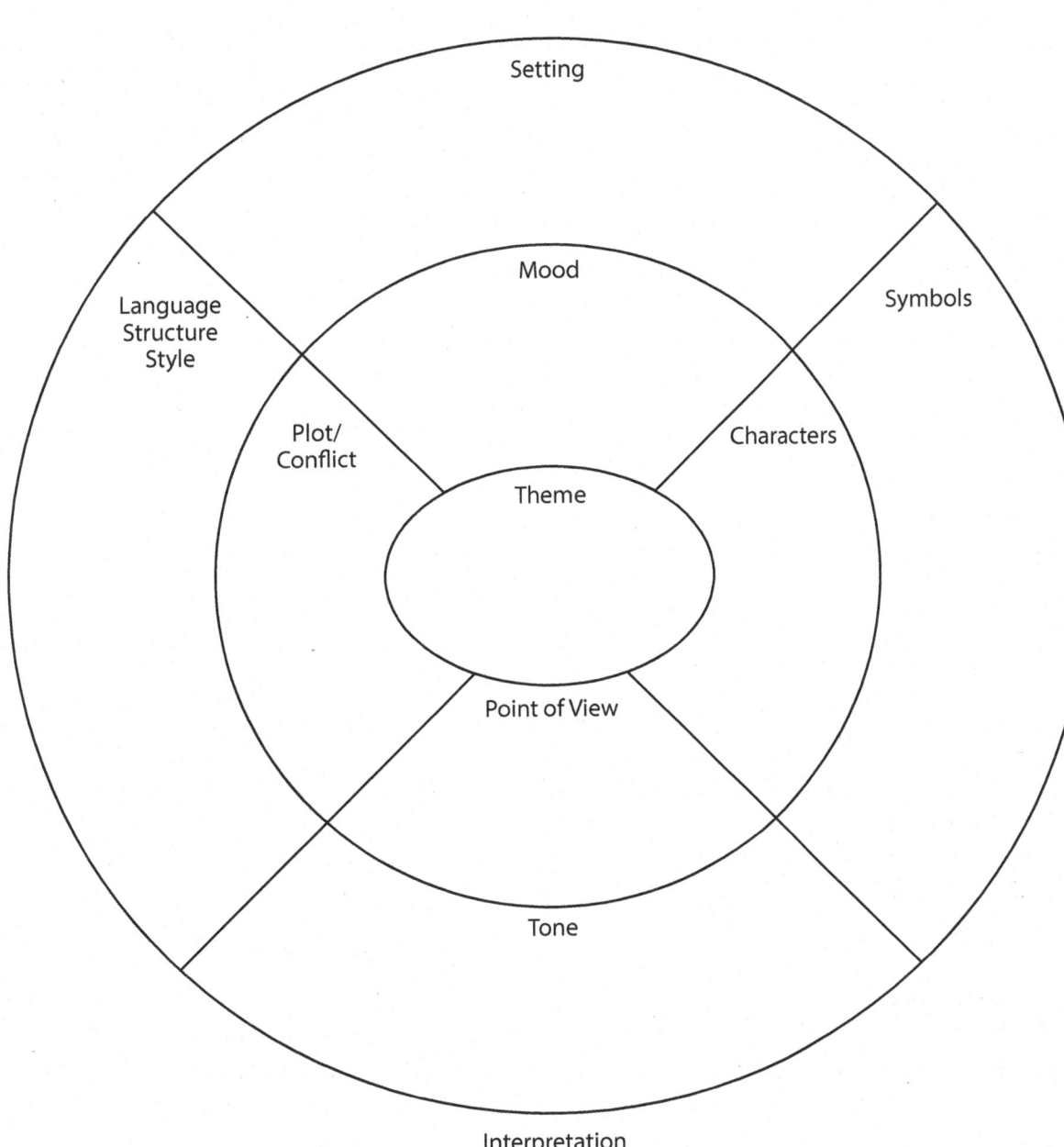

Created by Tamra Stambaugh, Ph.D., & Emily Mofield, Ed.D., 2015.

Name: _____ Date: _____

Handout 6.2
Big Idea Reflection

What?	**Concepts:** What concepts/ideas are in the text?	
	Generalizations: What broad statement can you make about one or more of these concepts? Make it generalizable beyond the text.	
	Issue: What is the main issue, problem, or conflict?	
So What?	**Insight:** What insight on life is provided from this text?	
	World/Community/Individual: How does this text relate to you, your community, or your world? What question does the author want you to ask yourself?	
Now What?	**Implications:** How should you respond to the ideas in the text? What action should you take? What are the implications of the text? What can you do with this information?	

Created by Emily Mofield, Ed.D., & Tamra Stambaugh, Ph.D., 2015.

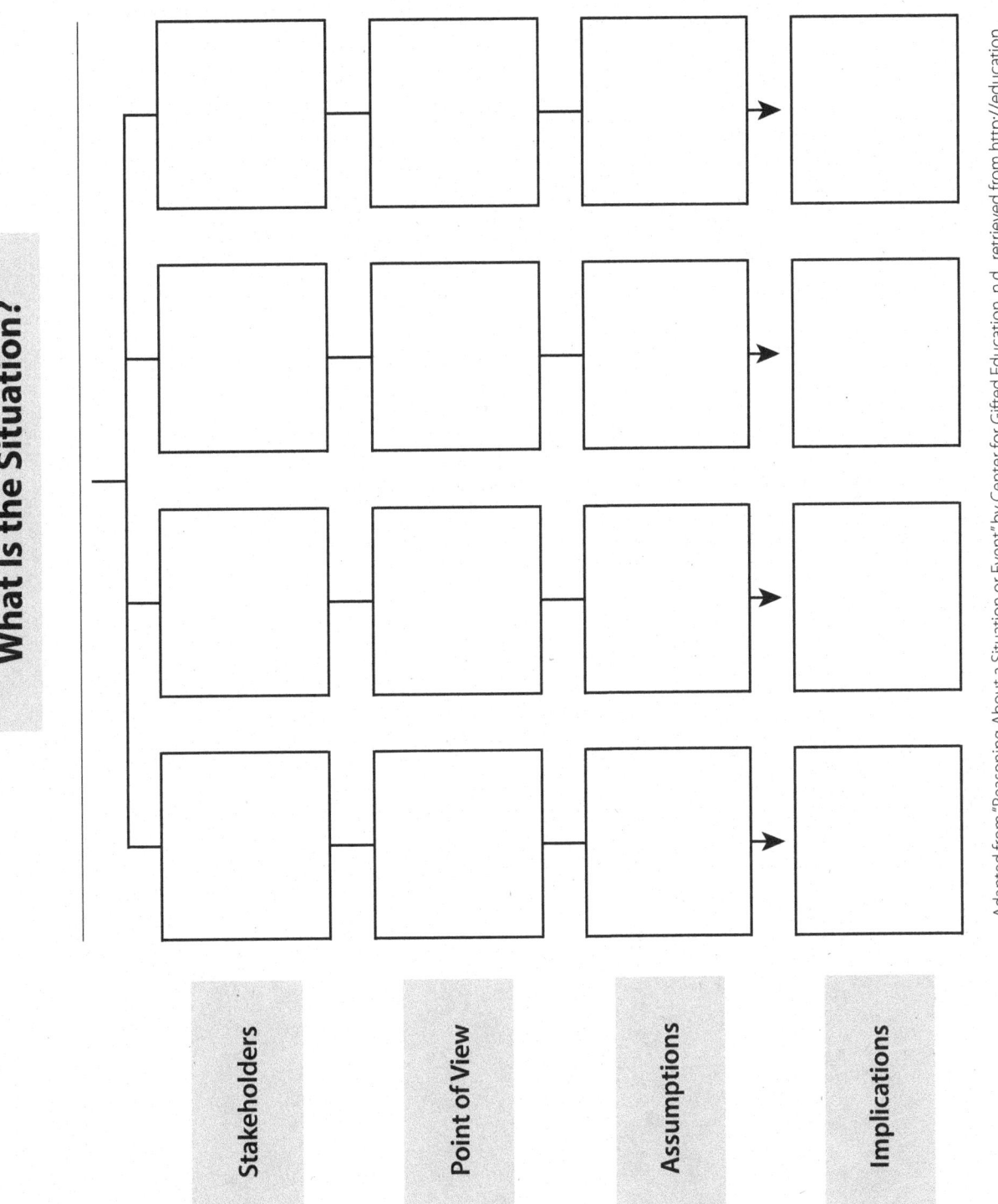

Lesson

"The Persistence of Memory" by Salvador Dali
The Power of Memory

Goals/Objectives

Content: To analyze and interpret texts and art, students will be able to:
- explain with evidence how literary or visual elements contribute to the overall meaning of a work,
- respond to interpretations of texts through a variety of contexts by justifying ideas and providing new information, and
- compare and contrast the impact of various texts, art, experiences, and real-world events on themes and generalizations.

Process: To develop thinking, writing, and communication skills, students will be able to:
- use evidence to develop appropriate inferences, and
- analyze societal or individual conflicts resulting from the struggle for power.

Concept: To understand the theme of power and related generalizations, students will be able to:
- defend "power may be used or abused" with evidence from text, media, or experience;
- explain how the generalizations "power is the ability to influence" and "power is connected to a source" are manifest within various fictional, historical, and personal contexts;
- explain how the omnipresence of power is shown through various art and literary forms within multiple contexts; and
- explain the relationship of power to other universal themes.

Accelerated CCSS ELA Standards

- SL.8.2
- SL.9-10.1
- SL.9-10.1c
- SL.9-10.1d
- SL.9-10.4
- W.9-10.4
- W.9-10.5
- RI.9-10.7

Perspectives of Power

Materials

- Copy of Salvador Dali's "Persistence of Memory" retrieved online
- Student copies of "Persistence of Memory" (optional, retrieved online)
- Other samples of surrealism such as "Son of Man" by René Magritte and "On the Other Side" by Angelina Kokovina to show on projector
- Handout 1.4: Concept Organizer (continued from previous lessons)
- Handout 7.1: Blank Visual Analysis Wheel
- Handout 7.2: Big Idea Reflection
- Rubric 1: Product Rubric (Appendix C)

Note: You may want to consult online descriptions of "Persistence of Memory" from the Museum of Modern Art (MoMA) in New York City.

Introductory Activities

1. Introduce surrealism, showing examples of surrealistic paintings.
    - Show "Son of Man" by René Magrite. Ask: *Do you like this painting? Why is this art? What makes art actually art? Does this painting relate to any ideas we have encountered in this unit so far?* (Students may make a connection with the concept of temptation from "Blue Beard.")
    - Show "On the Other Side" by Angelina Kokovina. Ask: *How is this painting like the previous painting?* (Sample response: They both portray unrealistic aspects of reality. They project dream-like states.)
    - Explain to students that these works are categorized as surrealism. Surrealism reflects ideas of the unconscious. Surrealistic artists claim that their works reveal the truest reality, the authentic self—the subconscious. Surrealistic art will portray paradoxical visual statements (visual inconsistencies that cannot exist in reality).
    - Show "Butterfly" by Salvador Dali. Ask: *How is this painting relevant to another lesson from this unit?* (Students may make a connection with "A Sound of Thunder" with the visual representation of a butterfly.)

2. Introduce Salvador Dali. Show a portrait of Dali (some are interesting, particularly the ones with his flamboyant moustache). Give some brief background information: *Dali is a famous Spanish Surrealist artist, who lived from 1904 to 1989. He was highly influenced by Freudian psychology (especially the role of the subconscious). He is known for being very eccentric and for his attention-seeking behaviors with the public.*

View Art

1. Show "Persistence of Memory" by Salvador Dali.
2. Ask every student to respond in round robin (no discussion yet) to the following. This round-robin response will allow students to see various aspects of the painting before analyzing it. Say: *I see something you don't see.* Ask students to say one thing they see in the painting that they notice.
3. Lead a discussion by asking the following questions:
   - What's interesting about the clocks? (Sample response: They are melting.)
   - Which clock is different? What is on the clock? (Sample response: Ants.)
   - What is on the clock on the table? (Sample response: Fly.) What could this mean?
   - What is the significance of the tree? Why did Dali paint it this way? (Sample response: No leaves, no life, hollow hole.)
   - What is the figure in the middle? Is this a favorable object?
   - What features does it have? (Sample response: Eyelashes—perhaps it is half asleep, half awake.)
   - What objects are in the shade and what is shown in the light? (Sample response: The landscape and small right pebble are in the light; the other surrealistic objects are in the shade—perhaps showing a distinction between reality and nonreality.)
   - How can we categorize the objects? (Sample response: Hard and soft objects; perhaps the hard objects are aspects of reality while the soft objects cannot exist in reality.)
   - Why is it important that a clock is on the ambiguous middle figure?
   - What title would you give this painting? Why?

Visual Analysis

1. Use Handout 7.1: Blank Visual Analysis Wheel to guide discussion on Dali's "Persistence of Memory." Focus on separate elements first, then emphasize more complex questions throughout (e.g., what *techniques* did Dali use to create these *images* and what is important about where they are in the painting?). Students can take notes on the wheel and draw arrows to illustrate connections between the various elements.
2. Sample questions and responses to lead analysis include the following. Some information is adapted from Authentic Society, available at: http://www.authenticsociety.com/about/thepersistenceofmemory_dali.
   - **Context/Purpose:**
     - *What is the context of this work?* This is one of Dali's most famous works, painted in 1931. Dali called his paintings "hand-dreamed photographs."

- *What do you think his purpose/motive is in creating this?* To express ideas about dreams, reality, and the power of memory on our subconscious (Students may not realize this until after analyzing the painting.).

- **Point of View/Assumptions:**
  - *What assumptions (beliefs taken for granted by the artist) does the artist have regarding his work? What does he assume about time?* He assumes the viewer will have various interpretations and reactions.

- **Images/Technique/Structure:**
  - **Images:** *What could the images (discussed earlier) symbolize?*
    - The ambiguous figure in the middle may symbolize a projection of lifelessness, like a dead fish brought up to shore. Some critics say this is Dali's face profile folded in half. Perhaps the viewer projects his or her feelings onto the ambiguous figure and it is whatever the viewer's subconscious projects onto it.
    - The melting pocketwatches may symbolize the melting of time; time is relative, not fixed. Some have theorized that Dali is reflecting Einstein's theory of relativity, but Dali himself rejected this and said his clocks were more like Camembert cheese melting. Only in dreams is time distorted, so this surrealistic dreamlike world portrays that time can stop in dreams.
    - The orange clock may symbolize a hard substance, the reality of time, and that time outside of dreams can quickly be eaten away.
    - The ants are "eating away" time, symbolizing humans' anxiety toward passing time.
    - The fly may symbolize that time is fleeting.
    - The time of day—sunset—may symbolize the end of life or approaching darkness.

  - **Technique:** *What techniques does the artist use to enhance visual effects? What colors are most prominent and how does this contribute to the meaning? How does his use of light contribute to his ideas?* He shows elements of softness, creating an effect of "melting." Unlike other artists, Dali paints to cast light into the spaces that are typically unseen (e.g., the valleys in the background), representative of illuminating the subconscious.
  - **Structure:** *What makes the structure of the painting different from typical landscape art?* Typical landscape art focuses on the beauty

of scenery, while the focus in this painting is on an ambiguous being and deformed objects against a naked landscape.

- **Emotions/Technique:**
  - *How would you categorize the mood of the painting and why?* Rotting, decaying, somber.
  - *How did he create this effect (technique)? What emotions are evoked?*

- **Artist Background/Technique/Structure:**
  - *Refer to information provided within the lesson. What is special about his use of techniques?* Note his use of visual paradoxes that cannot exist in reality.

- **Main Idea:**
  - *What is Dali conveying about life in this painting?* We must recognize the passing of time in our lives. Time will run out and all things will end. Memories persist in our sleep while time continues.
  - *What is Dali's main idea?* As humans, we must face the power of memory, time, the unconscious; the conflict of reality versus dreams.

- **Implications:**
  - *What are the implications of viewing this art?* The viewer's subconscious projects reality. This piece is one of the most famous pieces of art and is now at the Museum of Modern Art in New York City. His ideas allow viewers to think about reality in a different way.

- **Evaluation:**
  - *Do you like this art? Would you hang it in your home? Does it make you think? Was the artist successful in presenting his ideas?* Justify your answers with evidence.

Big Idea Reflection (Optional)

Use Handout 7.2: Big Idea Reflection to help students transfer knowledge of the art to real life.

- **Concepts:** Time, reality, memory, subconscious.
- **Generalizations:** What generalization about power do you see as most evident in the story? What other generalizations can be made?
- **Problem:** Reality versus dreams. Time is fleeting.
- **Insight:** Time is a powerful force in our lives.

Perspectives of Power

- **World/Community/Individual:** How do I value my time? Why do some personal memories persist more than others? What does this reveal about me? What anxieties do I have regarding the passage of time in my own life?
- **Implications:** How might I personally respond to the ideas in this painting?

In-Class Activities to Deepen Learning

1. Have students create a short story or poem to go with this artwork. Students may work in groups to develop their works.
2. Distribute black-and-white copies of the painting. Ask students to add their own color and additional images to add additional meaning to the work. Students should write a new explanation of how their alteration creates additional meaning.

Concept Connections

Discuss connections to power by asking the following questions. Students may reflect on concept connections using Handout 1.4: Concept Organizer, continued from previous lessons. Figure 7.1 may be helpful in guiding discussion.

- How is the subconscious related to power?
- What does this painting reveal about time and power?
- What is Dali's message about the use and abuse of time?

Choice-Based Differentiated Products

Students may choose one of the following independent products to complete (*Note*: Use Rubric 1: Product Rubric in Appendix C to assess student products):

- Apply a Visual Analysis Wheel to Dali's work "Disappearing Bust of Voltaire" (1941). Complete a Visual Analysis Wheel, and turn in a written response explaining how the artist's technique, structure, use of images, artist's background knowledge, and assumptions contribute to the message and implications of the work. Relate the work to the idea of power within your analysis.
- Think of a song that matches the mood of the painting "The Persistence of Memory." Explain why the song complements the painting with at least four supporting features of the music (specific lyrics, use of elements in music, etc.). Include at least one connection to the idea of power.
- Explore surrealism in another form (e.g., music, politics, philosophy). After browsing, develop five broad questions relating to surrealism and answer them in a visual presentation. In an essay or presentation, explain how this movement powerfully influenced culture and society.

Power is the ability to influence.	
Our subconscious has a powerful ability to influence our lives.	
Power is connected to a source.	
Power is connected to time.	
Power may be used or abused.	
Our use of time can be used or abused in our own lives. Do we appreciate time?	
Examine the relationship between power and another concept.	
Students may examine the connection to time, memory, subconscious, and/or anxiety.	

Figure 7.1. Sample student responses to power generalizations.

- Create your own piece of surrealistic art. Incorporate features of surrealism including portrayal of the power of subconscious thoughts, contrasts using paradoxical visual statements, and dream-like features.

ELA Practice Tasks

Assign the following task as a performance-based assessment for this lesson: *Relate "The Sound of Thunder" by Bradbury to Dali's "The Persistence of Memory." In what ways do they convey a similar message? In an essay, cite at least two examples from each work to support your answer.*

Formative Assessment

1. Ask students to respond to the following prompt in a single paragraph: *What is Dali's main idea in "The Persistence of Memory" and how is it supported?*
2. Use the scoring guidelines in Figure 7.2 to evaluate students' assessments.

	Message and Evidence
0	Provides no response.
1	Response is limited, vague, and/or inaccurate. Only the message is mentioned with little support.
2	Response lacks adequate explanation. Some parts of the response are correct, but the response only vaguely addresses the artist's main idea and evidence. Response lacks support.
3	Response is accurate and makes sense. Response includes 1–2 examples of support for the main idea.
4	Response is accurate, insightful, and well-written. Response includes 2–3 examples of support for the main idea.

Figure 7.2. Scoring guidelines for Lesson 7 formative assessment.

Name: _____ Date: _____

Handout 7.1
Blank Visual Analysis Wheel

Directions: Draw arrows across elements to show connections.

Art Piece: _____

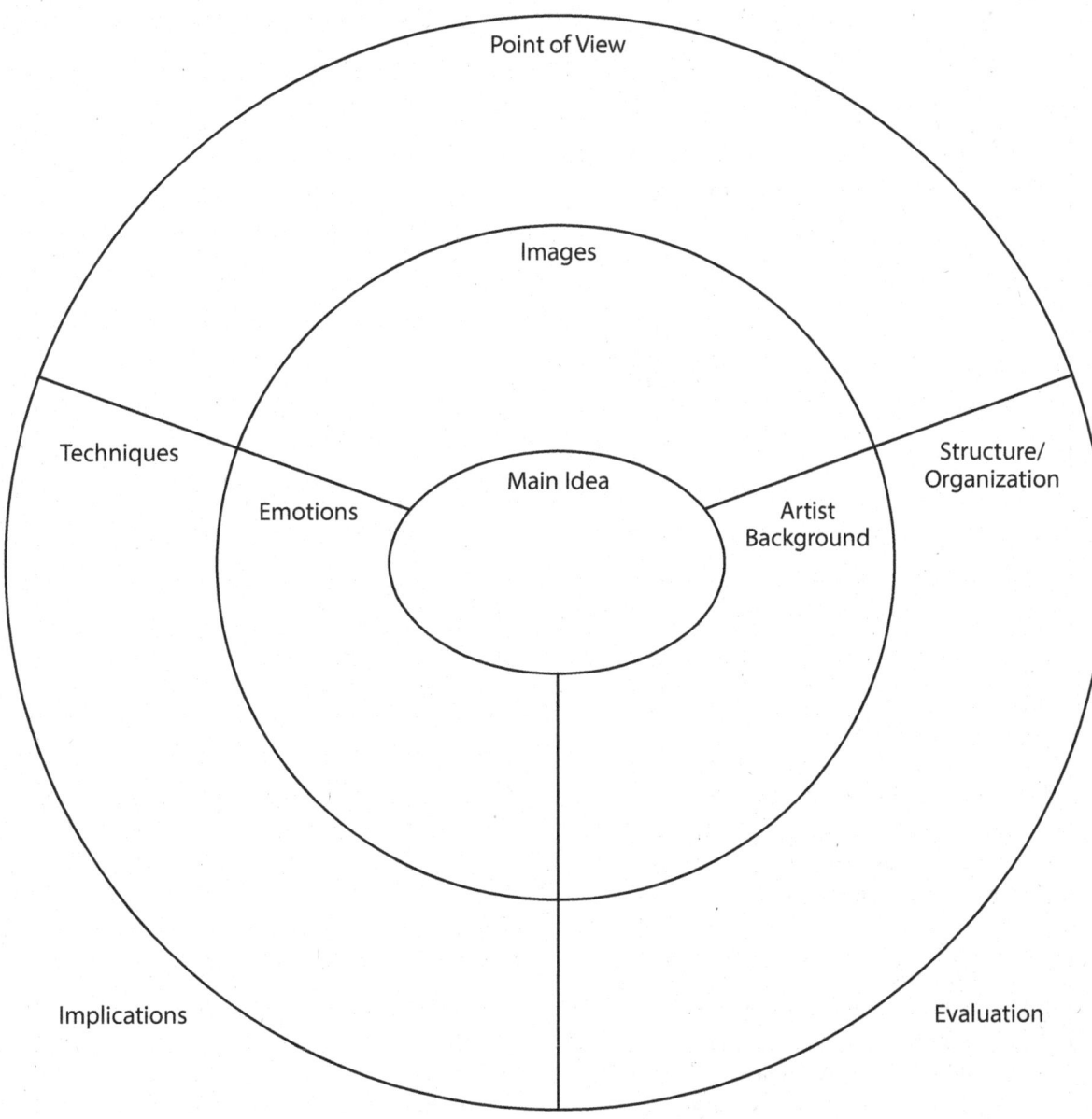

Created by Tamra Stambaugh, Ph.D., & Emily Mofield, Ed.D., 2015.

Name: _____ Date: _____

Handout 7.2
Big Idea Reflection

What?	**Concepts:** What concepts/ideas are in the text?	
	Generalizations: What broad statement can you make about one or more of these concepts? Make it generalizable beyond the text.	
	Issue: What is the main issue, problem, or conflict?	
So What?	**Insight:** What insight on life is provided from this text?	
	World/Community/Individual: How does this text relate to you, your community, or your world? What question does the author want you to ask yourself?	
Now What?	**Implications:** How should you respond to the ideas in the text? What action should you take? What are the implications of the text? What can you do with this information?	

Created by Emily Mofield, Ed.D., & Tamra Stambaugh, Ph.D., 2015.

Lesson 8

"The Wild Swans at Coole"
by W. B. Yeats
The Power of Nostalgia

Goals/Objectives

Content: To analyze and interpret texts and art, students will be able to:
- explain with evidence how literary or visual elements contribute to the overall meaning of a work,
- respond to interpretations of texts through a variety of contexts by justifying ideas and providing new information, and
- compare and contrast the impact of various texts, art, experiences, and real-world events on themes and generalizations.

Process: To develop thinking, writing, and communication skills, students will be able to:
- use evidence to develop appropriate inferences, and
- analyze societal or individual conflicts resulting from the struggle for power.

Concept: To understand the theme of power and related generalizations, students will be able to:
- defend "power may be used or abused" with evidence from text, media, or experience;
- explain how the generalizations "power is the ability to influence" and "power is connected to a source" are manifest within various fictional, historical, and personal contexts;
- explain how the omnipresence of power is shown through various art and literary forms within multiple contexts; and
- explain the relationship of power to other universal themes.

Accelerated CCSS ELA Standards

- RL.9-10.1
- RL.9-10.2
- RL.9-10.4
- RL.9-10.5
- RL.9-10.6
- W.9-10.4
- SL.9-10.1c
- SL.9-10.1d
- SL.9-10.4

Perspectives of Power

- SL.9-10.1

Materials

- Lyrics/Music "100 years" by Five for Fighting, available at http://www.azlyrics.com/lyrics/fiveforfighting/100years.html
- "Nothing Gold Can Stay" by Robert Frost available at, http://www.poets.org/poetsorg/poem/nothing-gold-can-stay
- Handout 1.4: Concept Organizer (continued from previous lessons)
- Handout 8.1: "The Wild Swans at Coole" by W. B. Yeats
- Handout 8.2: Blank Literary Analysis Wheel
- (Optional) Handout 8.3 Big Idea Reflection
- Rubric 1: Product Rubric (Appendix C)

Introductory Activities

1. Play the game, "What's in the bag?" Place a small mirror inside a bag. Students must ask yes/no questions to guess what is in the bag. When students guess "mirror," ask: *How is a mirror like poetry?*
2. Guide students to understand that one of the purposes of poetry and other literature is to reflect life or an aspect of the human experience.

Read Text

1. Distribute Handout 8.1: "The Wild Swans at Coole" by W. B. Yeats. As it is read during the first reading, students should underline words they do not know. Make sure students know these terms:
   - **Brimming:** Filled completely as if about to spill out
   - **Clamorous:** Noisy, loud

2. Ask: *What feelings can we associate with some of the words in this poem? What emotions do some of the words/lines evoke in us? Are the connotations positive or negative?*
3. Ask students to read the poem again with the purpose of understanding what the poem is actually about.
4. Assign pairs of students to paraphrase assigned stanzas.

Text-Dependent Questions

Select from the following text-dependent questions for leading a Socratic seminar or class discussion:

- What is this poem about? Is it about growing older or is it about losing love? (Hold a mini-debate about textual evidence that supports both sides.)
- Does the author enjoy watching the swans? How do you know?
- How does Yeats describe the swans? What do they represent?
- What emotions does the narrator have? How do these emotions change throughout the poem?
- What patterns do you notice? (Help students notice examples of alliteration, rhyme scheme, and patterns of "change" symbols such as autumn and twilight, etc.)

Optional: Show a video version of the poem to enhance understanding (many can be found on YouTube).

Literary Analysis

1. Guide students in analyzing the poem, using Handout 8.2: Blank Literary Analysis Wheel (in small groups or whole group). Lead students through a basic discussion of each literary element, then emphasize the interaction of the elements with more complex questions. Students can take notes on the wheel and draw arrows to illustrate connections between elements.
2. Focus on the following complex questions:
    - How does the setting serve as a symbol within the poem?
    - How do the symbols contribute to the theme(s) of the poem?
    - How does language shape the tone of the poem?

The following notes may be helpful in guiding students through the analysis:
- **Theme:** Themes of the poem may include losing the "ideal," change, nostalgia, or aging. Swans are usually monogamous—it is important that there are only 59 swans—one swan is without a partner; an "ideal" is missing.
- **Setting:** The season autumn gives a sense of change—moving from summer to winter, alluding to something dying or something being lost—twilight also conveys this meaning.
- **Symbols:** Symbols may include swans, the "ideal"/the something that can be lost; autumn/twilight, change/moving toward the end of something (e.g., moving toward winter/night); and the lake, time in your life.
- **Tone:** Yeats's tone toward the swans is admiring, nostalgic, and/or regretful.
- **Language:** Note the use of alliteration—"wander where they will"— that conveys a sense of movement.
- **Context (consider sharing after discussion of poem):** W. B. Yeats, a well-known Irish poet, wrote the poem in 1917 at Coole Lake in Coole, Ireland. Yeats had also had a relationship with a woman, Maud Goode, whom he

proposed to several times, and she said no. She married someone else in 1903. Also, the poem was written right after World War I (1914–1918). Ireland was now different from what it once was before World War I. What pieces of evidence in the poem show these influences?

Big Idea Reflection (Optional)

Use Handout 8.3: Big Idea Reflection to help students transfer knowledge of the poem to real life.

- **Concepts:** Nostalgia, regret, love, change, appreciation of past and present.
- **Generalizations:** What generalization about power do you see as most evident in the story? What other generalizations can be made?
- **Insight:** The "ideal, flawless" things in our life will eventually go away; change is a part of our lives . . . youth, beauty, childhood, family, love; "Don't cry because it's over, smile because it happened"—Dr. Seuss.
- **Problem:** Saying goodbye to something you hold dear; confronting a major change in your life.
- **World/Community/Individual:** Individual—What are the flawless ideals I want to hold on to in my life? Will they change? How can I spend my time most valuably in the present? Students may connect by realizing they are saying goodbye to childhood or middle school if moving on to high school. World—our own country is not the same after the 9/11 terrorist attacks. This relates to Yeats's ideas of Ireland changing.
- **Implications:** What can I do to prepare for upcoming change in my own life? What must I consider about the present before it is gone?

In-Class Activities to Deepen Learning

1. Ask students: *What connections can you make with this poem, Bradbury's "A Sound of Thunder," and Dali's "Persistence of Memory?"* Students should see the importance of appreciating the present, reflecting on the past, and contemplating the future in these works—the power and influence of time.
2. Have students show an interpretation of the poem in a creative way. They can present a real-world scenario skit and adapt it so that it not just a literal depiction of the poem; students could also present a human tableau.
3. Assign students a letter in W. B. Yeats's name. Have students write the letter on their paper and create a visual to depict their interpretation of the poem. For example, a student could draw a big Y to be the basis of a tree. The tree could be leafless to represent that something good is now gone and change has occurred.

4. Play the song "100 years" by Five for Fighting (available on YouTube) and/or share the poem "Nothing Gold Can Stay" by Robert Frost (available online). Use a Venn diagram or comparison chart to show specific ways these pieces are similar (see Figure 8.1).

Concept Connections

Use Handout 1.4: Concept Organizer to relate power generalizations to Yeats's poem. Students should list examples about how the work demonstrates some of these generalizations. Figure 8.2 provides possible responses for this lesson; various interpretations are encouraged.

Choice-Based Differentiated Products

Students may choose one of the following independent products to complete (*Note*: Use Rubric 1: Product Rubric in Appendix C to assess student products):

- Write a personal reflection that explains the swans, autumn, and lake in your own life. In what ways are these symbols a part of your life and how has this poem impacted your appreciation for the past and present?
- Think of a song that relates to the poem. In a paragraph or two, explain how the song relates to the poem, citing at least three specific lines from each piece. Relate at least one comparison to the idea of power of past, present, or future.
- Research more about W. B. Yeats's life and read another one of his poems. Conduct a literary analysis on the poem by completing the Literary Analysis Wheel. Write a reflection that describes how you see the influences of his life in his writings. Then, explain which poem is most personally meaningful to you and why.
- Using the same structure as Yeats's poem, write your own poem related to the power of nostalgia and change in your own life. Develop a visual (e.g., illustrations or a collage) to accompany the poem. This may include a collection of favorite memories.
- Paint a picture of the poem using specific details from Yeats's writing. Portray the main message and mood of the poem through your artistic techniques.

ELA Practice Tasks

Assign one of the following tasks as a performance-based assessment for this lesson:

Perspectives of Power

"Wild Swans at Coole"	Comparison	"Nothing Gold Can Stay"
"The trees are in their autumn beauty"	Both show concept of changing seasons, representing change stages in life	"Nature's first green is gold/Her hardest hue to hold"

Figure 8.1. Sample comparison chart.

Power is the ability to influence.
The power of thinking about the past influences us to savor the present.
Power is connected to a source.
The power of this poem is connected to reflecting upon the past and treasuring the present.
Power may be used or abused.
Power of reflection can be used to appreciate the present while we have the "swans" in our lives.
Examine the relationship between power and another concept.
The poem reveals the power of change—we should acknowledge that our lives will change, so appreciate the "ideals" or great things now.

Figure 8.2. Sample student responses to power generalizations.

- In a well-developed essay, compare how Yeats's "The Wild Swans at Coole" and Frost's "Nothing Gold Can Stay" both show the power of losing an ideal, citing relevant textual examples in each poem.
- How effective is Yeats in evoking nostalgia? In a review, support your response with relevant evidence from the poem.

Formative Assessment

1. Ask students to respond to the following prompt in a single paragraph: *What can you infer about the narrator's feelings about the past from the following: "Delight men's eyes when I awake some day to find they have flown away?" How does this relate to the central problem in the poem?*
2. Use the scoring guidelines in Figure 8.3 to evaluate students' assessments.

	Inference From Evidence
0	Provides no response.
1	Response is limited, vague, and/or inaccurate. There is no justification for answers given.
2	Response is accurate, but lacks adequate explanation. Response includes some justification about the conflict.
3	Response is accurate and makes sense. Response includes some justification about the conflict.
4	Response is accurate, insightful, interpretive, and well written. Response includes thoughtful justification about the conflict.

Figure 8.3. Scoring guidelines for Lesson 8 formative assessment.

Name: _____ Date: _____

Handout 8.1
"The Wild Swans at Coole" *by W. B. Yeats*

The trees are in their autumn beauty,
The woodland paths are dry,
Under the October twilight the water
Mirrors a still sky;
Upon the brimming water among the stones
Are nine-and-fifty swans.

The nineteenth autumn has come upon me
Since I first made my count;
I saw, before I had well finished,
All suddenly mount
And scatter wheeling in great broken rings
Upon their clamorous wings.

I have looked upon those brilliant creatures,
And now my heart is sore.
All's changed since I, hearing at twilight,
The first time on this shore,
The bell-beat of their wings above my head,
Trod with a lighter tread.

Unwearied still, lover by lover,
They paddle in the cold
Companionable streams or climb the air;
Their hearts have not grown old;
Passion or conquest, wander where they will,
Attend upon them still.

But now they drift on the still water.
Mysterious, beautiful;
Among what rushes will they build,
By what lake's edge or pool
Delight men's eyes when I awake some day
To find they have flown away?

Name: _____ Date: _____

Handout 8.2
Blank Literary Analysis Wheel

Directions: Draw arrows across elements to show connections.

Text: _____

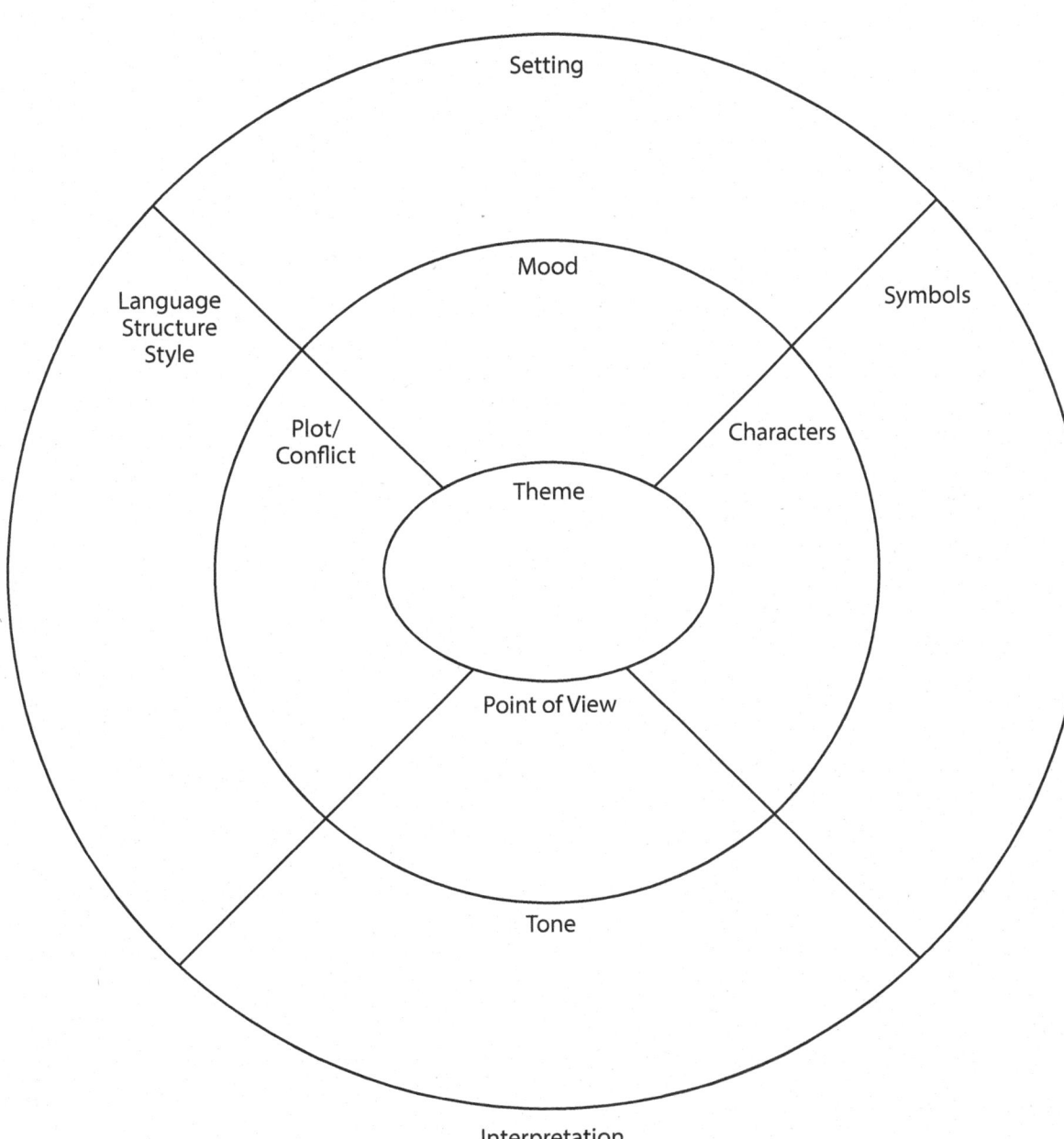

Created by Tamra Stambaugh, Ph.D., & Emily Mofield, Ed.D., 2015.

Name: _____ Date: _____

Handout 8.3
Big Idea Reflection

What?	**Concepts:** What concepts/ideas are in the text?	
	Generalizations: What broad statement can you make about one or more of these concepts? Make it generalizable beyond the text.	
	Issue: What is the main issue, problem, or conflict?	
So What?	**Insight:** What insight on life is provided from this text?	
	World/Community/Individual: How does this text relate to you, your community, or your world? What question does the author want you to ask yourself?	
Now What?	**Implications:** How should you respond to the ideas in the text? What action should you take? What are the implications of the text? What can you do with this information?	

Created by Emily Mofield, Ed.D., & Tamra Stambaugh, Ph.D., 2015.

POWER OF PERSONAL RESPONSE

Lesson 9

"The Pursuit of Disarmament"
by John F. Kennedy
The Power of Cooperation Versus Competition

Goals/Objectives

Content: To analyze and interpret texts and art, students will be able to:
- respond to interpretations of texts through a variety of contexts by justifying ideas and providing new information,
- explain verbally and in writing how a writer develops and supports his claim, and
- identify rhetorical devices that influence effective argumentation within primary source documents and justify why they are effective.

Process: To develop thinking, writing, and communication skills, students will be able to:
- reason through an issue by using multiple points of view, assumptions, and implications to defend a statement or idea;
- use evidence to develop appropriate inferences;
- evaluate the use of effective argumentation;
- analyze purposes, assumptions, and consequences of primary sources within a historical context; and
- analyze societal or individual conflicts resulting from the struggle for power.

Concept: To understand the theme of power and related generalizations, students will be able to:
- defend "power may be used or abused" with evidence from text, media, or experience;
- explain how the generalizations "power is the ability to influence" and "power is connected to a source" are manifest within various fictional, historical, and personal contexts;
- explain how the omnipresence of power is shown through various art and literary forms within multiple contexts; and
- explain the relationship of power to other universal themes.

Perspectives of Power

Accelerated CCSS ELA Standards

- RI.9-10.1
- RI.9-10.2
- RI.9-10.3
- RI.9-10.4
- RI.9-10.5
- RI.9-10.6
- RI.9-10.9
- SL.9-10.1
- SL.9-10.1c
- SL.9-10.1d
- SL.9-10.4
- RH.9-10.1
- RH.9-10.2
- RH.9-10.4
- RH.9-10.5
- RH.9-10.8
- W.9-10.5
- W.9-10.4

Materials

- (Optional) Video of Kennedy's speech, available at http://www.jfklibrary.org/Asset-Viewer/BWC7I4C9QUmLG9J6I8oy8w.aspx
- Two blue poker chips, two red poker chips
- Prisoner's Dilemma video, available at https://www.youtube.com/watch?v=jUTWcYXVR5w
- Handout 9.1: "The Pursuit of Disarmament" by John F. Kennedy
- Handout 9.2: Blank Rhetorical Analysis Wheel
- (Optional) Handout 9.3: Reasoning About a Situation or Event
- Rubric 1: Product Rubric (Appendix C)

Note: You may wish to do some basic background reading on game theory. This is a suggested source: http://sociology.about.com/od/Sociological-Theory/a/Game-Theory.htm

Introductory Activities

1. **Engage students in a quick debate.** Ask: *Which is more beneficial for society: competition or cooperation?* Students may stand on opposite sides of the room to debate their points of view.
2. Play the following game. Divide the class into two teams, each standing on opposite sides of the room. Assign a leader for each group and give each leader an envelope, a blue chip, and a red chip. Each team must unanimously decide whether to put a red chip or blue chip into the envelope. To win, a team must score 18 points or more. There will be only 10 rounds. During each round, the leader will come forward and present the chip decided. Explain that points will be awarded in the following manner:
   - If both teams select a blue chip, both teams receive 3 points.
   - If both teams select a red chip, both teams receive 0 points.

- If one team selects a blue chip and the other team selects a red chip, the team that selected the blue chip receives 0 points, while the team that selected the red chip receives 3 points.

Game Guidelines:
- Group leaders must participate in a conference with teammates prior to each round to ensure that the group will reach a unanimous decision.
- If the teacher discovers a decision made by a team is not unanimous, the team can lose 3 points.
- Play 10 rounds and keep score.

3. Reflect on the game. Ask students:
    - What strategy did you use to decide what color chip to play?
    - What can we learn about the nature of human nature in the game?
    - What does this reveal about the concepts of power? What is more powerful, cooperation or competition?
    - In what circumstances is cooperation a more powerful force?
    - What are the concepts related to each?

    (*Note:* The game is adapted from *Topic Activity Units 2011–12* by Kathy Frazier and Elaine Reynolds, 2011, Melbourne, FL: Future Problem Solving Program International, Inc.)

4. Explain that the game played is a simulation on game theory. Define game theory for students: *Game theory is the study of strategic decision-making in human interaction. Game theory illustrates that players must consider their opponents' strategies when determining their own strategies.*

5. Play Rock-Paper-Scissors.
    - **Series 1:** Ask students to play Rock-Paper-Scissors with a partner. After playing with one partner, the winners will continue with other partners while the loser sits "out" (those who tie are also considered "out"). Continue playing until there is one winner.
    - **Series 2:** Students play with only one partner for 15 tries and keep track of who wins.
    - Following both rounds, ask students: *How did you develop your strategy? Did you have a strategy? Was it different when you played the first time than when you played with just one partner? Would it have been smart to use the same methods throughout the game? Why is it better to apply a mixed-method approach?* Explain that this is a zero-sum game (one person's loss is equal to the other person's gain). Show students a matrix that demonstrates the strategy options (see Figure 9.1).

	Rock	Paper	Scissors
Rock	0, 0	-1, 1	-1, 1
Paper	1, -1	0, 0	1, -1
Scissors	-1, 1	1, -1	0, 0

Figure 9.1. Sample Rock-Paper-Scissors strategy matrix.

6. Show video to help students understand the "Prisoner's Dilemma." Several YouTube videos are available. "Prisoner's Dilemma" illustrates the interaction of cooperation and self-interest—the players are drawn into a bad outcome by each following his own best private interests. Then, re-enact the dilemma in another scenario with two students in the class.

7. Ask: *How is The Prisoner's Dilemma a paradox?* Explain that the paradox is that if the two individuals act for their own best interest, then neither will achieve the most ideal outcome. If one follows the logical process of helping oneself, then this person is in a worse state than if they had cooperated with each other. For further research, see The Concise Encyclopedia of Economics entry on game theory at http://www.econlib.org/library/Enc/GameTheory.html.

8. Explain that game theory takes place in everyday situations and on a global scale. The remaining part of the lesson will consider game theory and the implications of the Cuban Missile Crisis. The Cuban Missile Crisis was a confrontation between the United States and the Soviet Union from October 16, 1962, through October 28, 1962, over the Soviet Union's placement of nuclear missiles in Cuba. The options for the U.S. and Soviet Union were set up much like the Prisoner's Dilemma (see "Game Theory and the Cuban Missile Crisis" by Steven Brams, available at http://plus.maths.org/content/game-theory-and-cuban-missile-crisis).

Read Text

1. Distribute Handout 9.1: "The Pursuit of Disarmament" by John F. Kennedy. As students read Kennedy's speech, ask students to consider connections to game theory and the prisoner's dilemma (refer to definition of game theory).
2. You may wish to show the speech starting from 3:20, available at http://www.jfklibrary.org/Asset-Viewer/BWC7I4C9QUmLG9J6I8oy8w.aspx

Text-Dependent Questions

Select from the following text-dependent questions for leading a Socratic seminar or class discussion:
- What is Kennedy's main reason to speak of peace?
- What effect does the repetition of "it makes no sense . . . " have on the first paragraph?
- How does Kennedy present contrasting ideas in the second paragraph and what effect does this have on the listener?
- According to Kennedy, what is the role of the U.S. in influencing the Soviet Union?
- How does Kennedy bring the responsibility of peace to a more personal level?
- How does Kennedy address the opposing argument that peace is impossible?
- According to the speech, how does Kennedy define peace and how is this different from public assumptions about peace?
- What does Kennedy mean by "a warning to the American people not to fall into the same trap as the Soviets, not to see only a distorted and desperate view of the other side"?
- What are the implications of war and peace, according to Kennedy?
- Why does Kennedy acknowledge the accomplishments of the Soviet Union?
- How does Kennedy address the commonalities between the U.S. and Soviet Union? How does this support his main argument?
- Is Kennedy promoting the idea of competition or cooperation? Use textual evidence to support your answer.

Rhetorical Analysis

Have students complete Handout 9.2: Blank Rhetorical Analysis Wheel in pairs or in small groups. Explain that in order to evaluate an argument, they have to determine the author's purpose and main argument (claim). They will examine specific appeals (ethos, logos, and pathos) used to support the claim and how these appeals are developed by techniques, organization, and assumptions by the writer. Students may take notes on the wheel and draw arrows to illustrate connections between the various elements. Sample questions and responses to lead analysis include:
- **Context/Purpose:**
    - *What is the historical context?* This speech was given about 9 months after the Cuban Missile Crisis when Kennedy declared to the Soviet Union that the U.S. would not accept the existence of nuclear weapons in Cuba. The Soviet Union did not deploy the weapons, but war was perilously close.

- *What is Kennedy's purpose?* He aims to develop an argument against disarmament.

- **Claim:**
  - *What is Kennedy's main claim?* In examining our attitudes, let's continue to persevere in preserving peace.

- **Point of View/Assumptions:**
  - *What are Kennedy's assumptions?* Kennedy assumes that listeners will be open to self-examination and changed attitudes.
  - *What is Kennedy's point of view?* He does not want to be blind to differences but pay direct attention to the common interests (e.g., we breathe the same air).

- **Logos/Techniques/Structure:**
  - *What are his main points and how are they developed? How does he structure his argument to make sense?* He gives reasons to speak of peace, examines his own attitude of peace, reexamines the attitude toward the Soviet Union, and reexamines the attitude toward the Cold War. He structures his argument by making a claim and supporting it with three points (deductive). He uses repetition of "it makes no sense" to appeal to our reasoning. In the second paragraph, he develops major contrasts (e.g., destroy and never create) to develop reasoning. He uses metaphor (e.g., "poison carried by wind," etc.) and repetition of "peace" to develop points.

- **Pathos/Techniques:**
  - *How does Kennedy develop emotional appeals?* He grabs attention and evokes urgency ("billions of dollars . . . " "all destroyed within 24 hours . . . ") and challenges reflection.

- **Ethos/Techniques:**
  - *How does Kennedy develop credibility and trust?* He recognizes the opposing side ("Some say . . . "). He acknowledges Soviet accomplishments. He connects with the listener with "we" and "let us." He points out lies ("it is discouraging . . . ").

- **Implications:**
  - *What are the implications/consequences of this document?* It eased tension and opened the minds of Americans to reshape attitudes.

- **Evaluation:**
  - *How effective is the author in supporting his claim? Is there a balance of pathos, ethos, and logos appeals?* This is a well-balanced argument, particularly strong with ethos appeals in addressing opposing viewpoints. This is especially important within the urgent historical context of U.S.-Soviet tensions.

In-Class Activities to Deepen Learning

1. Ask students: *How does this speech relate to the concept of game theory?*
2. (Optional) Use Handout 9.3: Reasoning About a Situation or Event to discuss whether the U.S. should promote nuclear disarmament. Students should carefully consider the point of view of the Soviet Union (see Figure 9.2).

Concept Connections

Discuss connections to power by asking the following questions. Students may reflect on concept connections using Handout 1.4: Concept Organizer, continued from previous lessons. Figure 9.3 may be helpful in guiding discussion.
- How is self-gain relevant to power?
- Which is a stronger source of power—cooperation or competition?

Choice-Based Differentiated Products

Students may choose one of the following independent products to complete (*Note*: Use Rubric 1: Product Rubric in Appendix C to assess student products):
- Complete a Rhetorical Analysis Wheel on Kennedy's speech "Cuban Missile Crisis, Address to the Nation." How does this speech compare to "The Pursuit of Disarmament?" Which speech is more effective at using rhetorical elements to develop the claim? In addition, explain in a paragraph how the Cuban Missile Crisis relates to the concept of game theory, citing at least three quotes from the text.
- Read additional background research about the implications of game theory on the field of mathematics, biology, politics, or economics. Create a presentation that teaches the class 5–10 facts about what you learn. In addition, make up your own game that demonstrates the principles of game theory as it relates to one of these fields. Demonstrate to the class how to play and develop a matrix chart to show the "strategy" possibilities.
- Research more about game theory in society. Write an essay in which you describe ways in which you see at least three examples of game theory in

Perspectives of Power

Stakeholders	United States	Soviet Union
Point of View		
Assumptions		
Implications		

Figure 9.2. Sample point of view chart.

Power is the ability to influence.
The motivation of self-gain has tremendous influence on strategy.
Power is connected to a source.
While self-interest is often viewed as the most powerful source, cooperation is often the most beneficial for both parties.
Power may be used or abused.
Power can be used for the greater good or for personal gain.
Examine the relationship between power and another concept.
Student responses can relate to cooperation, conflict, self-preservation, and strategy.

Figure 9.3. Sample student responses to power generalizations.

contemporary society or in your own life. Present your ideas in a presentation for your class.
- Write a persuasive essay or editorial to convince others that cooperation or competition is a more powerful force in society, providing specific examples to support your ideas. Consider submitting the editorial to a local newspaper.

ELA Practice Tasks

Assign one of the following tasks as a performance-based assessment for this lesson:

	Effective Rhetoric
0	Provides no response.
1	Response is limited and vague. Response only partially answers the question. A rhetorical element is not mentioned.
2	Response is accurate with 1–2 rhetorical elements named. Response includes limited or no evidence from text. OR Response includes evidence from text, but does not relate to a rhetorical element.
3	Response is appropriate and accurate, describing 1–2 rhetorical elements to support effective argumentation. Response includes some evidence from the text.
4	Response is insightful and well supported, describing 2–3 rhetorical elements. Response includes evidence from the text.

Figure 9.4. Scoring guidelines for Lesson 9 formative assessment.

- In a comparison essay, compare how Susan B. Anthony and John F. Kennedy both use similar techniques in developing their arguments, citing at least three textual examples from each text.
- Write an editorial in response to Kennedy's speech. In your editorial, give a critique evaluating Kennedy's strategy to build his claims for peace. Cite relevant textual evidence.

Formative Assessment

1. Ask students to respond to the following prompt in a single paragraph: *How effective is Kennedy in developing his argument? Support your answer by referring to elements of effective argumentation.*
2. Use the scoring guidelines in Figure 9.4 to evaluate students' assessments.

Name: _____ Date: _____

Handout 9.1
"The Pursuit of Disarmament" *by John F. Kennedy*

... I speak of peace because of the new face of war. Total war makes no sense in an age where great powers can maintain large and relatively invulnerable nuclear forces and refuse to surrender without resort to those forces. It makes no sense in an age where a single nuclear weapon contains almost ten times the explosive force delivered by all the Allied air forces in the second world war. It makes no sense in an age when the deadly poisons produced by a nuclear exchange would be carried by wind and water and soil and seed to the far corners of the globe and to generations yet unborn.

Today the expenditure of billions of dollars every year on weapons acquired for the purpose of making sure we never need them is essential to the keeping of peace. But surely the acquisition of such idle stockpiles—which can only destroy and never create—is not the only, much less the most efficient, means of assuring peace.

I speak of peace, therefore, as the necessary rational end of rational men. I realize the pursuit of peace is not as dramatic as the pursuit of war—and frequently the words of the pursuers fall on deaf ears. But we have no more urgent task.

Some say that it is useless to speak of peace or world law or world disarmament—and that it will be useless until the leaders of the Soviet Union adopt a more enlightened attitude. I hope they do. I believe we can help them do it.

But I also believe that we must re-examine our own attitudes—as individuals and as a nation—for our attitude is as essential as theirs. And every graduate of this school, every thoughtful citizen who despairs of war and wishes to bring peace, should begin by looking inward—by examining his own attitude towards the possibilities of peace, towards the Soviet Union, towards the course of the cold war and towards freedom and peace here at home.

First: Examine our attitude towards peace itself. Too many of us think it is impossible. Too many think it is unreal. But that is a dangerous, defeatist belief. It leads to the conclusion that war is inevitable—that mankind is doomed—that we are gripped by forces we cannot control.

We need not accept that view. Our problems are man-made. Therefore, they can be solved by man. And man can be as big as he wants. No problem of human destiny is beyond human beings. Man's reason and spirit have often solved the seemingly unsolvable—and we believe they can do it again.

I am not referring to the absolute, infinite concepts of universal peace and goodwill of which some fantasies and fanatics dream. I do not deny the value of hopes and dreams but we merely invite discouragement and incredulity by making that our only and immediate goal.

Let us focus instead on a more practical, more attainable peace—based not on a sudden revolution in human nature but on a gradual evolution in human institutions—on a series of concrete actions and effective agreement which are in the interests of all concerned.

Name: _____   Date: _____

Handout 9.1, Continued

There is no single, simple key to this peace—no grand or magic formula to be adopted by one or two powers. Genuine peace must be the product of many nations, the sum of many acts. It must be dynamic, not static, changing to meet the challenge of each new generation. For peace is a process—a way of solving problems.

With such a peace, there will still be quarrels and conflicting interests, as there are within families and nations. World peace, like community peace, does not require that each man love his neighbor—it requires only that they live together with mutual tolerance, submitting their disputes to a just and peaceful settlement. And history teaches us that enmities between nations, as between individuals, do not last forever. However fixed our likes and dislikes may seem, the tide of time and events will often bring surprising changes in the relations between nations and neighbors.

So let us persevere. Peace need not be impracticable—and war need not be inevitable. By defining our goal more clearly—by making it seem more manageable and less remote—we can help all people to see it, to draw hope from it and to move irresistibly towards it.

And second: let us re-examine our attitude towards the Soviet Union. It is discouraging to think that their leaders may actually believe what their propagandists write.

It is discouraging to read a recent authoritative Soviet text on military strategy and find, on page after page, wholly baseless and incredible claims—such as the allegation that American imperialist circles are preparing to unleash different types of war . . . that there is a very real threat of a preventative war being unleashed by American imperialists against the Soviet Union . . . (and that) the political aims,—and I quote,—of the American imperialists are to enslave economically and politically the European and other capitalist countries . . . (and) achieve world domination . . . by means of aggressive war.

Truly, as it was written long ago: The wicked flee when no man pursueth. Yet it is sad to read these Soviet statements—to realize the extent of the gulf between us. But it is also a warning—a warning to the American people not to fall into the same trap as the Soviets, not to see only a distorted and desperate view of the other side, not to see conflict as inevitable, accommodation as impossible and communication as nothing more than an exchange of threats.

No government or social system is so evil that its people must be considered as lacking in virtue. As Americans, we find Communism profoundly repugnant as a negation of personal freedom and dignity. But we can still hail the Russian people for their many achievements—in science and space, in economic and industrial growth, in culture, in acts of courage.

Among the many traits the peoples of our two countries have in common, none is stronger than our mutual abhorrence of war. Almost unique among the major world powers, we have never been at war with each other. And no nation in the history of battle ever suffered more than the Soviet Union in the second world war. At least 20 million lost their lives. Countless millions of homes and families were burned or sacked. A third of the nation's territory, including two-thirds of its industrial base, was turned into a wasteland—a loss equivalent to the destruction of this country east of Chicago.

Today, should total war ever break out again—no matter how—our two countries will be the primary targets. It is an ironic but accurate fact that the two strongest powers are the two in the most danger of devastation. All we have built, all we have worked for, would be

Name: _____ Date: _____

Handout 9.1, Continued

destroyed in the first 24 hours. And even in the cold war—which brings burdens and dangers to so many countries, including this nation's closest allies—our two countries bear the heaviest burdens. For we are both devoting massive sums of money to weapons that could better be devoted to combat ignorance, poverty, and disease.

We are both caught up in a vicious and dangerous cycle with suspicion on one side breeding suspicion on the other, and new weapons begetting counter-weapons.

In short, both the United States and its allies, and the Soviet Union and its allies, have a mutually deep interest in a just and genuine peace and in halting the arms race. Agreements to this end are in the interests of the Soviet Union as well as ours—and even the most hostile nations can be relied upon to accept and keep those treaty obligations and only those treaty obligations which are in their own interest.

So let us not be blind to our differences, but let us also direct attention to our common interests and the means by which those differences can be resolved. And if we cannot end now our differences, at least we can help make the world safe for diversity. For, in the final analysis, our most basic common link is that we all inhabit this small planet. We all breathe the same air. We all cherish our children's futures. And we are all mortal.

Third: Let us re-examine our attitude towards the cold war, remembering that we are not engaged in a debate, seeking to pile up debating points.

We are not here distributing blame or pointing the finger of judgment. We must deal with the world as it is, and not as it might have been had the history of the last eighteen years been different . . . .

Name: _____ Date: _____

Handout 9.2
Blank Rhetorical Analysis Wheel

Directions: Draw arrows across elements to show connections.

Text: _____

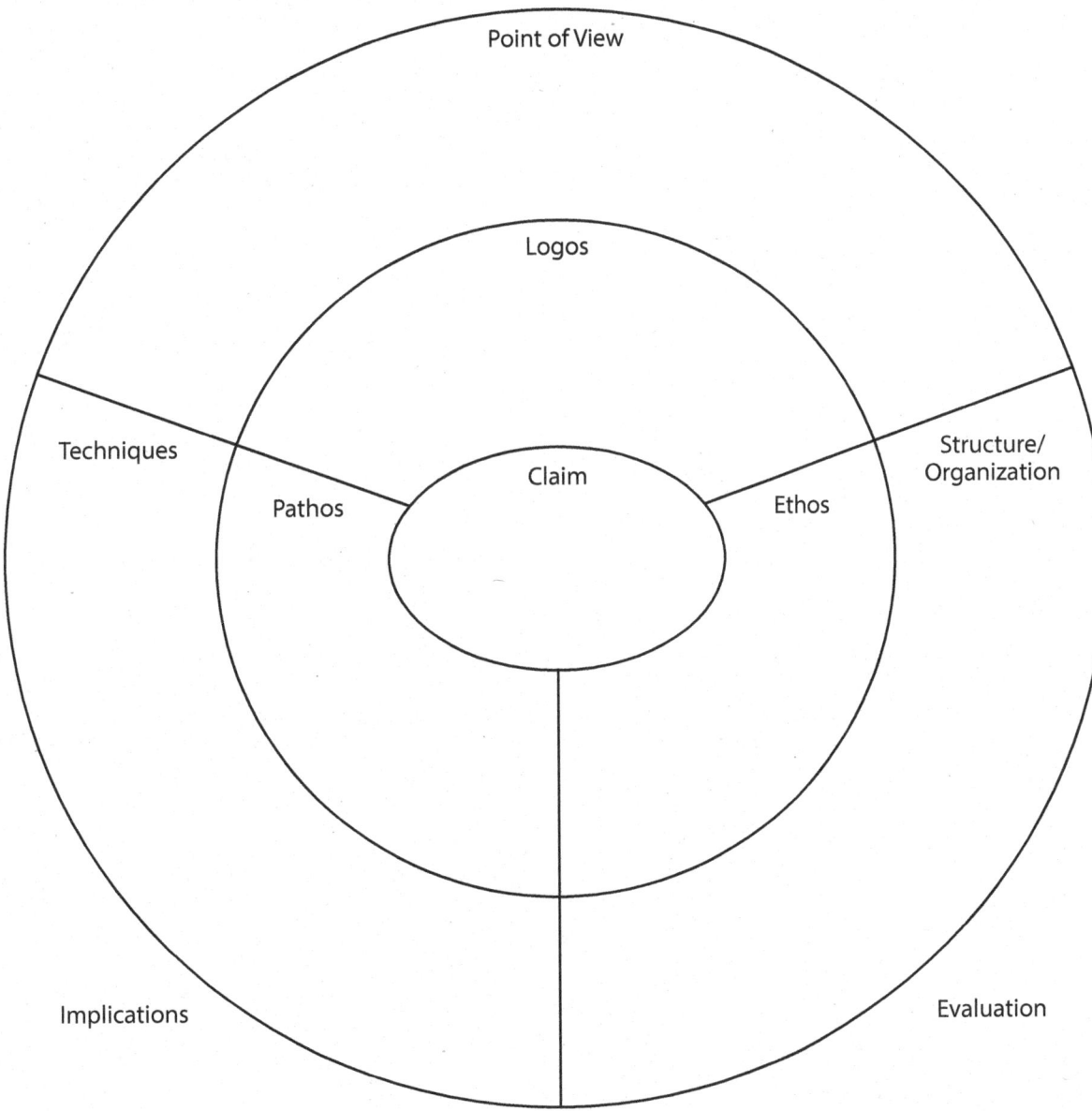

Created by Emily Mofield, Ed.D., & Tamra Stambaugh, Ph.D., 2015.

Name: _____ Date: _____

Handout 9.3
Reasoning About a Situation or Event

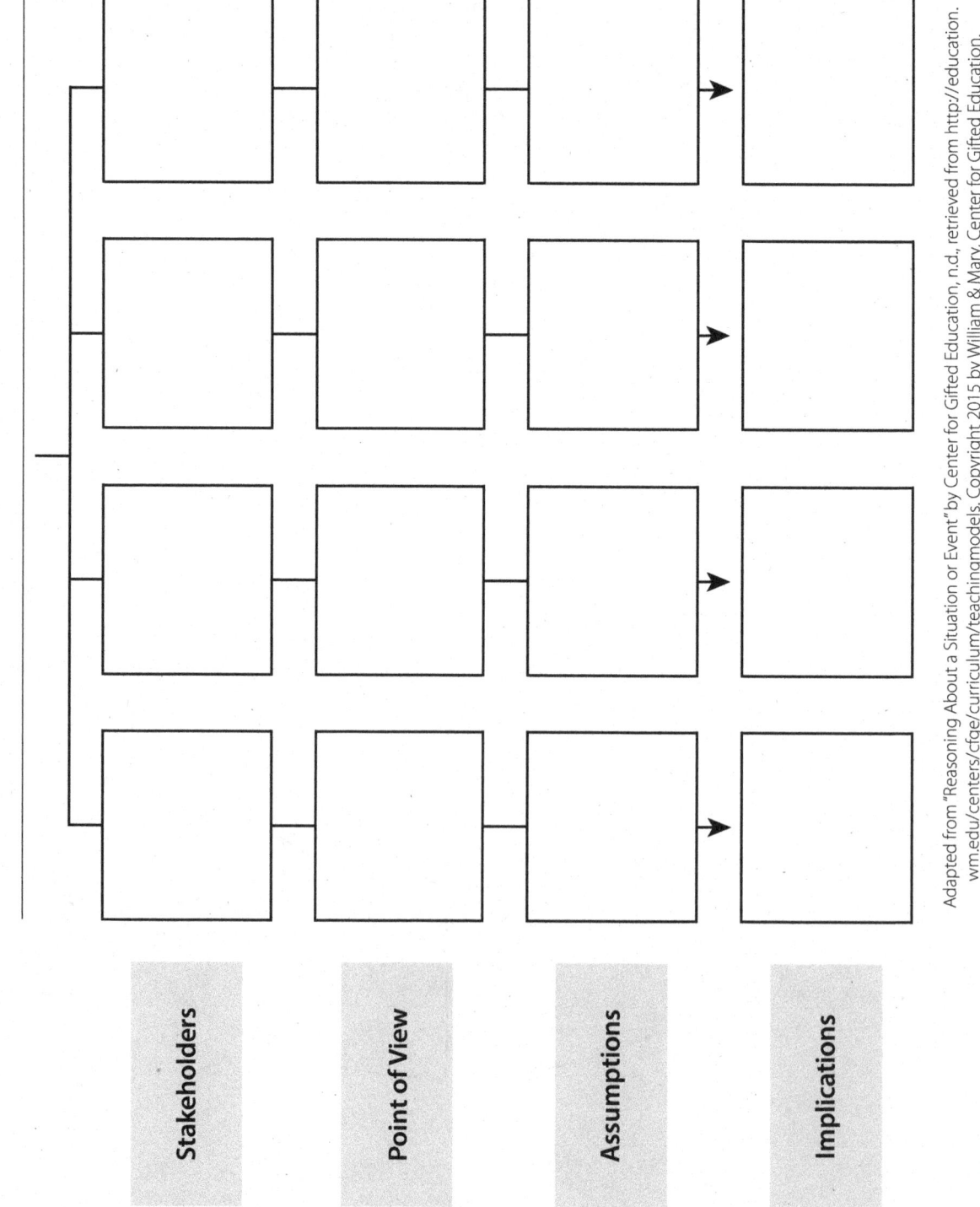

Lesson 10

"The Perils of Indifference"
by Elie Wiesel
The Power of Response

Goals/Objectives

Content: To analyze and interpret texts and art, students will be able to:
- respond to interpretations of texts through a variety of contexts by justifying ideas and providing new information,
- explain verbally and in writing how a writer develops and supports his claim, and
- identify rhetorical devices that influence effective argumentation within primary source documents and justify why they are effective.

Process: To develop thinking, writing, and communication skills, students will be able to:
- reason through an issue by using multiple points of view, assumptions, and implications to defend a statement or idea;
- use evidence to develop appropriate inferences;
- evaluate the use of effective argumentation;
- analyze purposes, assumptions, and consequences of primary sources within a historical context; and
- analyze societal or individual conflicts resulting from the struggle for power.

Concept: To understand the theme of power and related generalizations, students will be able to:
- defend "power may be used or abused" with evidence from text, media, or experience;
- explain how the generalizations "power is the ability to influence" and "power is connected to a source" are manifest within various fictional, historical, and personal contexts;
- explain how the omnipresence of power is shown through various art and literary forms within multiple contexts; and
- explain the relationship of power to other universal themes.

Accelerated CCSS ELA Standards

- RI.9-10.1
- RI.9-10.2
- RI.9-10.3
- RI.9-10.4
- RI.9-10.5
- RI.9-10.6
- RI.9-10.9
- SL.9-10.1
- SL.9-10.1c
- SL.9-10.1d
- SL.9-10.4
- RH.9-10.1
- RH.9-10.2
- RH.9-10.4
- RH.9-10.5
- RH.9-10.8
- W.9-10.5
- W.9-10.4

Materials

- (Optional) Photo of Elie Wiesel, retrieved online
- Handout 1.4: Concept Organizer continued from previous lessons
- Handout 10.1: "The Perils of Indifference" by Elie Wiesel
- Handout 10.2: Blank Rhetorical Analysis Wheel
- (Optional) Handout 10.3: Blank Visual Analysis Wheel
- (Optional) Handout 10.4: "First They Came for the Socialists" by Martin Niemöller
- (Optional) Handout 10.5: Big Idea Reflection
- Rubric 1: Product Rubric (Appendix C)

Introductory Activities

1. Begin class by asking students to make one million dots on a sheet of paper. Give students a few minutes. Encourage students to develop a strategy. After about 5 minutes, tell students that they will need to complete this for homework later. Ask them how long they think this will take. (Of course, you will not officially assign this for homework but you want them to understand the significance.)
   - Help students figure this out. If it takes 1 second to make 2 dots, then it will take 8,333 minutes, which is 138.8 hours, which is 5.7 days! Help students understand the magnitude of a million.
   - Explain to students that during the Holocaust, more than 6 million Jews were killed. To put things in perspective, 2,296 people were killed on September 11, 2001.

2. Ask students: *Who is to blame for the killing of the 6 million Jews?* Most students may say Hitler, but many may not consider bystanders.
   - Ask students to guess what percentage of people were bystanders, perpetrators, or rescuers of the victims of the Holocaust. Define bystander

effect: *The bystander effect is a social phenomenon in which the presence of other people reduces helping behavior.* Show the following percentages:
- Rescuers: Less than 5%
- Bystanders: 85%
- Perpetrators: about 10%

3. Ask students:
    - Why do you think so many people did nothing (as bystanders)?
    - What would have happened if more people helped as rescuers?
    - What would have happened to bystanders if they interfered? Would this have been the same or a different outcome if the bystanders had acted collectively? Individually?

4. Help students understand how systems worked to allow the Holocaust by reading the following text aloud from Hillberg (1985):

    > Organizing the transportation of victims from all over Europe to the concentration camps involved a countless number of railroad employees and clerical workers who had to work the trains and maintain the records. National Railroad tickets were marked for a one-way trip. Currency exchange at the borders had to be handled. Finance ministers of Germany moved to seize the pensions of victims from banks, yet the banks requested proof of death. Many building contracts and patents for ovens and gas chambers were required . . . . The railroads were an independent corporation which was fully aware of the consequences of its decisions. The civilian railroad workers involved in operating rails to Auschwitz were simply performing their daily tasks. These were individual people making individual decisions. They were not ordered or even assigned. Orders from the SS to the railroads were not even stamped "secret" because that would admit guilt of something abnormal in the bureaucracy. The many clerical workers who handled these orders were fully aware of the purpose of Auschwitz. (p. 183)

5. Ask students to define indifference. Then provide the dictionary definition: *Indifference is a lack of interest, concern, or sympathy.* As students read Handout 10.1, they should consider how Wiesel defines indifference and how may differ from the dictionary definition.

Read Text

Distribute Handout 10.1: "The Perils of Indifference" by Elie Wiesel. Explain that Elie Wiesel is a survivor of the Holocaust. Show his picture (retrieve online). He was in concentration camps in Auschwitz, Buna, and Buchenwald. He is a famous author, most notably for his memoir, *Night*.

Text-Dependent Questions

Select from the following text-dependent questions for leading a Socratic seminar or class discussion:
- What effect does Elie Wiesel give the reader when referring to himself in third person (in first few paragraphs)? Why is the narrative technique effective for the listener?
- Why does Elie Wiesel emphasize the idea of gratitude in the beginning of the speech? Is the gratitude only for liberation from the Holocaust?
- Of the questions Elie Wiesel asks, which one is most significant to the listener, and why? Why is it important that Elie Wiesel asks so many questions in his speech? (Sample response: It makes the listener question his or her own values directly.)
- According to Wiesel, which is worse, an unjust God or an indifferent one? What evidence supports Wiesel's reasoning?
- According to the text, why is indifference the friend of the enemy?
- What does Elie Wiesel mean by, "Indifference, then, is not only a sin, it is a punishment"? Be sure to examine the previous sentences.
- When and how does Wiesel's tone of gratitude change to an accusatory tone? Cite evidence of his accusatory tone.
- According to the text, how did America display indifference toward the treatment of the Jews?
- How does Wiesel build sympathy toward victims within the speech?
- What evidence of hope does Elie Wiesel provide concerning the future?
- What is significant about Wiesel's word choice when he refers to "profound fear and extraordinary hope"?
- When does Wiesel refer to Kosovo? What connection is Wiesel striving to make with regard to Kosovo and the Holocaust?
- Why does Wiesel begin and end with his reference to himself as a young boy? What effect does this have on his overall message?
- Is Wiesel ever offensive in his speech? Cite evidence to support your answer.
- Where in the speech does Wiesel shift his focus from the perils of indifference to more positive things? What point is Wiesel making, and does it support or weaken his main argument (e.g., paragraph 23)?
- How does Wiesel define "indifference"?

Rhetorical Analysis

Have students complete Handout 10.2: Blank Rhetorical Analysis Wheel in pairs or in small groups. Explain that in order to evaluate an argument, they have to determine the author's purpose and main argument (claim). They will examine specific appeals (ethos, logos, and pathos) used to support the claim and how these appeals are developed by techniques, organization, and assumptions by the writer. Students may take notes on the wheel and draw arrows to illustrate connections between the various elements. Some sample questions and responses to lead analysis include:

- **Context/Purpose:**
  - *What is the historical context?* Elie Wiesel presented this speech in Washington, DC (1999). The audience is indeed those mentioned at the beginning of the speech (e.g., Clinton), but more broadly, the speech is intended for everyone as individuals.
  - *What is Wiesel's purpose?* He aims to explain the perils of indifference and to persuade listeners to no longer be indifferent in the next century.

- **Message/Claim:**
  - *What is Wiesel's main claim?* People have the power to respond to evil if they are not indifferent.

- **Point of View/Assumptions:**
  - *What are Wiesel's assumptions?* Indifference is dangerous and the cause of great evil.
  - *What is Wiesel's point of view?* His point of view reveals courage to point out flaws of the United States (FDR). He has a negative point of view toward FDR; he does not entirely trust that the future will be better (hopeful and fearful).

- **Logos/Techniques/Structure:**
  - *How does he present his main points?* Introduction, explanation of indifference with examples, disapproval of FDR and negatives of the century, positives of the century, conclusion.
  - *What techniques are used to appeal to reason?* He establishes an ethical argument against indifference. His use of imagery (dusk/dawn, light/dark) helps establish his points. He uses several examples to support his ideas.
  - *How is the speech structured to make sense?* Parts of the speech are written as narrative where Elie is the main character. Overall, it is problem-solution, with the solution implied: listeners should respond to evil.

Perspectives of Power

- **Pathos/Techniques/Structure:**
  - *How does Wiesel develop emotional appeals? What techniques are used and where are they placed?* He evokes conviction in the audience through the use of rhetorical questions. He evokes guilt, urgency, and challenge among the audience. He uses language with positive and negative connotations. He appeals to fear and hope especially in the last paragraph. His narrative technique (referring to himself in third person at the beginning and end) evokes sympathy. Note the major shifts in tone throughout the text.

- **Ethos/Techniques/Structure:**
  - *How does Wiesel develop credibility and trust?* He is credible because he himself has experienced the effects of indifference. He establishes this with his narrative technique and personal references as a young boy. He develops credibility by expressing gratitude before pointing his finger to FDR.

- **Implications:**
  - *What are the implications/consequences of this speech?* He personally challenges us to examine the power of response.

- **Evaluation:**
  - *How effective is the author in supporting his claim?* This is a well-balanced ethical argument. His narrative techniques are particularly useful in appealing to our reason, emotions, and developing his credibility.

In-Class Activities to Deepen Learning (Optional)

1. Conduct a visual analysis on "The Family" by Samuel Bak (easily retrieved online). Hint: Blind and mute people connect to the inaction of bystanders. Use Handout 10.3: Blank Visual Analysis Wheel to record ideas.
2. Read, analyze, and discuss the quotation by Martin Niemöller: "First They Came for the Socialists" (Handout 10.4).
3. Explain that many of Dr. Seuss's books are books with hidden political messages (e.g., "The Sneetches" is about discrimination, "The Lorax" is about protecting the environment). Ask students to write a children's book with a message against indifference.
4. Have students connect Wiesel's speech to present times in small groups or pairs using Handout 10.5: Big Idea Reflection.

Concept Connections

Help students understand that indifference is the absence of power. Therefore the absence of power did not influence anyone into action; there is power in our response to injustice. Use Handout 1.4: Concept Organizer to relate power generalizations to the text. Students should list examples about how the work demonstrates some of these generalizations. Figure 10.1 provides possible responses for this lesson; various interpretations are encouraged.

Choice-Based Differentiated Products

Students may choose one of the following independent products to complete (*Note*: Use Rubric 1: Product Rubric in Appendix C to assess student products):

- Read another speech given by Elie Wiesel and complete a Rhetorical Analysis (using the Blank Rhetorical Analysis Wheel, see Appendix B). In a paragraph, note patterns and similarities about Elie Wiesel's techniques and methods.
- With teacher approval, develop your own experiment to test the bystander effect. Research more about bystander effects and experiments used to test it. Conduct your own research and present your results. Relate your findings to a concept generalization about power.
- Write your own speech that addresses an issue related to indifference. Consider topics such as bullying, political unrest in other parts of the world, the elderly, or orphaned children. Use effective rhetorical elements within your speech and relate your ideas to at least one concept generalization about power. Underline and label these techniques within your speech.
- Write a first person narrative piece from the perspective of a bystander or a victim related to the Holocaust or any other situation. In the narrative, be sure to explain thoughts and feelings of why you chose not to act (as a bystander) or your feelings as a victim.
- Consider your world. Whom do you feel you have a responsibility to care for and protect? How can you use your individual power to make a difference? Consider community issues such as bullying or more global issues such as the status of women and orphans in third-world countries or contemporary genocide. Develop and present an in-depth action plan to address the problem. Include who, what, when, where, and how the problem will be solved. Include how you will get others to assist your efforts and how you will promote your efforts and measure outcomes.

Perspectives of Power

> | |
> |---|
> | **Power is the ability to influence.** |
> | Doing nothing influences others to do nothing. |
> | **Power is connected to a source.** |
> | Power is connected to personal responsibility and action. |
> | **Power may be used or abused.** |
> | Being indifferent can actually promote abuse because it allows abuse to happen. |
> | **Examine the relationship between power and another concept.** |
> | Consider concepts: conformity, exclusion, inclusion, belonging, peer pressure, responsibility, fear, belonging. |

Figure 10.1. Sample student responses to power generalizations.

ELA Practice Tasks

Assign one of the following tasks as a performance-based assessment for this lesson:

- An ethical argument is one that argues whether something is right or wrong. What is Elie Wiesel's major ethical argument and how does he support it? Explain in a well-developed essay, citing evidence from the text.
- Which rhetorical appeal (logos, ethos, or pathos) does Elie Wiesel use most effectively? Support your answer with evidence from the text in a well-developed essay.
- Write an essay that explains the causes and effects of indifference, according to Elie Wiesel. Develop your essay with support that is grounded in evidence from the text.

Formative Assessment

1. Ask students to respond to the following prompt in a single paragraph: *How effective is Elie Wiesel in developing his argument? Support your answer by referring to elements of effective argumentation.*
2. Use the scoring guidelines in Figure 10.2 to evaluate students' assessments.

	Effective Rhetoric
0	Provides no response.
1	Response is limited and vague. Response only partially answers the question. A rhetorical element is not mentioned.
2	Response is accurate with 1–2 rhetorical elements named. Response includes limited or no evidence from text. OR Response includes evidence from text, but does not relate to a rhetorical element.
3	Response is appropriate and accurate, describing 1–2 rhetorical elements to support effective argumentation. Response includes some evidence from the text.
4	Response is insightful and well supported, describing 2–3 rhetorical elements. Response includes evidence from the text.

Figure 10.2. Scoring guidelines for Lesson 10 formative assessment.

Name: _____ Date: _____

Handout 10.1
"The Perils of Indifference" by Elie Wiesel

Mr. President, Mrs. Clinton, members of Congress, Ambassador Holbrooke, Excellencies, friends:

Fifty-four years ago to the day, a young Jewish boy from a small town in the Carpathian Mountains woke up, not far from Goethe's beloved Weimar, in a place of eternal infamy called Buchenwald. He was finally free, but there was no joy in his heart. He thought there never would be again. Liberated a day earlier by American soldiers, he remembers their rage at what they saw. And even if he lives to be a very old man, he will always be grateful to them for that rage, and also for their compassion. Though he did not understand their language, their eyes told him what he needed to know—that they, too, would remember, and bear witness.

And now, I stand before you, Mr. President—Commander-in-Chief of the army that freed me, and tens of thousands of others—and I am filled with a profound and abiding gratitude to the American people. "Gratitude" is a word that I cherish. Gratitude is what defines the humanity of the human being. And I am grateful to you, Hillary, or Mrs. Clinton, for what you said, and for what you are doing for children in the world, for the homeless, for the victims of injustice, the victims of destiny and society. And I thank all of you for being here.

We are on the threshold of a new century, a new millennium. What will the legacy of this vanishing century be? How will it be remembered in the new millennium? Surely it will be judged, and judged severely, in both moral and metaphysical terms. These failures have cast a dark shadow over humanity: two World Wars, countless civil wars, the senseless chain of assassinations (Gandhi, the Kennedys, Martin Luther King, Sadat, Rabin), bloodbaths in Cambodia and Algeria, India and Pakistan, Ireland and Rwanda, Eritrea and Ethiopia, Sarajevo and Kosovo; the inhumanity in the gulag and the tragedy of Hiroshima. And, on a different level, of course, Auschwitz and Treblinka. So much violence; so much indifference.

What is indifference? Etymologically, the word means "no difference." A strange and unnatural state in which the lines blur between light and darkness, dusk and dawn, crime and punishment, cruelty and compassion, good and evil. What are its courses and inescapable consequences? Is it a philosophy? Is there a philosophy of indifference conceivable? Can one possibly view indifference as a virtue? Is it necessary at times to practice it simply to keep one's sanity, live normally, enjoy a fine meal and a glass of wine, as the world around us experiences harrowing upheavals?

Of course, indifference can be tempting—more than that, seductive. It is so much easier to look away from victims. It is so much easier to avoid such rude interruptions to our work, our dreams, our hopes. It is, after all, awkward, troublesome, to be involved in another person's pain and despair. Yet, for the person who is indifferent, his or her neighbor are of no consequence. And, therefore, their lives are meaningless. Their hidden or even visible anguish is of no interest. Indifference reduces the Other to an abstraction.

Handout 10.1, Continued

Over there, behind the black gates of Auschwitz, the most tragic of all prisoners were the "Muselmanner," as they were called. Wrapped in their torn blankets, they would sit or lie on the ground, staring vacantly into space, unaware of who or where they were—strangers to their surroundings. They no longer felt pain, hunger, thirst. They feared nothing. They felt nothing. They were dead and did not know it.

Rooted in our tradition, some of us felt that to be abandoned by humanity then was not the ultimate. We felt that to be abandoned by God was worse than to be punished by Him. Better an unjust God than an indifferent one. For us to be ignored by God was a harsher punishment than to be a victim of His anger. Man can live far from God—not outside God. God is wherever we are. Even in suffering? Even in suffering.

In a way, to be indifferent to that suffering is what makes the human being inhuman. Indifference, after all, is more dangerous than anger and hatred. Anger can at times be creative. One writes a great poem, a great symphony. One does something special for the sake of humanity because one is angry at the injustice that one witnesses. But indifference is never creative. Even hatred at times may elicit a response. You fight it. You denounce it. You disarm it.

Indifference elicits no response. Indifference is not a response. Indifference is not a beginning; it is an end. And, therefore, indifference is always the friend of the enemy, for it benefits the aggressor—never his victim, whose pain is magnified when he or she feels forgotten. The political prisoner in his cell, the hungry children, the homeless refugees—not to respond to their plight, not to relieve their solitude by offering them a spark of hope is to exile them from human memory. And in denying their humanity, we betray our own.

Indifference, then, is not only a sin, it is a punishment.

And this is one of the most important lessons of this outgoing century's wide-ranging experiments in good and evil.

In the place that I come from, society was composed of three simple categories: the killers, the victims, and the bystanders. During the darkest of times, inside the ghettoes and death camps—and I'm glad that Mrs. Clinton mentioned that we are now commemorating that event, that period, that we are now in the Days of Remembrance—but then, we felt abandoned, forgotten. All of us did.

And our only miserable consolation was that we believed that Auschwitz and Treblinka were closely guarded secrets; that the leaders of the free world did not know what was going on behind those black gates and barbed wire; that they had no knowledge of the war against the Jews that Hitler's armies and their accomplices waged as part of the war against the Allies. If they knew, we thought, surely those leaders would have moved heaven and earth to intervene. They would have spoken out with great outrage and conviction. They would have bombed the railways leading to Birkenau, just the railways, just once.

And now we knew, we learned, we discovered that the Pentagon knew, the State Department knew. And the illustrious occupant of the White House then, who was a great leader—and I say it with some anguish and pain, because, today is exactly 54 years marking his death—Franklin Delano Roosevelt died on April the 12th, 1945. So he is very much present to me and to us. No doubt, he was a great leader. He mobilized the American people and the world, going into battle, bringing hundreds and thousands of valiant and brave soldiers

Handout 10.1, Continued

in America to fight fascism, to fight dictatorship, to fight Hitler. And so many of the young people fell in battle. And, nevertheless, his image in Jewish history—I must say it—his image in Jewish history is flawed.

The depressing tale of the St. Louis is a case in point. Sixty years ago, its human cargo—nearly 1,000 Jews—was turned back to Nazi Germany. And that happened after the Kristallnacht, after the first state sponsored pogrom, with hundreds of Jewish shops destroyed, synagogues burned, thousands of people put in concentration camps. And that ship, which was already in the shores of the United States, was sent back. I don't understand. Roosevelt was a good man, with a heart. He understood those who needed help. Why didn't he allow these refugees to disembark? A thousand people—in America, the great country, the greatest democracy, the most generous of all new nations in modern history. What happened? I don't understand. Why the indifference, on the highest level, to the suffering of the victims?

But then, there were human beings who were sensitive to our tragedy. Those non-Jews, those Christians, that we call the "Righteous Gentiles," whose selfless acts of heroism saved the honor of their faith. Why were they so few? Why was there a greater effort to save SS murderers after the war than to save their victims during the war? Why did some of America's largest corporations continue to do business with Hitler's Germany until 1942? It has been suggested, and it was documented, that the Wehrmacht could not have conducted its invasion of France without oil obtained from American sources. How is one to explain their indifference?

And yet, my friends, good things have also happened in this traumatic century: the defeat of Nazism, the collapse of communism, the rebirth of Israel on its ancestral soil, the demise of apartheid, Israel's peace treaty with Egypt, the peace accord in Ireland. And let us remember the meeting, filled with drama and emotion, between Rabin and Arafat that you, Mr. President, convened in this very place. I was here and I will never forget it.

And then, of course, the joint decision of the United States and NATO to intervene in Kosovo and save those victims, those refugees, those who were uprooted by a man, whom I believe that because of his crimes, should be charged with crimes against humanity.

But this time, the world was not silent. This time, we do respond. This time, we intervene.

Does it mean that we have learned from the past? Does it mean that society has changed? Has the human being become less indifferent and more human? Have we really learned from our experiences? Are we less insensitive to the plight of victims of ethnic cleansing and other forms of injustices in places near and far? Is today's justified intervention in Kosovo, led by you, Mr. President, a lasting warning that never again will the deportation, the terrorization of children and their parents, be allowed anywhere in the world? Will it discourage other dictators in other lands to do the same?

What about the children? Oh, we see them on television, we read about them in the papers, and we do so with a broken heart. Their fate is always the most tragic, inevitably. When adults wage war, children perish. We see their faces, their eyes. Do we hear their pleas? Do we feel their pain, their agony? Every minute one of them dies of disease, violence, famine.

Some of them—so many of them—could be saved.

Name: _____ Date: _____

Handout 10.1, Continued

And so, once again, I think of the young Jewish boy from the Carpathian Mountains. He has accompanied the old man I have become throughout these years of quest and struggle. And together we walk towards the new millennium, carried by profound fear and extraordinary hope.

Name: _____ Date: _____

Handout 10.2
Blank Rhetorical Analysis Wheel

Directions: Draw arrows across elements to show connections.

Text: _____

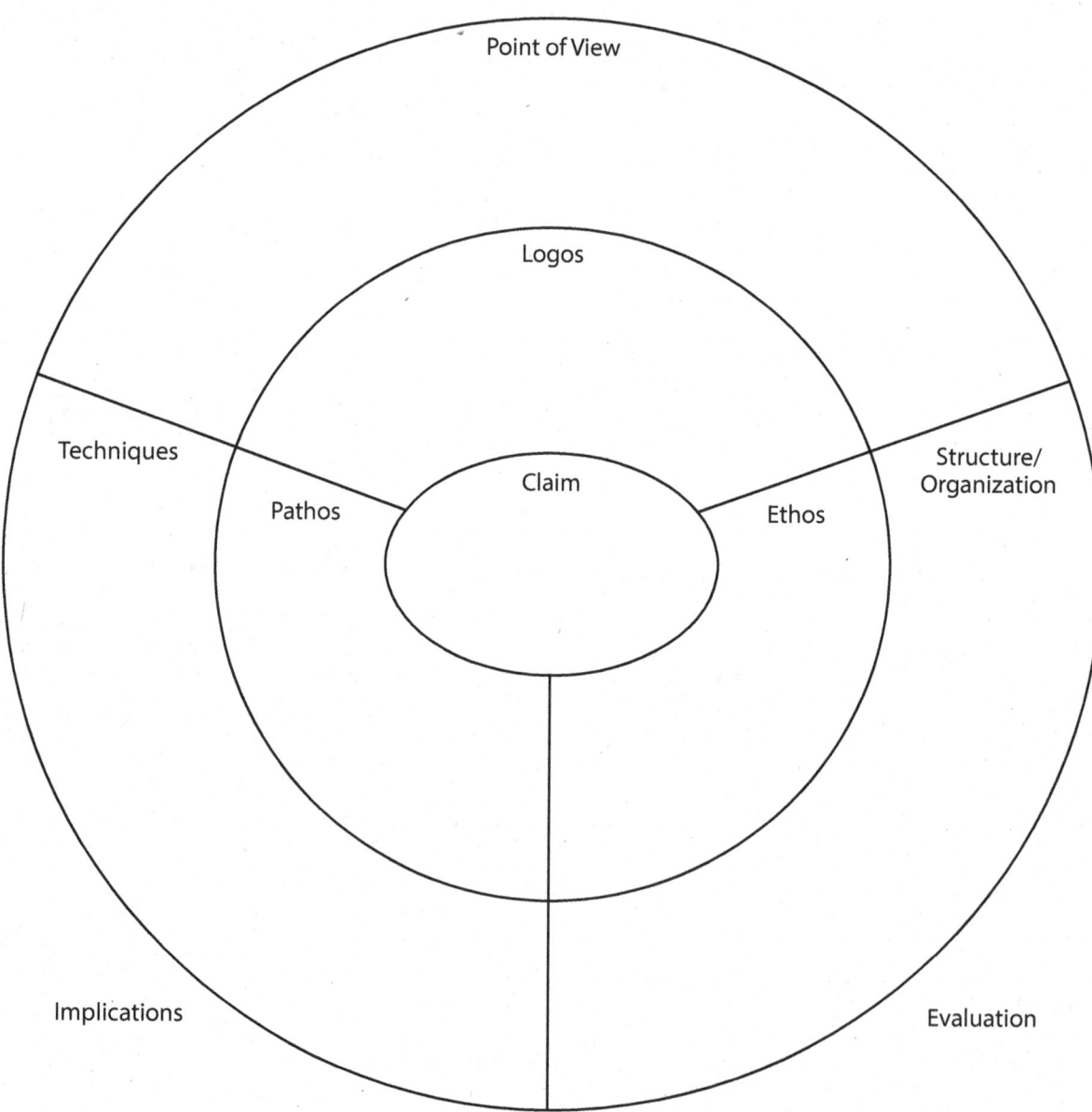

Created by Emily Mofield, Ed.D., & Tamra Stambaugh, Ph.D., 2015.

Perspectives of Power © Taylor & Francis Group

Name: _____ Date: _____

Handout 10.3
Blank Visual Analysis Wheel

Directions: Draw arrows across elements to show connections.

Art Piece: _____

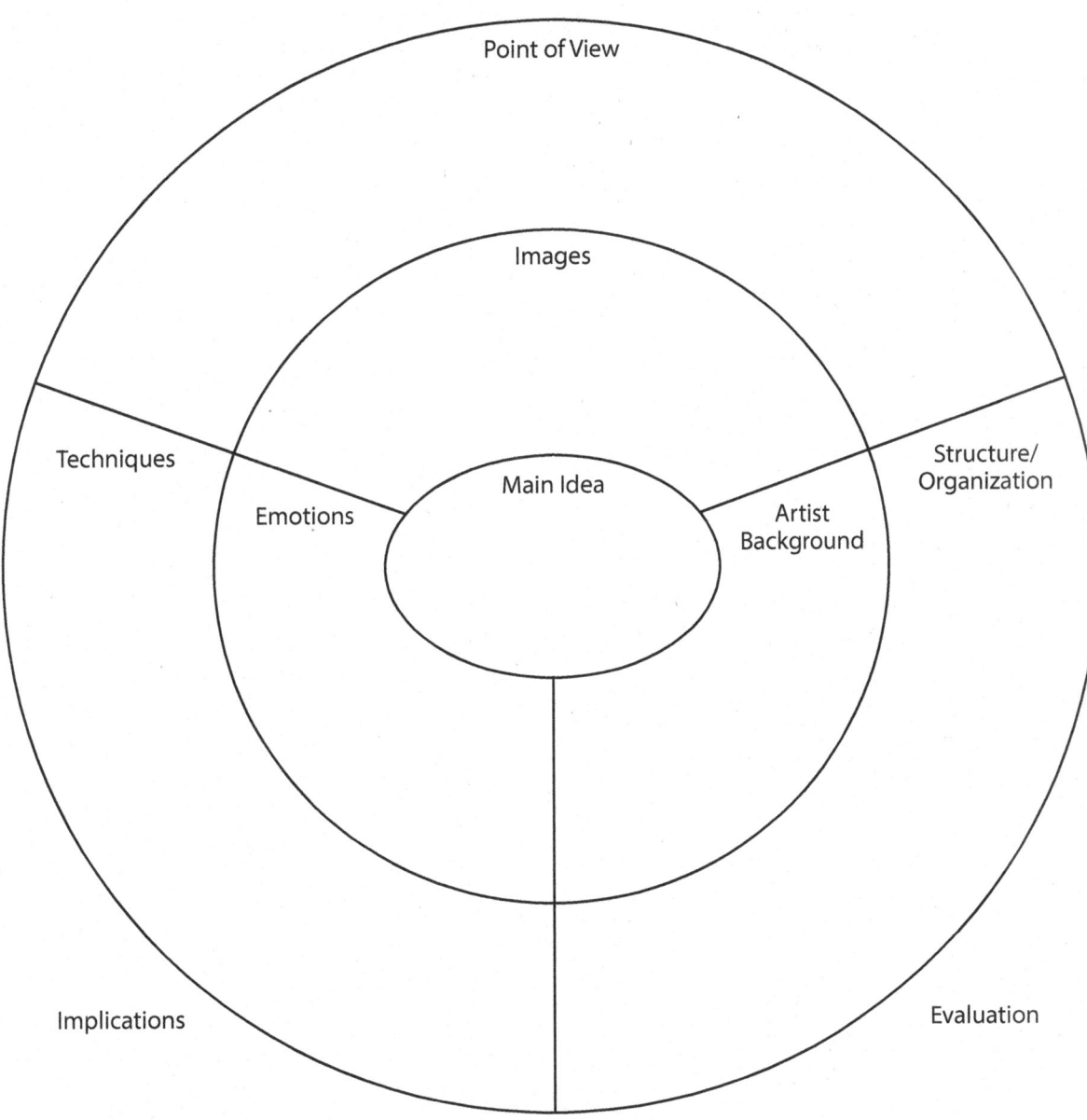

Created by Tamra Stambaugh, Ph.D., & Emily Mofield, Ed.D., 2015.

Name: _____   Date: _____

Handout 10.4
"First They Came for the Socialists" *by Martin Niemöller*

First they came for the Socialists, and I did not speak out—Because I was not a Socialist.

Then they came for the Trade Unionists, and I did not speak out—Because I was not a Trade Unionist.

Then they came for the Jews, and I did not speak out—Because I was not a Jew.

Then they came for me—and there was no one left to speak for me.

Name: _____ Date: _____

Handout 10.5
Big Idea Reflection

What?	**Concepts:** What concepts/ideas are in the text?	
	Generalizations: What broad statement can you make about one or more of these concepts? Make it generalizable beyond the text.	
	Issue: What is the main issue, problem, or conflict?	
So What?	**Insight:** What insight on life is provided from this text?	
	World/Community/Individual: How does this text relate to you, your community, or your world? What question does the author want you to ask yourself?	
Now What?	**Implications:** How should you respond to the ideas in the text? What action should you take? What are the implications of the text? What can you do with this information?	

Created by Emily Mofield, Ed.D., & Tamra Stambaugh, Ph.D., 2015.

Lesson 11

"We never know how high we are"
by Emily Dickinson
The Power of Risk

Goals/Objectives

Content: To analyze and interpret texts and art, students will be able to:
- explain with evidence how literary or visual elements contribute to the overall meaning of a work,
- respond to interpretations of texts through a variety of contexts by justifying ideas and providing new information, and
- compare and contrast the impact of various texts, art, experiences, and real-world events on themes and generalizations.

Process: To develop thinking, writing, and communication skills, students will be able to:
- use evidence to develop appropriate inferences, and
- analyze societal or individual conflicts resulting from the struggle for power.

Concept: To understand the theme of power and related generalizations, students will be able to:
- defend "power may be used or abused" with evidence from text, media, or experience;
- explain how the generalizations "power is the ability to influence" and "power is connected to a source" are manifest within various fictional, historical, and personal contexts;
- explain how the omnipresence of power is shown through various art and literary forms within multiple contexts; and
- explain the relationship of power to other universal themes.

Accelerated CCSS ELA Standards

- RL.9-10.1
- RL.9-10.2
- RL.9-10.4
- RL.9-10.5
- W.9-10.4
- SL.9-10.1c
- SL.9-10.1d
- SL.9-10.4
- SL.9-10.1

Materials

- Handout 11.1: Poems by Emily Dickinson and Edgar Masters
- Handout 11.2: Blank Literary Analysis Wheel
- Handout 11.3: Big Idea Reflection
- Handout 11.4: Reasoning About a Situation or Event (optional)
- Rubric 1: Product Rubric (Appendix C)

Introductory Activity

Play the game "What's in the bag?" Place a ruler or measuring tape inside a bag. Students must ask yes/no questions to guess what is in the bag. When students guess "ruler," ask: *How can we measure success? How can we measure the worth of a poem?* Guide students to see that success is difficult to measure; it depends on one's definition of success. Poems can be measured by looking at their literary elements and their effect on the overall meaning of the poem.

Read Poem

Distribute Handout 11.1: Poems by Emily Dickinson and Edgar Masters. Ask a student to read the poem "We never know how high we are" by Emily Dickinson. As it is read, students should underline words they do not know. Make sure students know these terms:
- **Statures:** Level of respect for a successful person; a person's height
- **Cubits:** Ancient unit of length (about 18 inches)
- **Warp:** To be twisted out of shape, usually due to dampness or heat

Text-Dependent Questions

Lead a close reading of Dickinson's poem. Select from the following text-dependent questions for leading a Socratic seminar or class discussion:
- What feelings can we associate with some of the words in this poem? What emotions do some of the words/lines evoke in us? Are the connotations positive or negative?
- Paraphrase Practice: (May be done in pairs or individuals). Recreate the poem in text message form in contemporary language. Consider using emojis to add to the tone.
- What is this poem about? Is it about the fear of failure or the fear of success? Hold a mini-debate.

- What patterns do you notice? (Help students notice examples of rhyme scheme, patterns of language relating to measurement—high, rise, statures, cubits.)

Literary Analysis

1. Guide students in analyzing the poem using Handout 11.2 Blank Literary Analysis Wheel. Lead students through a basic understanding of each element, then emphasize the interaction of the elements with more complex questions. Focus on the following complex questions:
   - How does the central conflict influence the theme?
   - How does Dickinson's point of view about success influence the tone?
   - How does Dickinson's use of metaphor contribute to the theme?

The following notes may be helpful in guiding students through the analysis:
- **Theme:** Themes of the poem may relate to fear, failure, success, and personal growth.
- **Conflict:** The central conflict of the poem may be "Should one pursue heroism in the face of failure?"
- **Symbols:** Symbols include: "touch the skies" = achievement of potential; cubits = self-evaluation; king = having wide success.
- **Tone:** Dickinson's tone is didactic and warning.
- **Context:** This was written by Dickinson who lived 1830–1886. The poem was first published in 1955. Dickinson lived in Amherst, MA. Her works were published posthumously.

Big Idea Reflection

Use Handout 11.3: Big Idea Reflection to help students transfer knowledge of Dickinson's poem to real life.
- **Concepts:** Success, failure, fear.
- **Generalizations:** In order to be powerful, one must face fear, power is connected to overcoming fear of success and failure.
- **Problem:** The conflict being afraid to take risks for fear of failure or even fear of success.
- **Insight:** The fear of success is just as threatening as the fear of failure because these two concepts are cyclical.
- **World/Community/Individual:** Individual—Am I afraid of failing? What things in life do I avoid because I am afraid to pursue them?
- **Implications:** What are the implications of the fear of failure on my own life? How can I address the issue of fear in my own life?

In-Class Activities to Deepen Learning

1. Ask students: *What connections can you make with Dickinson's poem and other works within the unit?* (e.g., this speaks to the power of personal response. Susan B. Anthony and Elie Wiesel are both examples of people who were "called to rise" in their era; they acted regardless of fear of success and fear of failure.)
2. Assign students a letter of Dickinson's (first or last) name. Have students write the letter on their paper use this as a basis to create a visual depicting their interpretation of the poem. For example, a student may draw a giant O and show the cyclical relationship between fear of failure and fear of success.
3. Have students create a bumper sticker with a pithy message to portray the idea of the poem.
4. Use Handout 11.4: Reasoning About a Situation or Event to discuss "Is this poem about the fear of failure or the fear of success?" Figure 11.1 includes sample responses.
5. Have students read "George Gray" by Edgar Masters (Handout 11.1). Use a Venn diagram or comparison chart to show specific ways these pieces are similar (see Figure 11.2).

Concept Connections

Discuss connections to power by asking the following questions. Figure 11.3 provides some sample responses. Students may reflect on concept connections using Handout 1.4: Concept Organizer, continued from Lesson 1.
- How does the power of fear influence our lives?
- How can the power of risk be used appropriately? According to Dickinson, how is the power of risk abused?

Choice-Based Differentiated Products

Students may choose one of the following independent products to complete (*Note*: Use Rubric 1: Product Rubric in Appendix C to assess student products):
- Write a personal reflection about the power of fear of failures or success in your life. Explain how this poem impacted you thinking about risk-taking and how you can take personal responsibility for success and failure in your future.
- Create a poem movie using Windows MovieMaker or other video publisher that illustrates the message of Dickinson's poem. Include music and images that match the tone and message of the poem. Include at least 8

Stakeholders	Those who interpret "fear of failure"	Those who interpret "fear of success"
Point of View	Evidence in poem to support this view	Evidence in poem to support this view
Assumptions	It is not worth taking the <u>risk</u> to do something great	It is not worth the <u>responsibility</u> to do something great
Implications	Avoidance of opportunities, thus missed success	Never have to face big responsibilities, thus will never have to face failure

Figure 11.1. *Is this poem about the fear of failure or the fear of success?* Sample responses.

"We never know how high"	Comparison	"George Gray"
"for fear to be a king"	Both show concept of fearing success	"Ambition called to me, but I dreaded the chances"

Figure 11.2. Sample poem comparison chart.

Power is the ability to influence.
The power of fear inhibits us from achieving our full potential.
Power is connected to a source.
Power is connected our personal choice to rise or not in the face of failure or success.
Power may be used or abused.
Our power to take a risk can be used to help the world (e.g., heroism), but the power to choose not to take a risk can allow for missed opportunities in our lives (thus, power is not used appropriately).
Examine the relationship between power and another concept.
Students should relate ideas to failure, success, risk, potential, etc.

Figure 11.3. Sample student responses to power generalizations.

	Concept/Theme
0	Provides no response.
1	Response is limited, vague, and/or inaccurate.
2	Response lacks adequate explanation. Response does not relate or create a generalization about power. Little or no evidence from text.
3	Response is accurate and makes sense. Response relates to or creates an idea about power with some relation to the text.
4	Response is accurate, insightful, and well-written. Response relates to or creates a generalization about power with evidence from the text.

Figure 11.4. Scoring guidelines for Lesson 11 formative assessment.

- slides/images in your poem movie. Capture the idea of "power" within your production.
- Write your own poem that relates to risk-taking, ambition, success, or failure. Develop a visual (e.g., illustrations or a collage) to accompany the poem. You may wish to include a collage of quotes about success and failure in your collage.

ELA Practice Tasks

Assign one of the following tasks as a performance-based assessment for this lesson:

- In a comparison essay, explain how "We never know how high we are" by Dickinson relates to Masters's "George Gray," citing at least three textual examples from each poem.
- What is the central conflict in the poem "We never know how high we are" and how should it be resolved? In an essay, support your answer with evidence from the text.

Formative Assessment

1. Ask students to respond to the following prompt in a single paragraph: *What does "We never know how high we are" reveal about the nature of power?*
2. Use the scoring guidelines in Figure 11.4 to evaluate students' assessments.

Name: _____ Date: _____

Handout 11.1
Poems *by Emily Dickinson and Edgar Masters*

"We never know how high we are" by Emily Dickinson

We never know how high we are
    Till we are called to rise;
And then, if we are true to plan,
    Our statures touch the skies—

The Heroism we recite
    Would be a normal thing,
Did not ourselves the Cubits warp
    For fear to be a King—

"George Gray" by Edgar Lee Masters

I have studied many times
The marble which was chiseled for me—
A boat with a furled sail at rest in a harbor.
In truth it pictures not my destination
But my life.
For love was offered me and I shrank from its disillusionment;
Sorrow knocked at my door, but I was afraid;
Ambition called to me, but I dreaded the chances.
Yet all the while I hungered for meaning in my life.
And now I know that we must lift the sail
And catch the winds of destiny
Wherever they drive the boat.
To put meaning in one's life may end in madness,
But life without meaning is the torture
Of restlessness and vague desire—
It is a boat longing for the sea and yet afraid.

Name: _____ Date: _____

Handout 11.2
Blank Literary Analysis Wheel

Directions: Draw arrows across elements to show connections.

Text: _____

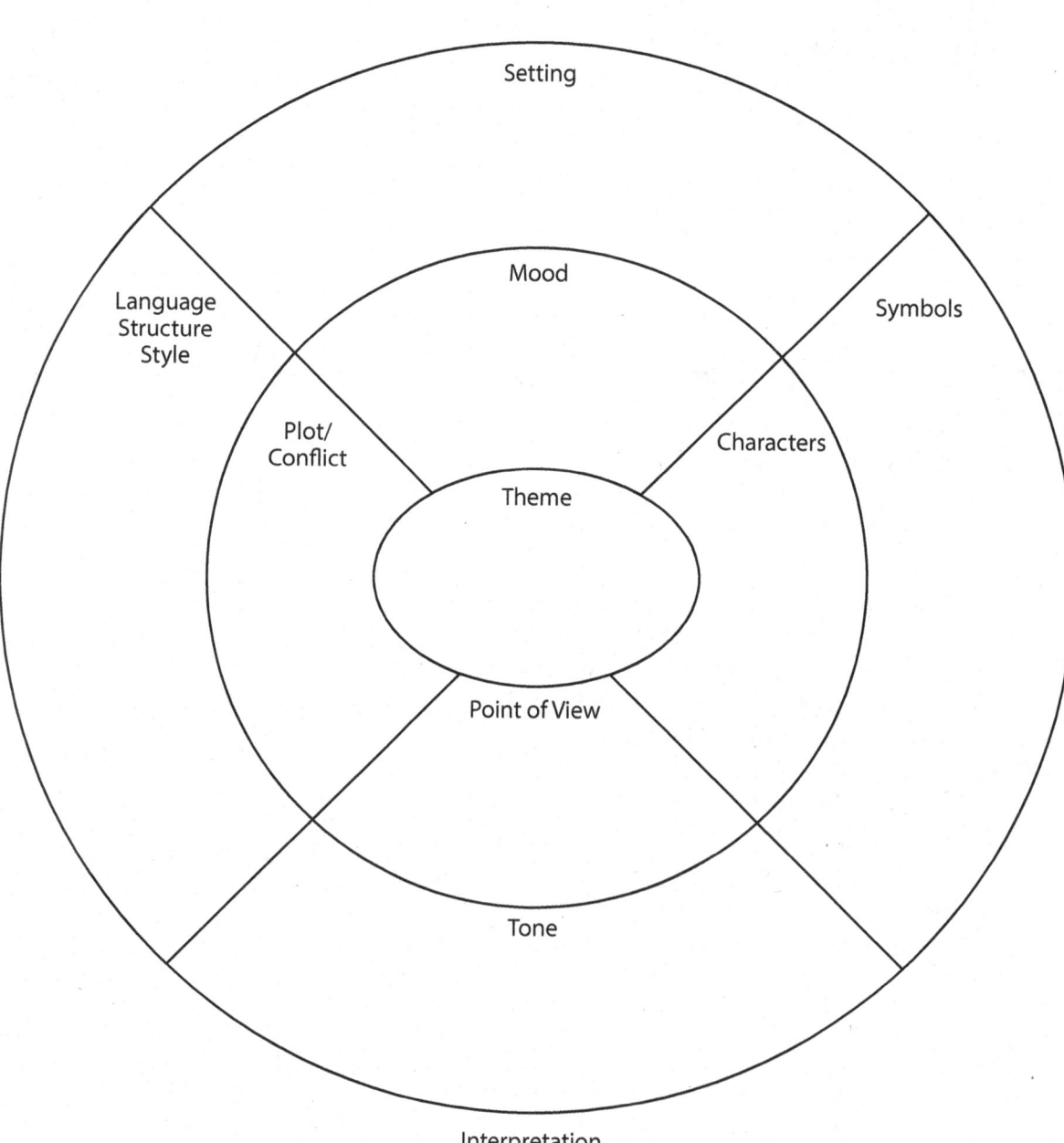

Created by Tamra Stambaugh, Ph.D., & Emily Mofield, Ed.D., 2015.

160
Perspectives of Power © Taylor & Francis Group

Name: _____ Date: _____

Handout 11.3
Big Idea Reflection

What?	**Concepts:** What concepts/ideas are in the text?	
	Generalizations: What broad statement can you make about one or more of these concepts? Make it generalizable beyond the text.	
	Issue: What is the main issue, problem, or conflict?	
So What?	**Insight:** What insight on life is provided from this text?	
	World/Community/Individual: How does this text relate to you, your community, or your world? What question does the author want you to ask yourself?	
Now What?	**Implications:** How should you respond to the ideas in the text? What action should you take? What are the implications of the text? What can you do with this information?	

Created by Emily Mofield, Ed.D., & Tamra Stambaugh, Ph.D., 2015.

Name: _____ Date: _____

Handout 11.4
Reasoning About a Situation or Event

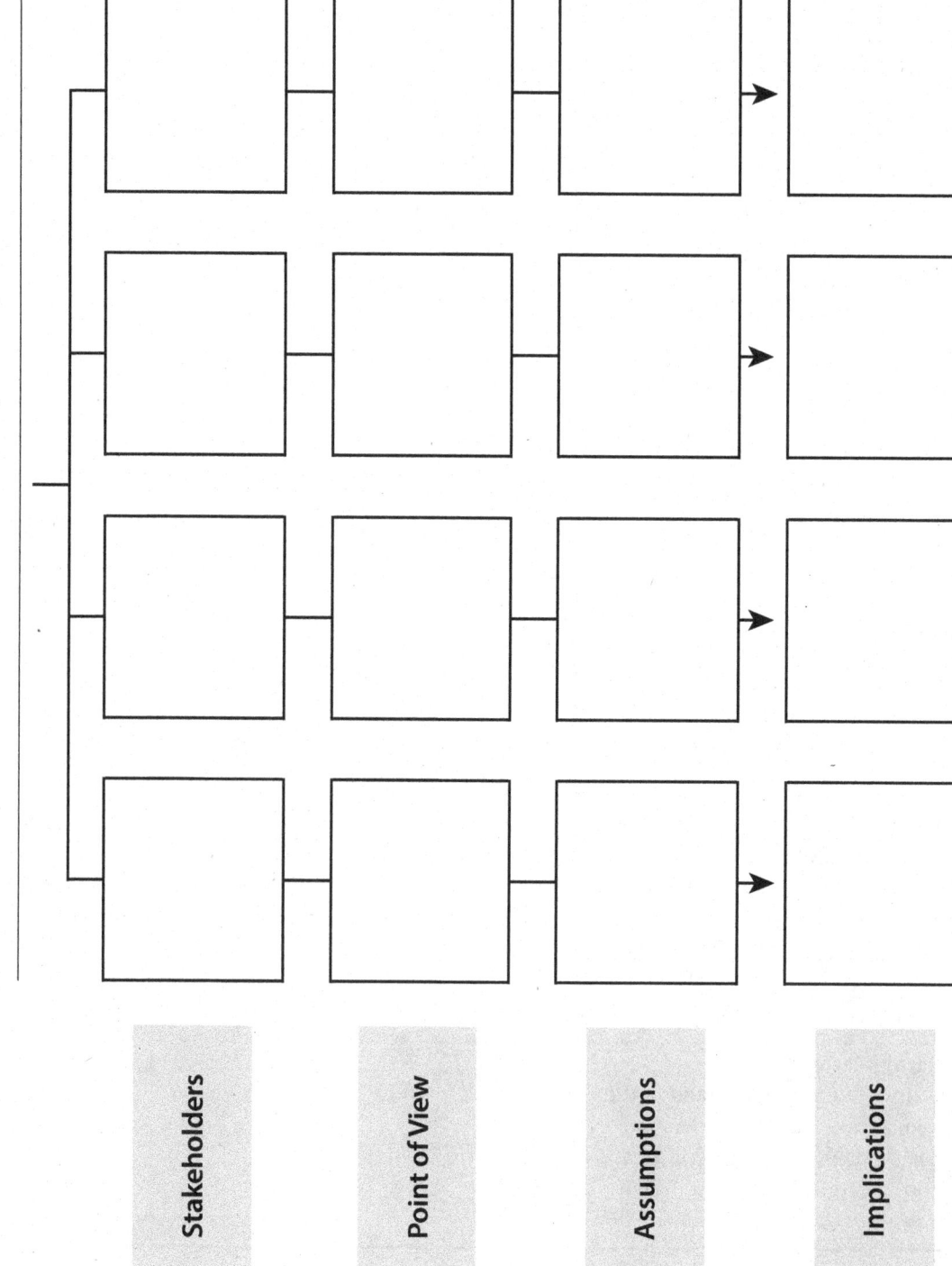

Adapted from "Reasoning About a Situation or Event" by Center for Gifted Education, n.d., retrieved from http://education.wm.edu/centers/cfge/curriculum/teachingmodels. Copyright 2015 by William & Mary, Center for Gifted Education.

CONCLUSION

Lesson 12

Final Reflection and Culminating Project

Goals/Objectives

Content: To analyze and interpret texts and art, students will be able to:
- explain with evidence how literary or visual elements contribute to the overall meaning of a work,
- respond to interpretations of texts through a variety of contexts by justifying ideas and providing new information, and
- compare and contrast the impact of various texts, art, experiences, and real-world events on themes and generalizations.

Process: To develop thinking, writing, and communication skills, students will be able to:
- use evidence to develop appropriate inferences, and
- analyze societal or individual conflicts resulting from the struggle for power.

Concept: To understand the theme of power and related generalizations, students will be able to:
- defend "power may be used or abused" with evidence from text, media, or experience;
- explain how the generalizations "power is the ability to influence" and "power is connected to a source" are manifest within various fictional, historical, and personal contexts;
- explain how the omnipresence of power is shown through various art and literary forms within multiple contexts; and
- explain the relationship of power to other universal themes.

Materials

- Students may need copies of Blank Literary Analysis Wheel, Big Idea Reflection, Blank Rhetorical Analysis Wheel, Blank Visual Analysis Wheel, Reasoning About a Situation or Event, and/or Handout 1.4: Concept

Organizer, depending on the project they choose (See Appendix B for models)
- Handout 12.1: *Perspectives of Power* Culminating Project
- Rubric 2: Culminating Project Rubric

Discussion

1. Remind students about the concept generalizations explored in this unit.
    - Power is the ability to influence.
    - Power is connected to a source.
    - Power can be used or abused.

2. Students should review their responses on concept organizers from previous lessons. Ask: *What patterns do you notice? What are the similarities? What are the major contrasts? What additional generalizations about power might you make based on the unit studied?*

Student Independent Reflection

Assign student reflections on Handout 12.1: Culminating Project (you may choose to assign all of them or part of them.)

Choice-Based Differentiated Products

1. Assign the culminating project (Handout 12.1). At teacher discretion, students can present parts of their projects to the class.
2. Use Rubric 2: Culminating Project Rubric (Appendix C) to assess student products.

ELA Practice Tasks

Assign one of the following tasks as a performance-based assessment for this lesson:
- How should power be used? After reading the texts and analyzing the art in this unit, write an essay to answer the question. Refer to at least four works from this unit to develop your response and cite specific evidence from the works.
- Refer to previous primary source documents analyzed within this unit. Write an argument essay in which you argue for which speaker makes the strongest argument to support his or her claim. Your essay should be grounded in evidence from across three unit texts. Use the Rhetorical Analysis Wheel as a guide for evaluation and writing.

Name: _____   Date: _____

Handout 12.1
Perspectives of Power Culminating Project

STUDENT REFLECTION

Directions: What other movies, stories, art, historical events, or current events involve these concepts in *Perspectives of Power*? Explain how one story or event demonstrates each concept.

1. Text/Event: _____
   Power is the ability to influence.

2. Text/Event: _____
   Power is connected to a source.

3. Text/Event: _____
   Power can be used or abused.

Name: _____ Date: _____

Handout 12.1, Continued

4. How does the theme of power relate to your own life? You may consider the power of oppression, the power of your past/present, the power of indifference, the power of personal responsibility or any other big idea from the unit.

CULMINATING PROJECT

Directions: Choose one activity to demonstrate your understanding of the content, processes, and concepts presented in this unit.

1. How powerful is media on your life and that of your peers? Develop your own research question related to this topic. Consider the influence of video games, social media, advertisements, TV programs, or any other media. Examples of specific questions: *How are girls stereotyped in Disney movies? Do video games promote violent behaviors? Are girls more likely to participate in cyberbullying?* The following must be included in your research investigation:
   - Define the purpose of your study and develop a specific research question.
   - Collect data on your topic by conducting a survey and/or analyzing the frequency of specific behaviors viewed in media.
   - Support your findings with relevant research from at least three online sources.
   - Present your findings in a 2–3 page research report and short visual media presentation (e.g., PowerPoint, video, Prezi, Glogster, etc.). Relate your findings to all three power generalizations from the unit.

2. Create your own short story that uses the following themes: Power of Oppression; Power of Past, Present, and Future; or Power of Personal Response. Complete a Blank Literary Analysis Wheel for your own story. Also provide concept support by completing Handout 1.4: Concept Organizer for the theme of power. Turn in your story, Literary Analysis Wheel, and Concept Organizer. Include development of dialogue, point of view, setting, plot elements, characterization, symbols, and theme within your story.

3. Study three pieces of visual art that you think relate to the theme of power in some way. Complete a visual analysis on each piece (these may also include political cartoons). Then, create a three-way Venn diagram on the pieces. Explain in a paragraph

Name: _____ Date: _____

Handout 12.1, Continued

    or two how each piece exemplifies the theme of power, citing evidence from the art. Show the pieces of art to the class and explain the themes to your classmates.

4. Find a *primary* source that relates to the lives of two individuals introduced in this unit: Emily Dickinson, Moyo Okediji, Charles Perrault, Ray Bradbury, W. B. Yeats, Susan B. Anthony, or Elie Wiesel, etc. (e.g., speeches, letters, diaries, autobiographies, interviews, essays they have written). Biographies or information written about them on the Internet are *not* primary sources. Then, using additional information from secondary sources, determine what is similar between the two individuals. In what ways are power themes evidenced in each of their life experiences and/or texts? Explain in a multiparagraph essay, citing evidence from your sources. Include a list of your sources.

5. Using Reasoning About a Situation or Event (Appendix B), evaluate the following question—How is power reflected in the human experience?—the situation. Choose four individuals from the unit (characters or real people). Complete the chart: Reasoning About a Situation or Event. Then, create a visual collage or multimedia movie to answer the question: How is power reflected in the human experience? Incorporate abstract symbols, words, pictures, and quotes about power, oppression, conflict, change, time, responsibility, or other related concepts. Also turn in a written description of symbols used.

6. Consider real-life applications of the lessons presented: modern-day slavery (e.g., human trafficking), treatment of women in foreign oppressive countries, indifference on global issues, present-day genocide, underachievement among gifted learners, taking risks in learning, addressing the repercussions of 9/11 terrorism attacks (related to "Wild Swans at Coole"). Develop a community service project or action plan related to addressing a problem surfaced within this unit. Complete the chart, Reasoning About a Situation or Event, concerning the stakeholders involved in the issue. Create a proposal for an action plan to address the issue as a community service project. Present your proposal to the class in a presentation. Turn in your chart, presentation, and proposal.

Culminating ELA Practice Tasks

Directions: Choose one task.

1. How should power be used? After reading the texts and analyzing the art in this unit, write an essay to answer the question from the perspectives of individuals studied in the unit. Refer to at least four works from this unit to develop your response and cite specific evidence from the works.

2. Refer to previous primary source documents analyzed within this unit. Write an argument essay in which you argue for which speaker makes the strongest argument to support his or her claim. Your essay should be grounded in evidence from across three unit texts. Use the Rhetorical Analysis Wheel for evaluation and writing.

Name: _____   Date: _____

Posttest
"The Fox, the Rooster, and the Dog" by Aesop

Directions: Read the text and write your responses to the questions below citing evidence from the text. After reading, complete the questions within 30 minutes.

   One moonlight night a Fox was prowling about a farmer's hen-coop, and saw a Rooster sitting high up beyond his reach. "Good news, good news!" he cried.
   "Why, what is that?" said the Rooster.
   "King Lion has declared a universal truce. No beast may hurt a bird henceforth, but all shall dwell together in brotherly friendship."
   "Why, that is good news," said the Rooster; "and there I see someone coming, with whom we can share the good tidings." And so saying he craned his neck forward and looked afar off.
   "What is it you see?" said the Fox.
   "It is only my master's Dog that is coming towards us. What, going so soon?" he continued, as the Fox began to turn away as soon as he had heard the news. "Will you not stop and congratulate the Dog on the reign of universal peace?"
   "I would gladly do so," said the Fox, "but I fear he may not have heard of King Lion's decree."

Name: _____ Date: _____

Posttest, Continued

QUESTIONS

1. How does the author's use of literary techniques (e.g., point of view, conflict, plot, language, symbolism, characterization, setting, etc.) contribute to the overall meaning of the passage?

2. "... I fear he may not have heard of King Lion's decree." What inferences can be made about Fox's motivation and conflict?

3. What does this story suggest about power? Use evidence from the story to support your answer.

Name: _____   Date: _____

Posttest Rubric
"The Fox, the Rooster, and the Dog" by Aesop

	0	1	2	3	4
Question 1: Content: Literary Analysis	Provides no response.	Response is limited and vague. There is no connection to how literary elements contribute to the meaning, main idea, or theme. A literary element is merely named.	Response is accurate with one to two literary techniques described with vague or no connection to a main idea or theme. Response includes limited or no evidence from text.	Response is appropriate and accurate describing at least two literary elements and a main idea or theme. Response is literal and includes some evidence from the text.	Response is insightful and well supported, describing at least two literary elements and the theme. Response includes abstract connections and substantial evidence from the text.
Question 2: Inference From Evidence	Provides no response.	Response is limited, vague, and/or inaccurate. There is no justification for answers given.	Response is accurate, but lacks adequate explanation. Response includes some justification for either the character's motivation or conflict.	Response is accurate and makes sense. Response includes some justification about the character's motivation and conflict.	Response is accurate, insightful, interpretive, and well written. Response includes thoughtful justification about the character's motivation and conflict.
Question 3: Concept/Theme	Provides no response.	Response is limited, vague, and/or inaccurate.	Response lacks adequate explanation. Response does not relate or create a generalization about power. Little or no evidence from text.	Response is accurate and makes sense. Response relates to or creates an idea about power with some relation to the text.	Response is accurate, insightful, and well written. Response relates to or creates a generalization about power with evidence from the text.

Note: Adapted from *Jacob's Ladder Reading Comprehension Program: Level 4* (p. 148) by T. Stambaugh & J. VanTassel-Baska, 2001, New York, NY: Taylor & Francis. Copyright 2001 by Taylor & Francis. Adapted with permission.

References

Assouline, S., Colangelo, N., VanTassel-Baska, J., & Lupkowski-Shoplik, A. (2015). (Eds). *A nation empowered: Evidence trumps the excuses holding American's students back.* Iowa City: University of Iowa, The Connie Belin & Jacqueline N. Blank International Center for Gifted Education and Talent Development.

Center for Gifted Education. (n.d.). Reasoning About a Situation or Event. *Teaching Models.* Retrieved from http://education.wm.edu/centers/cfge/curriculum/teachingmodels

Colangelo, N., Assouline, S., & Gross, M.U.M. (2004). *A nation deceived: How schools hold back America's brightest students* (Vol. II). Iowa City: University of Iowa, The Connie Belin & Jacqueline N. Blank International Center for Gifted Education and Talent Development.

Hilberg, R. (1985). *The destruction of European Jews.* New York, NY: Holmes & Meier.

Kulik, J. A., & Kulik, C.-L. C. (1992). Meta-analytic findings on grouping programs. *Gifted Child Quarterly, 36,* 73–77.

Morris, S. B. & DeShon, R. P. (2002). Combining effect size estimates in meta-analysis with repeated measures and independent-groups designs. *Psychological Methods, 7,* 105–125.

Rogers, K. B. (2007). Lessons learned about educating the gifted and talented: A synthesis of the research on educational practice. *Gifted Child Quarterly, 51,* 382–396.

Simulation Training Systems. (n.d.). *StarPower—Use & abuse of power, leadership & diversity.* Retrieved from http://www.stsintl.net/schools-and-charities/products/starpower

Smith, M. (1999). Moyo Okediji's "The Dutchman." Retrieved from http://www.unc.edu/courses/2005spring/engl/012/051/michasm

Stambaugh, T., & VanTassel-Baska, J. (2001). *Jacob's Ladder Reading Comprehension Program: Level 4.* Waco, TX: Prufrock Press.

Steenbergen-Hu, S., & Moon, S. M. (2011). The effects of acceleration on high-ability learners: A meta-analysis. *Gifted Child Quarterly, 55,* 39–53.

VanTassel-Baska, J. (1986). Effective curriculum and instruction models for talented students. *Gifted Child Quarterly, 30,* 164–169.

VanTassel-Baska, J., & Stambaugh, T. (2008). *What works: 20 years of curriculum research and development for high-ability learners.* Center for Gifted Education, College of William and Mary. Waco, TX: Prufrock Press.

Wright, J. (2006). "Decoding *The Matrix* Exploring Dystopian Characters through Film." *ReadWriteThink*. Retrieved from http://www.readwritethink.org/classroom-resources/lesson-plans/decoding-matrix-exploring-dystopian-926.html

Appendix A

Instructions for Using the Models

LITERARY ANALYSIS WHEEL INSTRUCTIONS

The Literary Analysis Model is used to guide students through analyzing how an author uses literary techniques to develop meaning within a work. The model allows students to see connections between multiple literary elements (e.g., setting impacts conflict, conflict reveals character motives and values, characterization impacts theme, etc.).

Using the Literary Analysis Wheel

The Literary Analysis Wheel can be used to guide students through an analysis of a short story, poem, or novel. First, guide students to identify elements of the wheel separately, then emphasize a deeper analysis by asking how elements relate to each other (e.g., point of view impacts theme, setting creates mood, etc.).

The Literary Analysis Wheel is meant to be interactive. The inner wheel conceptually spins so that its elements interact with each other and the outer wheel. Each element can relate to each other, regardless of its placement on the wheel.

The Literary Analysis Wheel Guide (Appendix B) shows specific prompts for each element of the wheel. The teacher may simply refer to the model during instruction or students may take notes on the Blank Literary Analysis Wheel using arrows to show how the various elements relate. It is suggested that students note the answers to the "simple" questions on the graphic organizer, and then discuss interactions with other elements. Consider making a poster of the Literary Analysis Wheel Guide and posting it in your classroom for students to refer to throughout the unit.

Once students are accustomed to using the wheel, encourage students to develop their own questions about the relationship between elements.

Students can make their own interactive paper-plate model of the wheel. Two different colored papers may be used for the inner and outer circles, secured with a brass paper fastener. Students may use the wheels as visuals in small groups.

Perspectives of Power

Sample questions for literary analysis. The following questions can be asked to support students in analyzing literature. Note that complexity is added by combining elements.

- **Simple:**
  - **Character:** *What are the values and motives of the characters? What evidence supports this? How does the author reveal character?*
  - **Setting:** *What is the time and place of the story?*
  - **Tone:** *What is the author's attitude toward the subject? With what attitude does the author approach the theme?*
  - **Symbols:** *How do objects or names represent more abstract ideas?*
  - **Point of View:** *What is the narrator's point of view (first person, third person objective, third person limited, third person omniscient)?*
  - **Language/Style/Structure:** *What figurative language and imagery does the author use? What is the author's style?*
  - **Plot/Conflict:** *What are the significant internal and external conflicts of the story? What are the significant parts of the plot?*
  - **Mood:** *What is the feeling the reader gets from the story? How is this established?*
  - **Theme:** *What is the author's main message that can be generalized to broader contexts? (The theme is the author's point of view on a given subject.)*

- **Complex:**
  - Setting+
    - *How does the setting influence the development of the theme?*
    - *How does the setting affect the mood?*
    - *What language does the author use to describe the setting (e.g., use of imagery, similes, etc.)?*
    - *How does the setting enhance conflict? How does the setting provoke plot events?*
    - *How is the setting symbolic of a larger idea (e.g., autumn, twilight)?*
    - *How does the setting affect and change the characters?*
    - *How does the setting help reveal the author's tone/attitude toward the theme/subject?*
    - *What conflicts could only happen in this setting? How does this influence the plot and theme?*

  - Symbols+
    - *How do symbols help develop the theme?*
    - *How does the author use figurative language to establish symbolism?*
    - *How do symbols relate to key plot elements and conflicts?*

Appendix A: Instructions for Using the Models

- *How do symbols contribute to establishing the mood?*
- *Is the setting symbolic of a larger idea (e.g., twilight, autumn)?*
- *How does the author's use of symbols reveal the author's tone?*
- *How are characters symbolic of archetypes? What symbols are associated with the characters?*

* Character+
  - *How do the characters' actions/beliefs/attitudes/struggles influence the theme?*
  - *How do the qualities of the characters affect the conflict as it relates to significant parts of the plot?*
  - *How do the characters' actions and responses establish mood?*
  - *What characters' thoughts/feelings are hidden and/or revealed by the narrator's point of view? How does this impact the reader's experience of the story?*
  - *How does the author use language to develop character? Consider dialect, descriptions, use of figurative language, and names.*
  - *Are characters revealed by symbols?*
  - *How does the setting affect character actions?*
  - *How does the author's tone toward the subject influence the development of characters?*

* Tone+
  - *How does the author's tone help establish the theme? What attitude does the author take in approaching the theme?*
  - *How is the author's tone revealed in the narrator's point of view (e.g. the narrator's words and feelings will reveal the attitude of how the author approaches the theme)?*
  - *What words/phrases does the author use to establish tone? How does the tone change throughout the story? How is this established through the author's style?*
  - *How is the author's tone revealed in the plot and conflicts? What specific textual evidence supports this?*
  - *How do the characters' conflicts reveal the author's tone toward a subject?*
  - *How does the author's tone aid in developing the mood of the story?*
  - *How do symbols help reveal the author's tone?*
  - *How do character actions, values, and conflicts reveal the author's tone?*
  - *How does the setting help reveal the author's tone/attitude toward the subject?*

Perspectives of Power

- Point of View+
    - How does the narrator's point of view shape the theme?
    - How does the narrator's point of view establish mood (e.g., the reader depends on the narrator's perspective in telling the story, so the reader feels the way the narrator does about what is being described)?
    - How does the narrator's point of view affect the way the reader views the significant conflicts and plot events?
    - What is the style of the narrator? How does the narrator's point of view (specifically, voice and diction) affect the story?
    - How is the author's tone revealed in the narrator's point of view (e.g. the narrator's words and feelings will reveal the attitude of how the author approaches the theme)?
    - What character thoughts are revealed or hidden because of the narrator's point of view? How does this impact the reader's experience of the story?

- Language/Style/Structure+
    - How does the author's use of figurative language or imagery contribute to literary elements?
    - How does the dialect of the characters contribute to our understanding of literary elements?
    - How does the author's style and sentence structure enhance the mood?

- Mood+
    - How does the mood help develop the theme? What if the mood were different, how would this change the theme of the story?
    - How does the author's point of view help create mood?
    - How does the author's tone create mood for the reader?
    - How do the character's actions, thoughts, and conflicts contribute to the mood?
    - How does the setting contribute to the mood?
    - How does the author use specific language to develop the mood?
    - How do specific symbols help establish the mood?

- Plot/Conflict+
    - How does the plot develop the theme? How would the theme be different if the story had a different ending?
    - How does the conflict reveal the character's values and motives?
    - How does setting impact the conflict and plot?

- *What insight about the conflict does the reader have (or not have) as a result of the narrator's point of view?*
- *How do symbols represent aspects of the conflict (also consider foreshadowing devices)?*
- *How do character actions, thoughts, and conflicts reveal the author's tone?*
- *How does the plot and conflict reveal and/or change the mood?*
- *How does the author's style contribute to the development of the plot? Why does the author use more language/description on certain aspects of the plot than others?*

- Theme+
  - *How does the plot impact the theme? How would the theme change if key parts of the plot or ending were changed?*
  - *How does the theme impact the development of the plot? If the author wanted to show a different theme, how would he have to change the plot of the story? How would the characters' values, motives, and actions change?*
  - *How do the literary elements contribute to the development of the theme?*

- **Interpretation:**
  - *Taken altogether, what is your interpretation of the work (e.g., what is the explanation or meaning of this work given the author's use of various literary elements)? How did literary elements combine to create meaning? Support your interpretation by referring to the interaction of multiple elements in shaping your understanding of the work.*

Example Literary Analysis Lesson

Read the poem "I like to see it lap the Miles" by Emily Dickinson (see Handout 1.1).

Step 1: Text-dependent questions. Lead students through a close reading of text. (*Note:* Do not give away that the poem is about a train; students should continue to hypothesize and discuss with textual evidence).

- According to the poem, does the author enjoy watching this object? How do you know? (Sample response: Yes, the first line of the poem states, "I like to see it . . .")
- According to the poem, does the author like the object itself? How do you know? (Sample response: No, negative connotations about the object—supercilious, complaining, horrid, hooting—are combined with its omnip-

otence. It carves out the quarry to fit its own needs, to "fit its sides"—which is not welcomed in Dickinson's world.)
- What feelings can we associate with some of the words in this poem (horrid, hooting, omnipotent, supercilious, complaining, docile, punctual)? Are the connotations positive or negative?
- How do these connotations change and what effect does it have on the poem? (Sample response: They change from negative to positive.)
- After a second reading, students should respond to a partner: What is this poem about? (Most may say a horse, but help students understand that it is being compared to a horse, continue to guide them as they "discover" it is a railway train.) What evidence is there to support your idea? (The poem is about a train that is compared to a horse. Ask students to highlight or underline all comparisons of the train symbolized through a horse. Note that a train was referred to as an "iron horse" during the time period.)

Step 2. Literary Analysis Wheel, separate elements. Lead students through a simple analysis by completing the separate parts of the wheel.
- **Setting:** What is the setting? What words are used to describe the setting?
- **Character:** Considering the train as a character, what are the train's values and motives? (Sample response: The train is the "iron horse," which is proud and powerful, changing the landscape to fit its own needs. The train's values are to be efficient and strong, with a motivation to arrive punctually at its destination.)
- **Point of View:** What is Dickinson's point of view toward the object? How do you know? (Sample response: She sees both the negative and positive qualities.) (*Note:* Because this is a poem, we are considering the author's point of view—however, in short stories and novels, consider first person, third limited, omniscient, and objective point of view.)
- **Language:** Do you notice any specific figurative language or sound devices throughout the poem? (Sample response: Alliteration: "like," "lap," "lick;" "stop," "step;" personification: "lick," "stop," "feed itself;" simile: "neigh like Boangeres;" rhythm: unaccented-accented syllable pattern.)
- **Symbol:** What does the horse imagery represent? Why is the symbol of a horse used? How is the allusion to Boangeres a symbol? (Sample response: The horse is a symbol for the iron horse—a train. Boangeres was a vociferous disciple—loud and annoying—symbolic of the train.)
- **Tone:** What is Dickinson's attitude toward the train? What is the tone? (Sample response: Her tone is ambiguous—it is both positive and negative—she hates it but is also in awe of its power. At times her tone can also be unwelcoming and unapproving. Note how this is affected by her point of view and language.)

Appendix A: Instructions for Using the Models

- **Conflict:** What is the significant conflict in the poem? (Sample response: Technology vs. nature.)
- **Theme:** What is the author's main message? (Sample response: Themes may relate to the the power of change, power of technology, or the intrusion of technology on nature.)
- **Mood:** Since this is a poem, it would be a stretch to be able to describe the mood based on the few lines that are given. It is suggested that this is not part of the poem analysis.

Step 3. Combined elements for complexity. Discuss how multiple elements interact to establish an overall interpretation of the poem.

- *How does Dickinson's use of language help develop our understanding of the character and the narrator's point of view?* She uses both positive ("docile," "omnipotent") and negative ("horrid," "Boangeres," "supercilious") connotations to show an ambiguous point of view—she loves and hates the train at the same time. The positive and negative connotations about the character help establish Dickinson's point of view.
- *How does the use of language help develop symbolism?* The horse imagery ("neigh," "feed itself at tanks," "stable") establishes the idea of "the iron horse." The *st-* alliteration helps create the sound a horse might make. The rhythm of the poem almost sounds like a train. The entire poem is a metaphor (horse compared to train) and supported through similes (e.g., "neigh like Boangeres") and personification ("lick the valleys," "feed itself," "step").
- *How does setting help establish our understanding of the train's character? How does the setting help us understand the conflict?* The train can be considered as the main character, the "iron horse," who is proud and powerful, changing the landscape to fit its own needs. It pares a quarry to meet its own needs. The use of "shanties" in the setting implies how the train condescendingly looks down upon human things. The train "licks" the valleys up, revealing how it authoritatively takes layers off the landscape.
- *How does the tone and conflict establish the theme of the poem?* Dickinson's tone and attitude toward the new technology establishes the conflict of nature versus technology. This clearly establishes the theme of the power and intrusion of technology on our lives.
- *If Dickinson were to change the theme to "overcoming obstacles," how would this affect how she describes the setting and character?* The character (the train) would be described more positively or even heroic. The setting would not showcase the train's domination; rather, it might be a hindrance to a train. Consider how the story "The Little Engine That Could" shows a contrasting theme (e.g., the setting poses an obstacle for the train instead of

the train imposing on nature; rather than the train having "power" over the setting, the setting poses "power" over the train).

VISUAL ANALYSIS WHEEL INSTRUCTIONS

The Visual Analysis Model is used to guide students through analyzing how an artist develops a main idea in art. Students analyze specific techniques, organization, and the artist's point of view toward the idea. Additionally, students examine prominent images and symbolism, the author's background, and emotions portrayed and evoked in the art. The model allows students to see the connection between multiple concepts (e.g., images are organized intentionally to create the main idea, point of view is influenced by the artist's background, specific techniques are used to evoke emotion, etc.).

Using the Visual Analysis Wheel

The Visual Analysis Wheel can be used to guide student through an in-depth analysis of art or visual media. It is meant to be interactive. The inner circle conceptually spins so that it interacts with elements on the outer circle.

The Visual Analysis Wheel Guide (Appendix B) shows specific prompts to guide students in thinking through each separate element. The teacher may simply refer to the model during instruction or students may take notes on the Blank Visual Analysis Wheel using arrows to show how the elements relate. It is suggested that students first note the answers to each concept separately on the graphic organizer, and then discuss how they influence each other.

Students can make their own interactive paper-plate model of the wheel. Two different colored papers may be used for the inner and outer circles, secured with a brass paper fastener. Students may use the wheels as visuals in small groups.

Sample questions for visual analysis. The following questions can be asked for analyzing art. Note that complexity is added by combining different elements.

- **Purpose:**
  - *What is the purpose of the art?*

- **Context:**
  - *What year was this art created? What artistic movements may have influenced this work? What type of art is this? What historical events are happening at the time this was made? Is there a specific audience for which the art was created?*

Appendix A: Instructions for Using the Models

- **Main Idea/Message:**
  - *What is the main idea of this art? What is the message of the art?*

- **Techniques:**
  - *What specific techniques does the artist use? (Consider color, shape, brushstroke, patterns, contrast.)*

- **Point of View/Assumptions:**
  - *What is the artist's point of view toward the topic?*
  - *What assumptions does the artist make?*
  - *What is the artist's unstated premise or belief? What does the artist take for granted about the audience?*

- **Structure:**
  - *How does the artist organize ideas?*
  - *What is the central part of the painting?*
  - *Where is your eye drawn first? Why?*

- **Images/Symbols:**
  - *What are the main images?*
  - *Do they symbolize a deeper meaning? How?*

- **Images/Structure:**
  - *Why does the artist intentionally place the objects where they are?*

- **Images/Point of View/Assumptions:**
  - *What do the artist's images reveal about his or her point of view/assumptions about the topic displayed?*

- **Images/Techniques:**
  - *What specific techniques does the artist use to create the main images of the art?*

- **Images/Purpose/Context:**
  - *How does the historical context influence the artist's choice of images in his art?*
  - *How does the audience for which this is intended influence the artist's choice of images?*

Perspectives of Power

- **Emotions:**
  - *What emotions does this art evoke in you?*
  - *What emotions does this art reveal/portray?*

- **Emotions/Point of View/Assumptions:**
  - *How does the artist's point of view toward the topic influence your emotional reaction to the art?*

- **Emotions/Technique:**
  - *What techniques does the artist use to portray and evoke emotion from his or her art?*

- **Emotions/Structure:**
  - *Are parts of the art more emotionally powerful than others? How did the artist organize his or her painting to evoke or portray emotion?*

- **Emotions/Purpose/Context:**
  - *How does the historical situation influence how the artist expresses or evokes emotion?*

- **Artist Background:**
  - *What do you know about the artist's personal life? Who influenced his or her work? How did his or her work influence others?*

- **Artist Background/Technique:**
  - *What techniques does the artist use that are unique to his or her style?*

- **Artist Background/Point of View/Assumptions:**
  - *How does the artist's background influence his or her point of view/assumptions about the topic?*

- **Artist Background/Structure:**
  - *Does the artist's background influence the way he or she organizes his or her art?*

- **Artist Background/Purpose/Context:**
  - *How is the artist influenced by the historical context of his or her time? How does the artist influence the historical context of his or her time?*

- **Implications:**
  - *What are the short- and long-term consequences of this art?*
  - *What are the implications for you after viewing this art?*

- **Evaluation:**
  - *Do you like this art? Why or why not? Use specific elements for the wheel in your answer.*
  - *What does this art make you think? Would you hang this in your home? Why or why not?*
  - *What elements of this art are most important to consider and why?*

Example Visual Analysis Lesson

Students view the lithograph "Relativity" by M. C. Escher (available online). Do not reveal the title.

Step 1: Close viewing questions. Lead students through an initial viewing of the art.

- What detail of this art is interesting to you? (Ask every student; short response.)
- How many staircases are there? (Sample response: Seven; some overlap.)
- How many sources of gravity are in this picture? (Sample response: Three.)
- What behaviors do you see of the people?
- What is the focal point of the picture? Justify your answer.
- How does Escher produce "dual effects" on this painting? (Sample response: The ceiling is also a floor.) Note that although two people may be on the same staircase, they exist in two separate dimensions. Do they know of each other's existence? (Sample response: One is going up, one is going down, but they are going in the same direction.)
- Round-robin: If you had to give the lithograph a title, what title would you give it? (Ask every student; short response.)
- Share with your neighbor why you chose this title (or if time permits, elicit this as whole group).
- Share the real title of the lithograph. "Relativity." Why do you think Escher gave it this title?

Step 2. Visual Analysis Wheel, separate elements. Lead students through completing relevant parts of the Visual Analysis Wheel during discussion. Focus first on the separate elements.

- **Purpose/Context:**
  - *What is the context of this art?* Lithograph printed in 1953.
  - *What do you think his purpose/motive is in creating this?* To express an idea of reality. (*Note:* Students may not be able to determine this until after discussing the art to some extent.)

- **Point of View/Assumptions:**
  - *What is Escher's point of view toward reality?* Escher is revealing that there are multiple realities existing simultaneously. We might also interpret this as multiple perceptions of truth existing at the same time. The only time people are in social contexts are "outside." Perhaps he is saying the only way to get out of the boring coming and going of life is to acknowledge others' perspectives.

- **Images:**
  - *What do you believe are the most prominent images in the picture? Why? How might they be symbols for something deeper?* Staircases = journey in life; featureless people = unaware people, emotionless; windows to outside = ways to get out of isolation.

- **Emotions:**
  - *What emotions does this evoke in you? What emotions are revealed?* The featureless people reveal a lack of emotion, indicating that people are coming and going in life in an emotionless state.

- **Artist Background:**
  - *What do you know about the artist's background? How is the artist influenced by the historical context of his time?* M. C. Escher (1898–1972) was a famous 20th-century Dutch artist who is known for developing impossible structures within his art. He made more than 448 lithographs (original prints) and woodcarvings, and more than 2,000 drawings. Escher also wrote many poems and essays, and he studied architecture, though he never graduated from high school. He used many mathematical aspects in his works. Most of Escher's works involve his own fascination with the concept of reality. His works showing paradoxes, tessellations, and impossible objects have had influence on graphic art, psychology, philosophy, and logic.

- **Main Idea:**
  - *What is Escher conveying about life in this painting? What is Escher's main idea?* Truth/reality is relative; each person has his own reality and may be unaware of others' realities.

- **Implications:**
  - *What are the implications of this art on you the viewer?*

Appendix A: Instructions for Using the Models

- **Evaluation:**
  - *Do you like this art? Would you hang it in your home? Does it make you think? Was the artist successful in presenting his ideas? Justify your answers with evidence.*

Step 3. Combined elements for complexity. Combine elements to develop more complex questions. Students may draw arrows on their wheels to show how elements relate (images + techniques, etc.).

- **Images/Technique:**
  - *What techniques does Escher use to enhance images?* The people are all identical and featureless. There are three sources of gravity and six staircases. The outside world is park-like. Some appear to be climbing upside down, but according to their gravity, they are climbing the staircase normally. Parts of the picture look two-dimensional, other parts look three-dimensional. He includes paradoxes (two people standing on same staircase in separate realities). The basements add a surreal effect.

- **Images/Structure:**
  - *How does Escher intentionally place the objects in the painting to reveal meaning?* He purposefully draws two people standing on the same step (top center); they coexist yet they are in different gravity worlds. *What does this reveal about life?* We are preoccupied with our own journeys, we do not acknowledge others' points of view.

- **Artist Background/Technique:**
  - *What techniques does Escher use that are unique to his style?* Escher creates impossible realities within this work (three gravity worlds existing as one). He is known for creating paradoxes in his art.

- **Emotions/Structure/Technique:**
  - *How did the artist organize his art to portray or evoke emotion? What techniques were used to evoke or portray emotion?* It is interesting that the staircase structure is an upside-down triangle. Perhaps this is to give a more chaotic feel to the picture. Those within the staircases are "lost" in a world of coming and going, living life unaware beyond their own self-centered world. His technique of painting featureless people portrays a lack of emotion. The lack of emotion interplays with a main idea that the people are not aware of each other's existence, particularly in the other gravity worlds.

RHETORICAL ANALYSIS WHEEL INSTRUCTIONS

The Rhetorical Analysis Model is used to analyze how an author develops and supports an argument. Students examine how a writer achieves his or her purpose by analyzing how several elements work together to create an effective argument. This includes thinking about the rhetorical situation (e.g., purpose, context, audience), means of persuasion (e.g., ethos, logos, and pathos appeals), and rhetorical strategies (e.g., techniques, evidence, structure, etc.). The author develops a claim through the use of three rhetorical appeals: logos (reasoning), pathos (emotion), and ethos (credibility) in response to the situation. These rhetorical appeals are developed by point of view, specific strategies, techniques, and organization. The model allows students to see connections between multiple elements (e.g., credibility is influenced by point of view, specific techniques are used to evoke emotion, structure develops strong logos appeals, etc.).

Overview of Aristotle's Rhetorical Appeals

Aristotle's rhetoric includes logos, ethos, and pathos appeals. This enhances a writer's ability to persuade an audience.
- **Logos:** How the author establishes good reasoning to make his message make sense. This includes major points, use of evidence, syllogisms, examples, evidence, facts, statistics, etc. Text focused.
- **Pathos:** How the author appeals to the audience's emotion. Audience focused.
- **Ethos:** How the author develops credibility and trust. Author focused.

Using the Rhetorical Analysis Wheel

The Rhetorical Analysis Wheel can be used to analyze how an author develops a claim through rhetorical appeals, techniques, and structure. Students also think through the point of view, assumptions, purpose, and implications of the document. It is meant to be interactive. The inner circle conceptually spins so that it interacts with elements on the outer circle.

The Rhetorical Analysis Wheel Guide (Appendix B) shows specific prompts to guide students in thinking through each separate element. The teacher may simply refer to the model during instruction or students may take notes on the Blank Rhetorical Analysis Wheel using arrows to show how elements relate. It is suggested that students first note the answers to each element separately on the graphic organizer, and then discuss how they influence each other. Consider making a poster of the Rhetorical Analysis Wheel Guide to refer to throughout the unit.

Appendix A: Instructions for Using the Models

Students can make their own interactive paper-plate model of the wheel. Two different colored papers may be used for the inner and outer circles, secured with a brass paper fastener. Students may use the wheels as visuals in small groups.

Sample questions for rhetorical analysis. The following questions can be asked for analyzing argument. Note that complexity is added by combining elements.

- **Purpose:**
  - *What is the author's purpose?*

- **Context/Audience:**
  - *Who is the audience and what is the historical situation?*
  - *What is the main problem in the historical context?*

- **Claim:**
  - *What is the main claim or message of the text?*

- **Techniques:**
  - *What specific techniques does the writer use to develop his or her claim?* Here are some examples of specific techniques that may be asked:
    - **Language:** Consider how specific word choice and style develops tone.
    - **Positive and negative connotations of words:** Consider how words evoke feelings.
    - **Personification:** Human qualities given to nonhuman objects/ideas.
    - **Simile:** A figure of speech that compares two unlike things using "like" or "as."
    - **Metaphor:** A direct comparison between two unlike things.
    - **Hyperbole:** An extreme exaggeration.
    - **Allusion:** A reference to a historical or Biblical work, person, or event. The writer assumes the reader can make connections between the allusion and text being read.
    - **Imagery:** Formation of mental images that appeal to the senses.
    - **Parallelism:** Using similar grammatical structures in order to emphasize related ideas.
    - **Repetition:** Repeating the same wording for emphasis, clarity, or emotional impact.
    - **Contrast:** A striking difference of ideas for effect.
    - **Rhetorical question:** A question asked by the writer, but not expected to be answered aloud. It evokes reflection.
    - **Liberty rhetoric:** Using patriotic appeals for freedom.
    - **War rhetoric:** Reasoning to convince war is necessary.

Perspectives of Power

- **Syllogism:** A form of deductive logic—a conclusion drawn from two premises. Example: If x=y and y=z, then x=z. If citizens can vote and if women are citizens, then women should be allowed to vote.
- **Use of evidence, facts, statistics, examples, and counterclaims (strongly connects with logos):** Explicit support for the argument.

- **Point of View/Assumptions:**
  - *What is the writer's point of view toward the topic?*
  - *What assumptions does the writer make?*
  - *What is the writer's unstated premise or belief? What does the writer take for granted about the audience?*

- **Structure/Organization:**
  - *How does the writer organize ideas (e.g., problem-solution, point by point, chronologically, sequentially, compare/contrast)?*
  - *Where is the thesis? Why is it here?*
  - *Does the writer structure his message deductively or inductively?*

- **Logos (Focus on Text):**
  - *What reasoning is used to help the argument make sense? What are the main points?*
  - *Are statements easy to accept or does the writer need to provide more evidence?*
  - *What research, facts, statistics, or expert opinions are used? Are these sufficient?*
  - **Logos/Structure**
    - *How does the structure of the document help the writer's argument make sense?*

  - **Logos/Point of View:**
    - *Does the writer assume that the audience already accepts a premise?*
    - *What do the writer's examples and facts (or lack of) reveal about his or her assumptions about the audience?*

  - **Logos/Techniques:**
    - *Which techniques are used to help the writer logically form his or her argument (e.g., syllogisms, comparisons, parallelisms, use of statistics, examples, etc.)?*

Appendix A: Instructions for Using the Models

- **Logos/Context:**
  - *How do the problem, context, and audience influence the writer's approach in developing a logical argument? Because the historical situation is what it is, how does this influence the way the writer organizes his reasoning?*

- **Pathos (Focus on Audience):**
  - *How does the writer appeal to the audience's emotions (guilt, fear, pride, etc.)?*
  - *What word connotations or imagery does the writer use to evoke emotion in the audience?*
  - *How do pathos appeals help the writer establish his claim?*
  - **Pathos/Point of View:**
    - *How does the writer's tone and point of view impact the desired emotional response?*
    - *How does the writer's bias influence the desired emotional response?*

  - **Pathos/Technique:**
    - *What techniques does the writer use to evoke emotion among the audience (e.g., repetition, liberty rhetoric, war rhetoric, similes, hyperbole, symbolism, rhetorical questions)?*

  - **Pathos/Structure:**
    - *Where does the writer place the emotional appeals? Why is this important? Do pathos appeals change throughout the text? How? Why? How does this enhance or take away from the argument?*

  - **Pathos/Context:**
    - *How does the historical situation/problem influence how the writer uses pathos appeals? How do pathos appeals help the writer accomplish his desired effect?*

- **Ethos (Focus on Writer):**
  - *Is the writer credible?*
  - *How does the writer establish trust?*
  - *Are sources credible?*
  - *Does the writer respect an opposing viewpoint?*
  - *Does the writer address counterclaims? How?*
  - *How do ethos appeals help the writer establish an effective argument?*

- **Ethos/Technique:**
  - *What techniques does the writer use to establish credibility (e.g., uses reliable sources, discusses character/reputation, etc.)?*

- **Ethos/Point of View:**
  - *Does the writer's bias take away from his or her credibility?*
  - *Do the writer's assumptions about the opposing point of view reduce his or her credibility?*

- **Ethos/Structure:**
  - *Where in the document does the writer develop his or her credibility? Why is it significant he or she places his or her ethos appeals here?*
  - *Where does the writer address counterclaims? How does he or she address the counterclaim, and how does this enhance or reduce his or her credibility?*

- **Ethos/Context:**
  - *Why is it important for the writer to develop trust with this audience in this historical situation?*
  - *What must the writer consider about the audience when establishing his or her credibility?*

- **Implications:**
  - *What are the short- and long-term implications/consequences of this document?*

- **Evaluation:**
  - *How effective is the writer in developing his or her claim? To what extent is the purpose fulfilled?*
  - *Is there a balance of pathos, ethos, and logos appeals?*
  - *Is there too much bias or emotional manipulation? Is there adequate evidence to support the claim(s)? Is the evidence credible, rational, and organized logically?*

Students should consider the author's purpose (to entertain, inform, persuade, express) when determining how effective the argument is. For example, it may not be necessary to provide counterarguments if the purpose of the text is not to persuade. Students should also consider the balance of logos, ethos, and pathos appeals.

Appendix A: Instructions for Using the Models

Example Rhetorical Analysis Lesson

Students should read the excerpt from Franklin D. Roosevelt's Second Inaugural Address (see p. 199).

Step 1: Text-dependent questions. Lead students through a close reading of the text for initial comprehension. You may also ask students to paraphrase sections of the text into their own words.

- According to Roosevelt, what brings an ever richer life to Americans?
- Why does Roosevelt personify Comfort, Opportunism, and Timidity? How are these "voices" considered distractions?
- What are some of the positive aspects of the current state of affairs?
- According to the text, why is prosperity dangerous?
- What is meant by "prosperity already tests the persistence of our progressive purpose"?
- Which one of Roosevelt's "I see" statements is most powerful?
- According to the text, how do we test our progress?
- What is Roosevelt's solution to the problems of tens of millions?
- What four words are most important to the text? Can you put these four words together in a sentence to summarize FDR's main message?

Step 2: Teach elements of rhetorical analysis. Teach students some basic principles of a rhetorical analysis:

- **Modes of Rhetoric (Logos, Pathos, Ethos):** Explain Aristotle's modes of rhetoric (see p. 188).
- **Techniques:** Students will consider how these appeals are developed through different techniques used by the author. Go over a few techniques with students (see p. 189). Note that language, positive and negative connotations, personification, repetition, and rhetorical questions are used.
- **Structure/Organization:** Students should consider where the appeals are placed within the documents and why they are there. They should also consider the overall structure of the document as it often supports the logos appeal (it helps the author's rationale "make sense" by putting ideas in this order). Why is it important that the points are placed structurally where they are? Throughout the analysis, the elements of logos, ethos, and pathos interact with structure, techniques and point of view.

Step 3: Rhetorical Analysis Wheel: Separate Elements. Lead students through completing relevant parts of the Rhetorical Analysis Wheel. Students do not need to write detailed explanations on the organizer, just notes. Focus first on the separate elements.

Perspectives of Power

- **Purpose:**
  - *What is Roosevelt's purpose in delivering this message?* To persuade the American people to carry on toward progress by moving forward together.

- **Message/Claim:**
  - *What is Roosevelt's main claim? What is the main idea he is proving?* America will carry on toward progress by addressing concerns of all.

- **Point of View/Assumptions:**
  - *What is Roosevelt's point of view toward progress? What are his assumptions?* FDR believes Americans should cautiously handle prosperity; it can distract Americans from progressing because of the self-interest involved. He assumes that government involvement into the affairs of people is welcomed, justified, and of goodwill.

- **Structure:**
  - *What is the overall structure of the speech?* Problem-solution.

- **Techniques:**
  - *What are some techniques you notice within the speech?* Rhetorical questions, personification, etc.

- **Logos:**
  - *What are the main points? How does the author support his claim with evidence and facts? What are the main "reasons" that support the claim?* **Logos/Reasoning:** FDR notes that America has progressed, but not arrived, and the American people should be warned by the disasters of prosperity. He lists positive state of affairs, lists negative state of affairs, and explains a hopeful future via government involvement. He provides evidence of a negative state of affairs ("I see millions . . . ").

- **Pathos:**
  - *What emotion(s) does the author attempt to evoke in the audience (pathos)?* FDR appeals to a sense of sympathy ("I see millions . . . ") and pride ("If I know aught of the will of our people . . . ").

- **Ethos:**
  - *Is the author credible? How does the author establish trust? Is evidence credible?* FDR is speaking at his second inaugural address and acknowledges the progress made during his presidency. He also refers to the

government as effective and competent to build trust. Evidence is not supported with specific credibility, and he is somewhat biased with his enthusiasm for a competent government addressing problems.

- **Implications:**
  - *What are the short- and long-term implications/consequences of this document?* This speech set the stage for many of FDR's initiatives. During his second term, Congress passed the Housing Act, laws were made to establish minimum wage (Fair Labor Standards Act), and more than 3.3 million jobs were developed through WPA (Works Progress Administration).

Step 4: Combined elements for complexity. Combine elements to develop more complex questions. Students may draw arrows on their wheels to show how elements relate (pathos + techniques, etc.).

- **Logos/Techniques:**
  - *What techniques are used to develop the reasoning in his argument?* He sets up the first point by asking a rhetorical question ("Shall we pause now and turn our back . . . "), uses personification to introduce the idea that we should be warned by the disasters of prosperity ("Comfort says . . . timidity says . . . "), addresses a counterclaim and acknowledges that we have progressed ("true, we have come far . . . "), and explains how progress today is more difficult in light of prosperity.

- **Logos/Structure:**
  - *How is the argument structured logically?* Problem-solution. It is also organized inductively. His main claim is that Americans will carry on by addressing the concerns of all. He provides evidence first and then makes this claim.

- **Pathos/Techniques:**
  - *What techniques are used to develop pathos appeals?* He uses repetition ("I see millions . . . ") to develop sympathy. He develops a sense of urgency with "at this very moment . . . " He uses loaded language ("meager," "indecent," "poverty," "denying work," "ill-housed," "ill-clad," "ill-nourished") for sympathy and pride ("goodwill," "effective government," "uncorrupted by cancers of injustice," "strong," "will to peace," "long-cherished ideals").

- **Pathos/Structure:**
  - *Where does he place pathos appeals (structure)? Why? Do they change? Why?* The pathos appeals are in line with the problem-solution logos structure. As he develops the problem, he evokes sympathy. As he develops the solution, he evokes pride.

- **Ethos/Techniques/Structure:**
  - *What techniques are used to establish ethos appeals and why are they placed where they are?* He includes "we," and "us" throughout the speech to connect with the audience. As he uses "we," he establishes that he has been a part of the present gains. The "we" language shifts to "I"—revealing that the audience can really trust him because he himself sees the problems. He shifts again to "we" when connecting the audience to the goodwill of the nation.

- **Evaluation:**
  - *How effective is the author in supporting his claim? Is there a balance of pathos, ethos, and logos appeals? Is the claim fully supported?* Roosevelt is effective in supporting the claim that America will continue on toward progress by addressing the concerns of all. There is a balance of logos, ethos, and pathos appeals. FDR gives sufficient evidence of the problem with the repeated "I see" statements, though the credibility of this evidence is not specific, but general.

Text Analysis Example, Simplified Version

Some teachers of younger grades may wish to focus on how the author supports a central idea by using relevant and sufficient evidence. This model does not focus on the rhetorical appeals (logos, ethos, and pathos) to support a claim, rather it focuses on why the author chose to use specific points to advance a central idea.

The following are simple and complex questions that could be used:

- **Purpose:**
  - *What is Roosevelt's purpose in delivering this message?* To persuade the American people to carry on toward progress by moving forward together.

- **Central Idea:**
  - *What is FDR's central idea (main message)?* We will carry on toward progress by addressing concerns of all.

Appendix A: Instructions for Using the Models

- **Point of View/Assumptions:**
  - *What is FDR's point of view toward progress? What are his assumptions?* FDR believes Americans should cautiously handle prosperity; it can distract us from progressing because of the self-interest involved. He assumes that government involvement into the affairs of people is welcomed, justified, and of goodwill.

- **Point 1/Evidence:**
  - *What is one important point FDR makes to develop his central idea?* **Point 1:** We should we warned by the disasters of prosperity. **Evidence:** "Comfort says, 'tarry a while.' Opportunism . . . ' To hold progress today, however, is more difficult . . . ."
  - *How does this point develop his central idea?* This explains the state of affairs—the nation has made great progress and experienced prosperity, but prosperity can also present a problem. He asks the nation to consider the nature of progress.
  - *What techniques are used to develop this point?* He personifies comfort, opportunism, and timidity to explain that the nation is at a place of decision in the face of prosperity. He describes symptoms of prosperity with negative word connotations ("dulled conscience, irresponsibility . . .").
  - *Why is it important the author discusses this point at this particular part of the speech (structure)?* This allows him to introduce the problem of prosperity. This sets him up to explain to the audience that not everyone is reaping the benefits of prosperity, which is important in developing his central idea.

- **Point 2/Evidence:**
  - *What is another important point FDR uses to develop his central idea?* **Point 2:** He explains a negative state of affairs. **Evidence:** "I see millions . . . ill-housed, ill-clad, ill-nourished."
  - *How does this point develop the central idea?* It explains the problem of poverty, that the concerns of all citizens are not addressed even within a time of prosperous progress.
  - *What techniques are used to develop his point?* He uses both repetition ("I see millions") and loaded language ("meager," "indecent," "poverty," "denying work," "ill-housed," "ill-clad," "ill-nourished") to develop sympathy (pathos appeal).
  - *Why is it important that the author discusses this point at this particular part of the speech (structure)?* At this part of the speech, he is developing

Perspectives of Power

the problem before he offers a solution. As he develops the problem, he evokes sympathy.

- **Point 3/Evidence:**
  - *What is another important point FDR uses to develop his central idea?* **Point 3:** FDR explains a hopeful future via government involvement. **Evidence:** "But it is not in despair I paint you that picture . . . government is competent . . . ."
  - *How does this point develop the central idea?* It explains how the nation can address the concerns of all of its citizens, even those in poverty.
  - *What techniques are used to develop his point? How does this technique develop his point?* He revisits the personified comfort, opportunism and timidity to remind the audience about the problem of prosperity within his solution for more government involvement. He uses positive word connotations when referring to the government and the American people ("men and women of good will," "warm hearts of dedication," "competent," "effective"). He refers to the government as effective and competent to build trust (ethos appeal).
  - *Why is this point where it is in the document (structure)? How does it help develop the central idea?* This point includes his closing where he offers a solution for the American people—come together with the government to address the problems of both comfortable prosperity and poverty.

- **Structure:**
  - *What is the overall structure of the document?* Problem-solution.

- **Implications:**
  - *What are implications/consequences of this document?* This speech set the stage for many of FDR's initiatives. During his second term, Congress passed the Housing Act, laws were made to establish minimum wage (Fair Labor Standards Act), and more than 3.3 million jobs were developed through WPA (Works Progress Administration).

- **Evaluation:**
  - *How effective is the author in using sufficient, relevant evidence to develop a central idea?* Roosevelt is somewhat effective in supporting the central idea that America will continue on toward progress by addressing the concerns of all. He speaks of the problem of progress and prosperity in general terms, but allows the audience to consider the problem through the present context. He provides a sufficient amount of evi-

dence for stating the problems of poverty through the repetition of "I see" statements, and he effectively explains how the government and the American people can work together to address the concerns of all.

FRANKLIN D. ROOSEVELT'S SECOND INAUGURAL ADDRESS

Delivered January 20, 1937

. . . Among men of good will, science and democracy together offer an ever-richer life and ever-larger satisfaction to the individual. With this change in our moral climate and our rediscovered ability to improve our economic order, we have set our feet upon the road of enduring progress.

Shall we pause now and turn our back upon the road that lies ahead? Shall we call this the promised land? Or, shall we continue on our way? For "each age is a dream that is dying, or one that is coming to birth."

Many voices are heard as we face a great decision. Comfort says, "Tarry a while." Opportunism says, "This is a good spot." Timidity asks, "How difficult is the road ahead?"

True, we have come far from the days of stagnation and despair. Vitality has been preserved. Courage and confidence have been restored. Mental and moral horizons have been extended.

But our present gains were won under the pressure of more than ordinary circumstances. Advance became imperative under the goad of fear and suffering. The times were on the side of progress.

To hold to progress today, however, is more difficult. Dulled conscience, irresponsibility, and ruthless self-interest already reappear. Such symptoms of prosperity may become portents of disaster! Prosperity already tests the persistence of our progressive purpose.

Let us ask again: Have we reached the goal of our vision of that fourth day of March 1933? Have we found our happy valley?

I see a great nation, upon a great continent, blessed with a great wealth of natural resources. Its hundred and thirty million people are at peace among themselves; they are making their country a good neighbor among the nations. I see a United States which can demonstrate that, under democratic methods of government, national wealth can be translated into a spreading volume of human comforts hitherto unknown, and the lowest standard of living can be raised far above the level of mere subsistence.

Perspectives of Power

But here is the challenge to our democracy: In this nation I see tens of millions of its citizens—a substantial part of its whole population—who at this very moment are denied the greater part of what the very lowest standards of today call the necessities of life.

I see millions of families trying to live on incomes so meager that the pall of family disaster hangs over them day by day.

I see millions whose daily lives in city and on farm continue under conditions labeled indecent by a so-called polite society half a century ago.

I see millions denied education, recreation, and the opportunity to better their lot and the lot of their children.

I see millions lacking the means to buy the products of farm and factory and by their poverty denying work and productiveness to many other millions.

I see one-third of a nation ill-housed, ill-clad, ill-nourished.

But it is not in despair that I paint you that picture. I paint it for you in hope—because the nation, seeing and understanding the injustice in it, proposes to paint it out. We are determined to make every American citizen the subject of his country's interest and concern; and we will never regard any faithful law-abiding group within our borders as superfluous. The test of our progress is not whether we add more to the abundance of those who have much; it is whether we provide enough for those who have too little.

If I know aught of the spirit and purpose of our Nation, we will not listen to comfort, opportunism, and timidity. We will carry on.

Overwhelmingly, we of the Republic are men and women of good will; men and women who have more than warm hearts of dedication; men and women who have cool heads and willing hands of practical purpose as well. They will insist that every agency of popular government use effective instruments to carry out their will.

Government is competent when all who compose it work as trustees for the whole people. It can make constant progress when it keeps abreast of all the facts. It can obtain justified support and legitimate criticism when the people receive true information of all that government does.

If I know aught of the will of our people, they will demand that these conditions of effective government shall be created and maintained. They will demand a nation uncorrupted by cancers of injustice and, therefore, strong among the nations in its example of the will to peace.

Today we reconsecrate our country to long-cherished ideals in a suddenly changed civilization. In every land there are always at work forces that drive men apart and forces that draw men together. In our personal ambitions we are individualists. But in our seeking for economic and political progress as a nation, we all go up, or else we all go down, as one people.

Appendix B

Blank Models and Guides

Perspectives of Power

BLANK LITERARY ANALYSIS WHEEL

Directions: Draw arrows across elements to show connections.

Text: _____

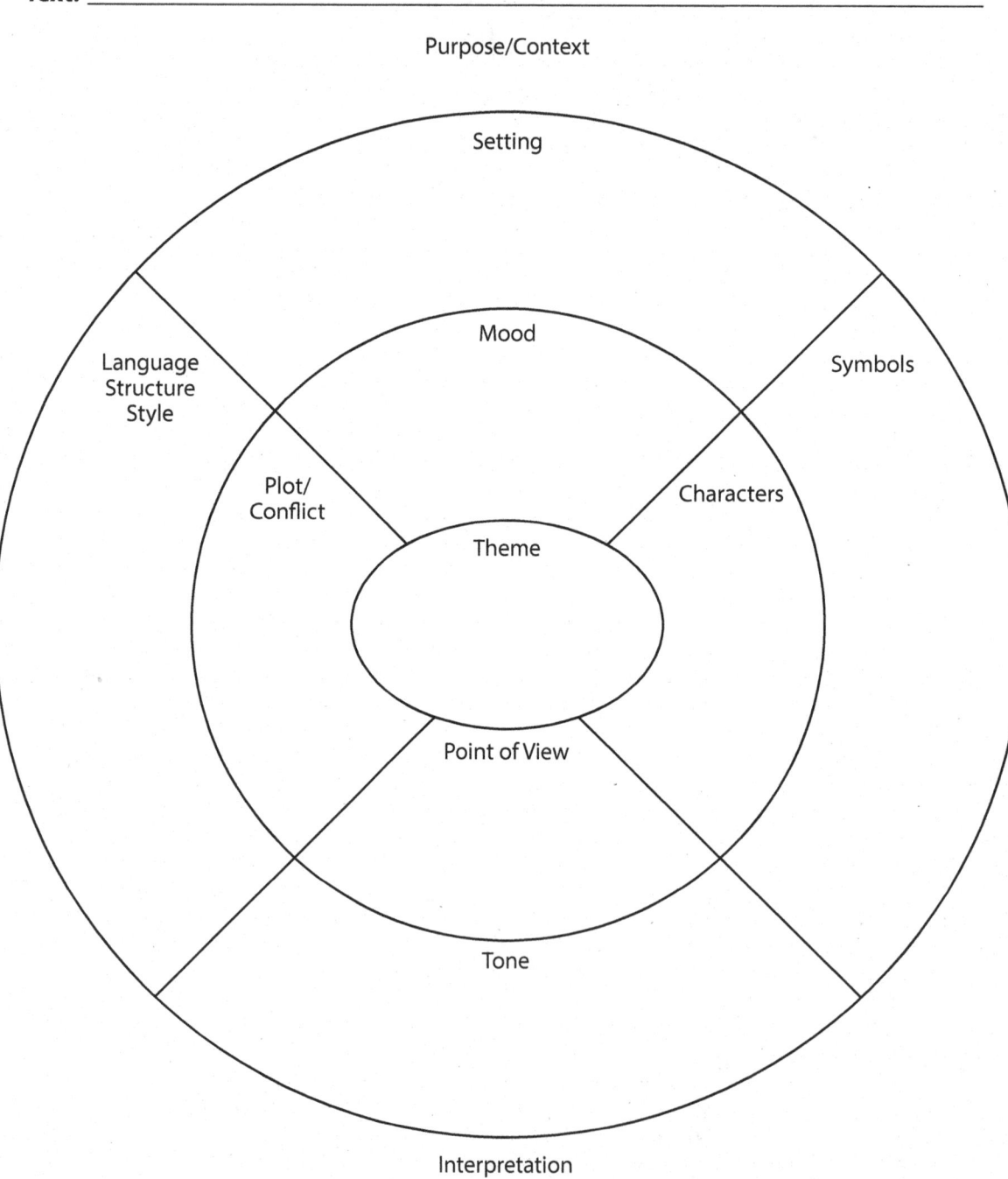

Created by Tamra Stambaugh, Ph.D., & Emily Mofield, Ed.D., 2015.

Appendix B: Blank Models and Guides

LITERARY ANALYSIS WHEEL GUIDE

Text: _____

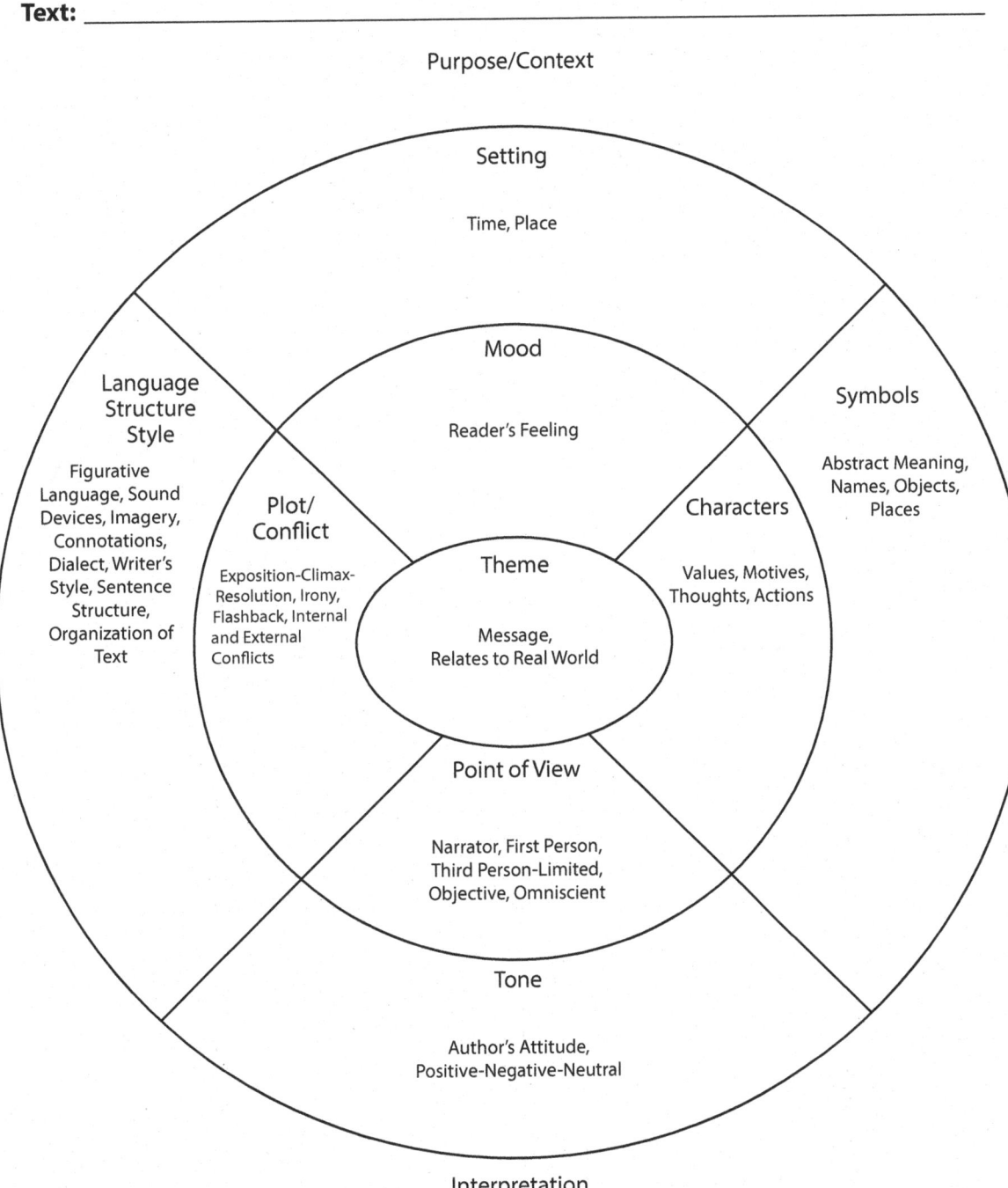

Created by Emily Mofield, Ed.D., & Tamra Stambaugh, Ph.D., 2015.

Perspectives of Power

BLANK VISUAL ANALYSIS WHEEL

Directions: Draw arrows across elements to show connections.

Art Piece: _____

Purpose/Context

Point of View

Images

Techniques

Emotions

Main Idea

Artist Background

Structure/Organization

Implications

Evaluation

Created by Tamra Stambaugh, Ph.D., & Emily Mofield, Ed.D., 2015.

Appendix B: Blank Models and Guides

VISUAL ANALYSIS WHEEL GUIDE

Art Piece: _____

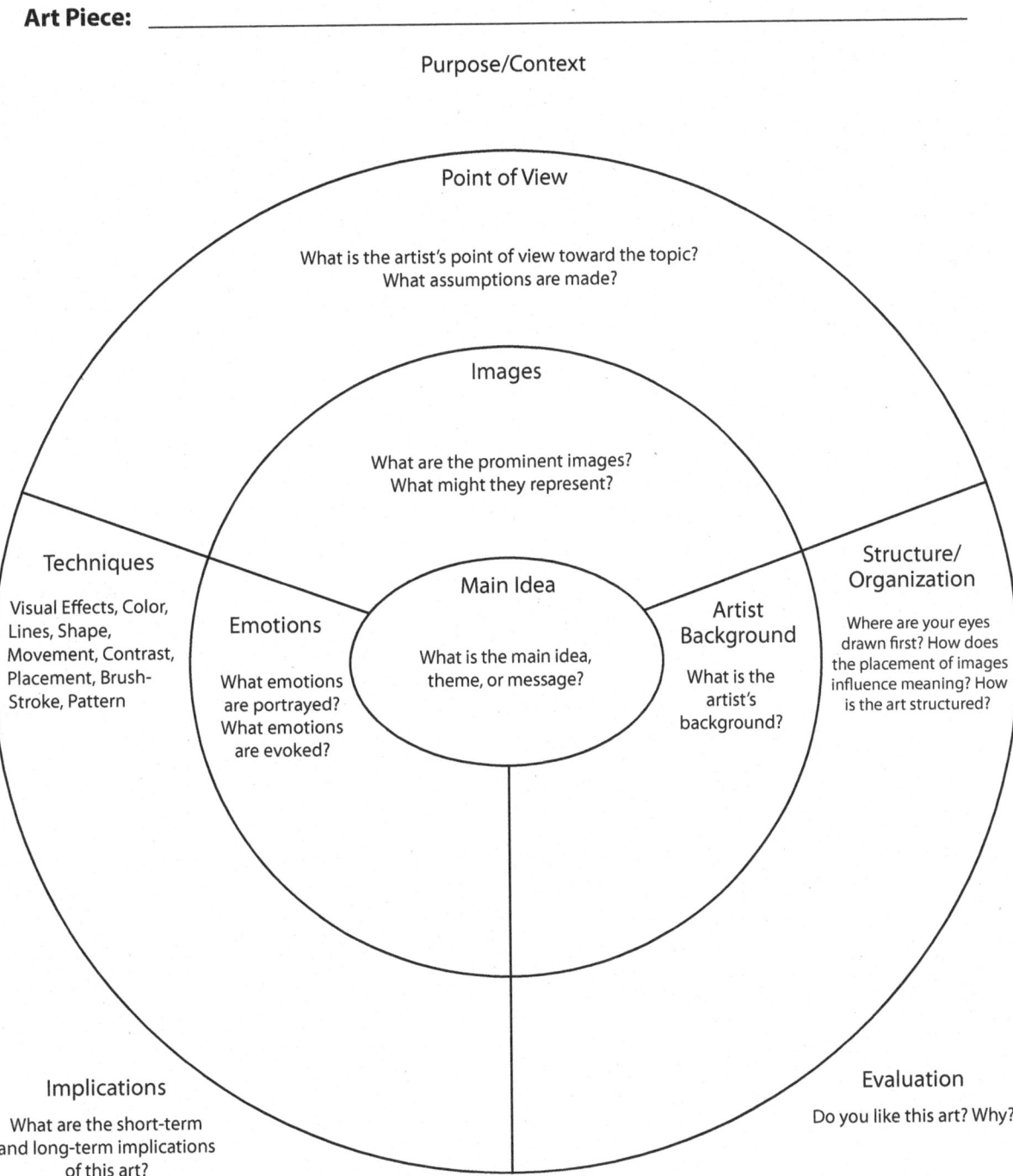

Created by Tamra Stambaugh, Ph.D., & Emily Mofield, Ed.D., 2015.

Perspectives of Power

BLANK RHETORICAL ANALYSIS WHEEL

Directions: Draw arrows across elements to show connections.

Text: _____

Purpose/Context

Point of View

Logos

Techniques

Pathos | Claim | Ethos

Structure/Organization

Implications

Evaluation

Created by Emily Mofield, Ed.D., & Tamra Stambaugh, Ph.D., 2015.

Appendix B: Blank Models and Guides

RHETORICAL ANALYSIS WHEEL GUIDE

Text: _____

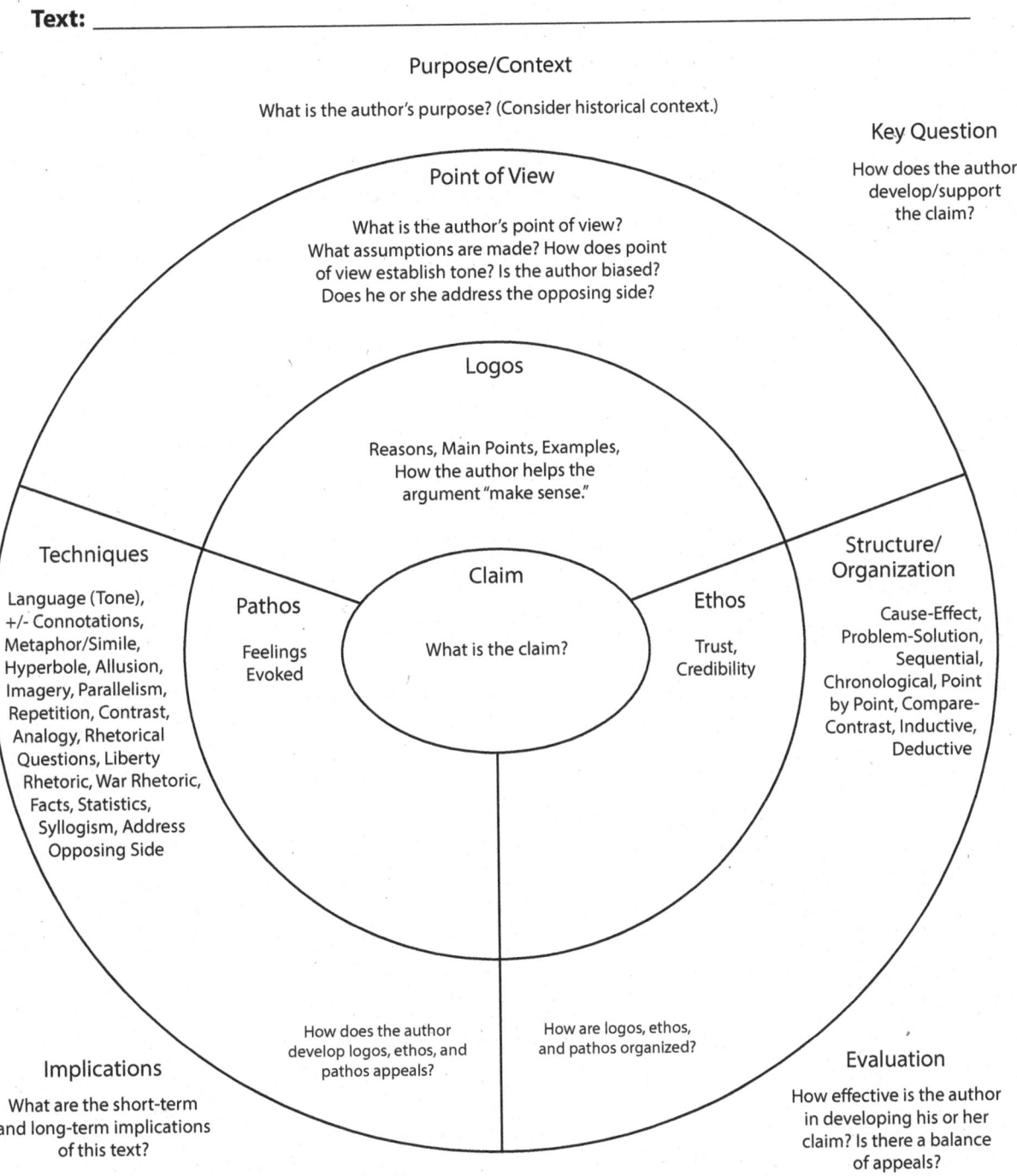

Created by Emily Mofield, Ed.D., & Tamra Stambaugh, Ph.D., 2015.

Perspectives of Power

BLANK TEXT ANALYSIS WHEEL

Directions: Draw arrows across elements to show connections.

Text: _____

- Purpose/Context
- Point of View
- Point #1
- Evidence
- Techniques
- Central Idea
- Point #2
- Point #3
- Structure/Organization
- Evidence
- Evidence
- Implications
- Evaluation

Created by Emily Mofield, Ed.D., & Tamra Stambaugh, Ph.D., 2015.

Appendix B: Blank Models and Guides

TEXT ANALYSIS WHEEL GUIDE

Text: _____

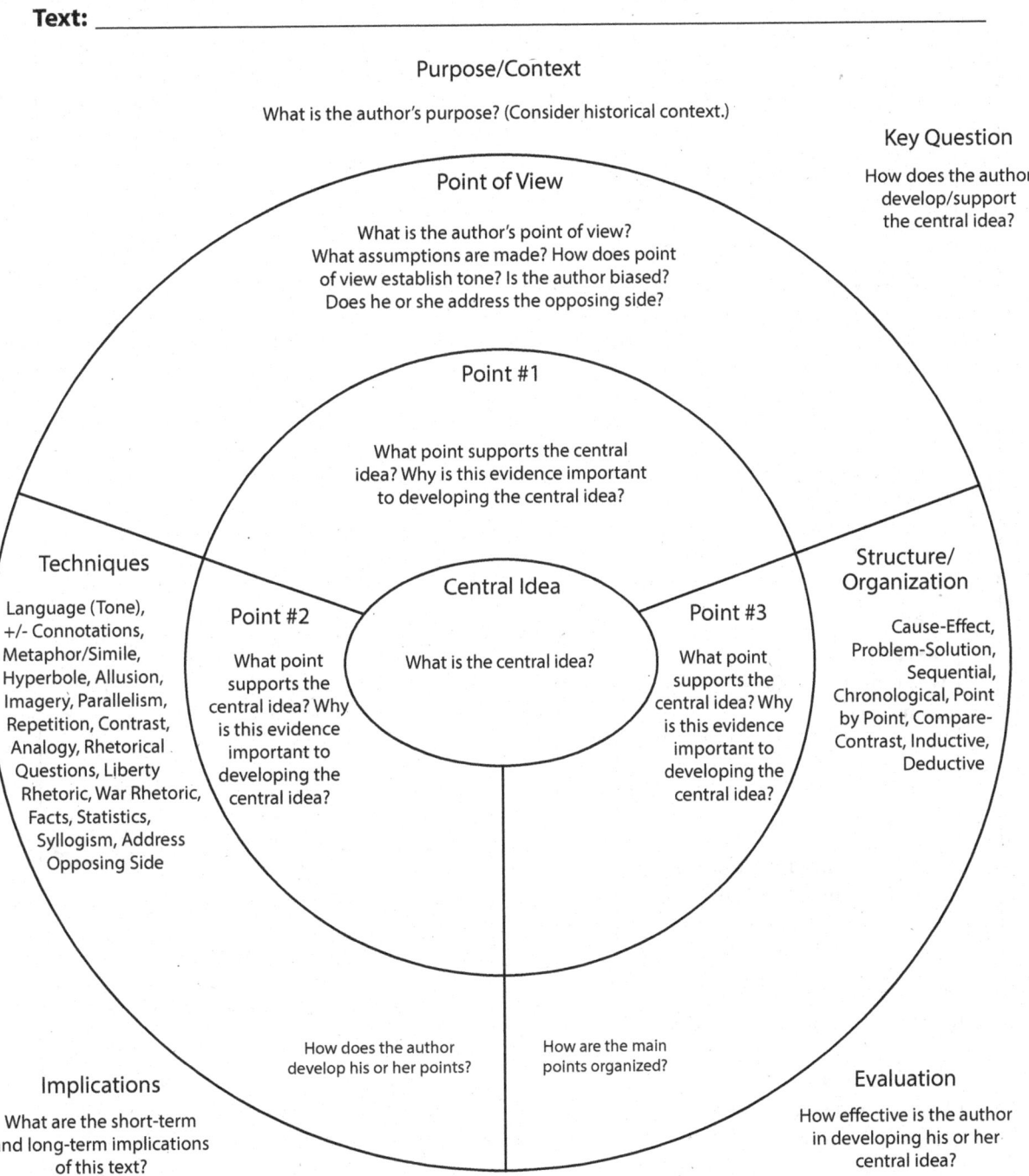

Created by Emily Mofield, Ed.D., & Tamra Stambaugh, Ph.D., 2015.

Perspectives of Power

BIG IDEA REFLECTION

What?	**Concepts:** What concepts/ideas are in the text?	
	Generalizations: What broad statement can you make about one or more of these concepts? Make it generalizable beyond the text.	
	Issue: What is the main issue, problem, or conflict?	
So What?	**Insight:** What insight on life is provided from this text?	
	World/Community/Individual: How does this text relate to you, your community, or your world? What question does the author want you to ask yourself?	
Now What?	**Implications:** How should you respond to the ideas in the text? What action should you take? What are the implications of the text? What can you do with this information?	

Created by Emily Mofield, Ed.D., & Tamra Stambaugh, Ph.D., 2015.

Appendix B: Blank Models and Guides

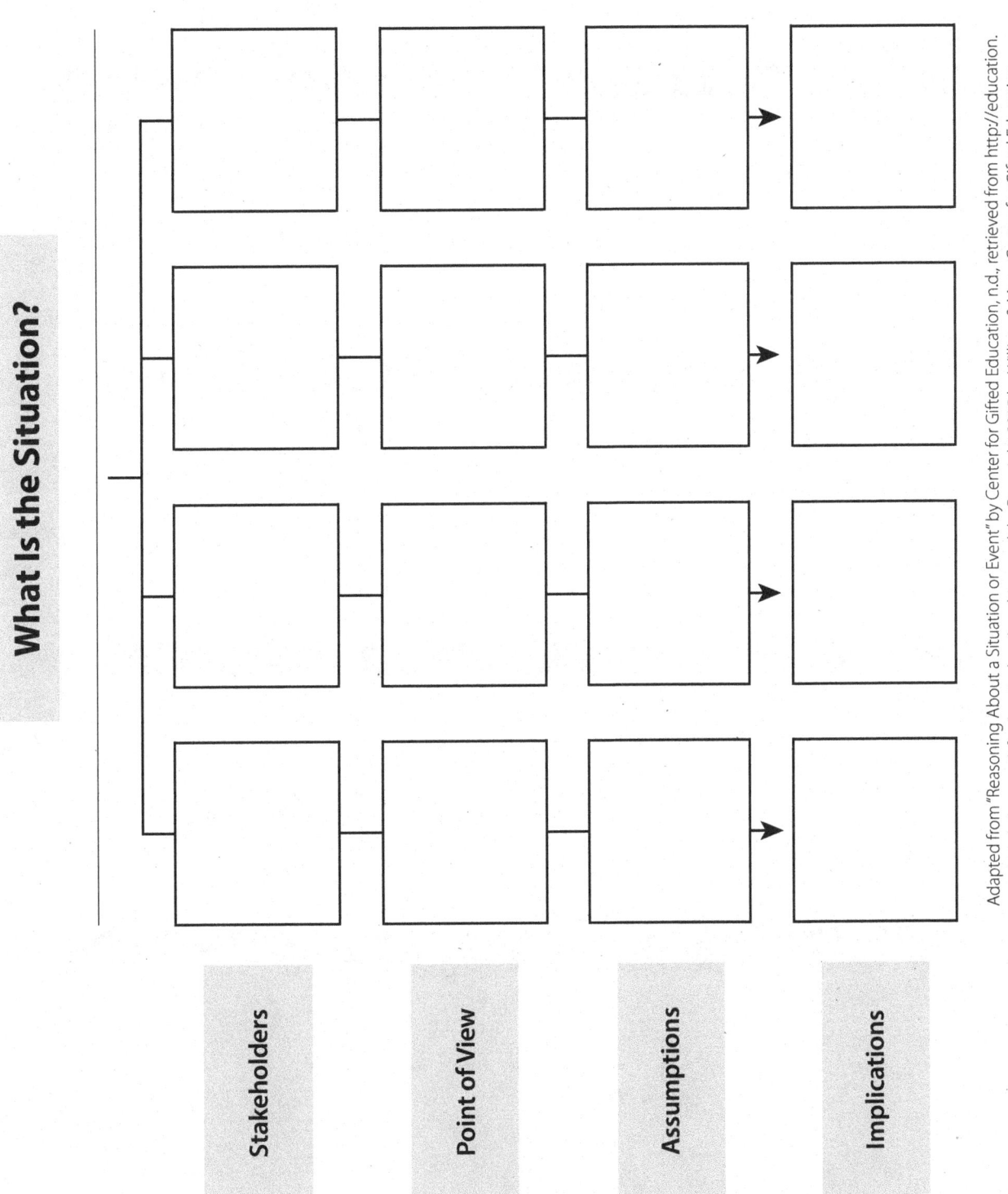

CONCEPT ORGANIZER

Literature, Art, or Media:	Literature, Art, or Media:	Literature, Art, or Media:
Power is the ability to influence.		
Power is connected to a source.		
Power may be used or abused.		
Examine the relationship between power and another concept.		

Appendix C
Rubrics

RUBRIC 1: PRODUCT RUBRIC

Name: _____ Date: _____ Lesson: _____

	Unacceptable/ Needs Improvement	Fair	Acceptable	Excellent
Completion	Not turned in or late.	Missing key pieces.	Completed but lacks thought and professionalism.	Satisfactorily meets all requirements and expectations of the task.
Concept/ Content	Limited or vague connection.	Little connection from lesson content is made to the theme of power.	Accurately relates lesson content and concept of power to assignment.	Insightfully relates lesson content and concept of power to assignment.
Thinking	Limited or vague evidence.	Reasoning is inaccurate/ Lacks originality, logical conclusions, or substantial claims.	Demonstrates some evidence of higher level thinking (creativity, evaluation, or analysis).	Demonstrates substantial evidence of higher level thinking (creativity, analysis, or evaluation with evidence).
Student-Developed Criteria				

Comments:

RUBRIC 2: CULMINATING PROJECT RUBRIC

Name: _____ Date: _____

	Unacceptable/ Needs Improvement	Fair	Acceptable	Exemplary
Completion	Not turned in or late.	Missing key pieces	Completed but lacks thought and professionalism.	Satisfactorily meets all requirements and expectations of the task.
Evidence	Limited or no evidence.	Little support or elaboration to support ideas and generalizations.	Gives support/elaboration to support ideas.	Gives meaningful support/elaboration to support ideas and generalizations.
Concept	Limited or vague connection.	Little connection from unit content is made to the theme of power.	Accurately relates ideas of power to assignment.	Insightfully relates the theme of power to assignment.
Content	Limited or no content application.	Vague connections are made to content.	Some connections are made to content with some evidence.	Synthesizes content across lessons with substantial support and evidence.
Process	Limited or vague evidence.	Reasoning is inaccurate/ Lacks originality, logical conclusions, or substantial claims.	Demonstrates some evidence of higher level thinking (creativity, evaluation, or analysis).	Provides insightful evidence to support higher level thinking (creativity, evaluation, or analysis) in developing complex conclusions.
Student-Developed Criteria				

Comments:

About the Authors

Emily Mofield, Ed.D., is a consulting teacher for gifted education for Sumner County Schools in Tennessee and is involved in supporting several projects with Vanderbilt Programs for Talented Youth. She has also taught as a gifted education language arts middle school teacher for 10 years. Her work is devoted to developing challenging differentiated curriculum for gifted learners and addressing their social/emotional needs. Emily regularly presents professional development on effective differentiation for advanced learners. She is a national board certified teacher in Language Arts and has been recognized as the Tennessee Association for Gifted Children Teacher of the Year.

Tamra Stambaugh, Ph.D., is an assistant research professor in special education and executive director of Programs for Talented Youth at Vanderbilt University Peabody College. She received her Ph.D. in Educational Policy, Planning, and Leadership with an emphasis in gifted education from the College of William and Mary. She is the coauthor/editor of several books including *Serving Gifted Students in Rural Settings* (coedited with Susannah Wood), *Comprehensive Curriculum for Gifted Learners* (with Joyce VanTassel-Baska), *Overlooked Gems: A National Perspective on Low-Income Promising Students* (with Joyce VanTassel-Baska), *Leading Change in Gifted Education* (with Bronwyn MacFarlane), the *Jacob's Ladder Reading Comprehension Program Series* (with Joyce VanTassel-Baska and Kim Chandler), and *Practical Solutions for Underrepresented Gifted Students: Effective Curriculum* (with Kim Chandler), as well as numerous book chapters and research articles. Stambaugh's research interests focus on talent development support structures for gifted students and key curriculum and instructional interventions that support gifted learners—especially those students from rural backgrounds and those from poverty.

Common Core State Standards Alignment

Lesson	Common Core State Standards in ELA/Literacy
Lesson 1	RL.9-10.1 Cite strong and thorough textual evidence to support analysis of what the text says explicitly as well as inferences drawn from the text.
	RL.9-10.2 Determine a theme or central idea of a text and analyze in detail its development over the course of the text, including how it emerges and is shaped and refined by specific details; provide an objective summary of the text.
	RL.9-10.3 Analyze how complex characters (e.g., those with multiple or conflicting motivations) develop over the course of a text, interact with other characters, and advance the plot or develop the theme.
	RL.9-10.4 Determine the meaning of words and phrases as they are used in the text, including figurative and connotative meanings; analyze the cumulative impact of specific word choices on meaning and tone (e.g., how the language evokes a sense of time and place; how it sets a formal or informal tone).
	RL.9-10.5 Analyze how an author's choices concerning how to structure a text, order events within it (e.g., parallel plots), and manipulate time (e.g., pacing, flashbacks) create such effects as mystery, tension, or surprise.
	W.9-10.4 Produce clear and coherent writing in which the development, organization, and style are appropriate to task, purpose, and audience.
	SL.9-10.1c Propel conversations by posing and responding to questions that relate the current discussion to broader themes or larger ideas; actively incorporate others into the discussion; and clarify, verify, or challenge ideas and conclusions.

Perspectives of Power

Lesson	Common Core State Standards in ELA/Literacy
Lesson 1, *continued*	SL.9-10.1d Respond thoughtfully to diverse perspectives, summarize points of agreement and disagreement, and, when warranted, qualify or justify their own views and understanding and make new connections in light of the evidence and reasoning presented.
	SL.9-10.4 Present information, findings, and supporting evidence clearly, concisely, and logically such that listeners can follow the line of reasoning and the organization, development, substance, and style are appropriate to purpose, audience, and task.
Lesson 2	RI.9-10.7 Analyze various accounts of a subject told in different mediums (e.g., a person's life story in both print and multimedia), determining which details are emphasized in each account.
	SL.8.2 Analyze the purpose of information presented in diverse media and formats (e.g., visually, quantitatively, orally) and evaluate the motives (e.g., social, commercial, political) behind its presentation.
	SL.9-10.1 Initiate and participate effectively in a range of collaborative discussions (one-on-one, in groups, and teacher-led) with diverse partners on grades 9–10 topics, texts, and issues, building on others' ideas and expressing their own clearly and persuasively.
	W.9-10.4 Produce clear and coherent writing in which the development, organization, and style are appropriate to task, purpose, and audience.
	W.9-10.5 Develop and strengthen writing as needed by planning, revising, editing, rewriting, or trying a new approach, focusing on addressing what is most significant for a specific purpose and audience.
	SL.9-10.1c Propel conversations by posing and responding to questions that relate the current discussion to broader themes or larger ideas; actively incorporate others into the discussion; and clarify, verify, or challenge ideas and conclusions.
	SL.9-10.1d Respond thoughtfully to diverse perspectives, summarize points of agreement and disagreement, and, when warranted, qualify or justify their own views and understanding and make new connections in light of the evidence and reasoning presented.
	SL.9-10.4 Present information, findings, and supporting evidence clearly, concisely, and logically such that listeners can follow the line of reasoning and the organization, development, substance, and style are appropriate to purpose, audience, and task.
Lesson 3	RL.9-10.1 Cite strong and thorough textual evidence to support analysis of what the text says explicitly as well as inferences drawn from the text.

Common Core State Standards Alignment

Lesson	Common Core State Standards in ELA/Literacy
Lesson 3, *continued*	RL.9-10.2 Determine a theme or central idea of a text and analyze in detail its development over the course of the text, including how it emerges and is shaped and refined by specific details; provide an objective summary of the text.
	RL.9-10.3 Analyze how complex characters (e.g., those with multiple or conflicting motivations) develop over the course of a text, interact with other characters, and advance the plot or develop the theme.
	RL.9-10.4 Determine the meaning of words and phrases as they are used in the text, including figurative and connotative meanings; analyze the cumulative impact of specific word choices on meaning and tone (e.g., how the language evokes a sense of time and place; how it sets a formal or informal tone).
	RL.9-10.6 Analyze a particular point of view or cultural experience reflected in a work of literature from outside the United States, drawing on a wide reading of world literature.
	RL.9-10.9 Analyze how an author draws on and transforms source material in a specific work (e.g., how Shakespeare treats a theme or topic from Ovid or the Bible or how a later author draws on a play by Shakespeare).
	W.9-10.4 Produce clear and coherent writing in which the development, organization, and style are appropriate to task, purpose, and audience.
	SL.9-10.1 Initiate and participate effectively in a range of collaborative discussions (one-on-one, in groups, and teacher-led) with diverse partners on grades 9–10 topics, texts, and issues, building on others' ideas and expressing their own clearly and persuasively.
	SL.9-10.1c Propel conversations by posing and responding to questions that relate the current discussion to broader themes or larger ideas; actively incorporate others into the discussion; and clarify, verify, or challenge ideas and conclusions.
	SL.9-10.1d Respond thoughtfully to diverse perspectives, summarize points of agreement and disagreement, and, when warranted, qualify or justify their own views and understanding and make new connections in light of the evidence and reasoning presented.
	SL.9-10.4 Present information, findings, and supporting evidence clearly, concisely, and logically such that listeners can follow the line of reasoning and the organization, development, substance, and style are appropriate to purpose, audience, and task.
Lesson 4	RI.9-10.1 Cite strong and thorough textual evidence to support analysis of what the text says explicitly as well as inferences drawn from the text.

Lesson	Common Core State Standards in ELA/Literacy
Lesson 4, *continued*	RI.9-10.2 Determine a central idea of a text and analyze its development over the course of the text, including how it emerges and is shaped and refined by specific details; provide an objective summary of the text.
	RI.9-10.3 Analyze how the author unfolds an analysis or series of ideas or events, including the order in which the points are made, how they are introduced and developed, and the connections that are drawn between them.
	RI.9-10.4 Determine the meaning of words and phrases as they are used in a text, including figurative, connotative, and technical meanings; analyze the cumulative impact of specific word choices on meaning and tone (e.g., how the language of a court opinion differs from that of a newspaper).
	RI.9-10.5 Analyze in detail how an author's ideas or claims are developed and refined by particular sentences, paragraphs, or larger portions of a text (e.g., a section or chapter).
	RI.9-10.6 Determine an author's point of view or purpose in a text and analyze how an author uses rhetoric to advance that point of view or purpose.
	RI.9-10.9 Analyze seminal U.S. documents of historical and literary significance (e.g., Washington's Farewell Address, the Gettysburg Address, Roosevelt's Four Freedoms speech, King's "Letter from Birmingham Jail"), including how they address related themes and concepts.
	W.9-10.4 Produce clear and coherent writing in which the development, organization, and style are appropriate to task, purpose, and audience.
	W.9-10.5 Develop and strengthen writing as needed by planning, revising, editing, rewriting, or trying a new approach, focusing on addressing what is most significant for a specific purpose and audience.
	SL.9-10.1 Initiate and participate effectively in a range of collaborative discussions (one-on-one, in groups, and teacher-led) with diverse partners on grades 9–10 topics, texts, and issues, building on others' ideas and expressing their own clearly and persuasively.
	SL.9-10.1c Propel conversations by posing and responding to questions that relate the current discussion to broader themes or larger ideas; actively incorporate others into the discussion; and clarify, verify, or challenge ideas and conclusions.
	SL.9-10.1d Respond thoughtfully to diverse perspectives, summarize points of agreement and disagreement, and, when warranted, qualify or justify their own views and understanding and make new connections in light of the evidence and reasoning presented.

Common Core State Standards Alignment

Lesson	Common Core State Standards in ELA/Literacy
Lesson 4, *continued*	SL.9-10.4 Present information, findings, and supporting evidence clearly, concisely, and logically such that listeners can follow the line of reasoning and the organization, development, substance, and style are appropriate to purpose, audience, and task.
	RH.9-10.1 Cite specific textual evidence to support analysis of primary and secondary sources, attending to such features as the date and origin of the information.
	RH.9-10.2 Determine the central ideas or information of a primary or secondary source; provide an accurate summary of how key events or ideas develop over the course of the text.
	RH.9-10.4 Determine the meaning of words and phrases as they are used in a text, including vocabulary describing political, social, or economic aspects of history/social science.
	RH.9-10.5 Analyze how a text uses structure to emphasize key points or advance an explanation or analysis.
	RH.9-10.9 Compare and contrast treatments of the same topic in several primary and secondary sources.
	RH.9-10.8 Assess the extent to which the reasoning and evidence in a text support the author's claims.
	RH.9-10.6 Compare the point of view of two or more authors for how they treat the same or similar topics, including which details they include and emphasize in their respective accounts.
Lesson 5	RL.9-10.1 Cite strong and thorough textual evidence to support analysis of what the text says explicitly as well as inferences drawn from the text.
	RL.9-10.2 Determine a theme or central idea of a text and analyze in detail its development over the course of the text, including how it emerges and is shaped and refined by specific details; provide an objective summary of the text.
	RL.9-10.3 Analyze how complex characters (e.g., those with multiple or conflicting motivations) develop over the course of a text, interact with other characters, and advance the plot or develop the theme.
	RL.9-10.4 Determine the meaning of words and phrases as they are used in the text, including figurative and connotative meanings; analyze the cumulative impact of specific word choices on meaning and tone (e.g., how the language evokes a sense of time and place; how it sets a formal or informal tone).
	W.9-10.4 Produce clear and coherent writing in which the development, organization, and style are appropriate to task, purpose, and audience.

Lesson	Common Core State Standards in ELA/Literacy
Lesson 5, *continued*	W.9-10.5 Develop and strengthen writing as needed by planning, revising, editing, rewriting, or trying a new approach, focusing on addressing what is most significant for a specific purpose and audience.
	SL.9-10.1 Initiate and participate effectively in a range of collaborative discussions (one-on-one, in groups, and teacher-led) with diverse partners on grades 9–10 topics, texts, and issues, building on others' ideas and expressing their own clearly and persuasively.
	SL.9-10.1c Propel conversations by posing and responding to questions that relate the current discussion to broader themes or larger ideas; actively incorporate others into the discussion; and clarify, verify, or challenge ideas and conclusions.
	SL.9-10.1d Respond thoughtfully to diverse perspectives, summarize points of agreement and disagreement, and, when warranted, qualify or justify their own views and understanding and make new connections in light of the evidence and reasoning presented.
	SL.9-10.4 Present information, findings, and supporting evidence clearly, concisely, and logically such that listeners can follow the line of reasoning and the organization, development, substance, and style are appropriate to purpose, audience, and task.
Lesson 6	RL.9-10.1 Cite strong and thorough textual evidence to support analysis of what the text says explicitly as well as inferences drawn from the text.
	RL.9-10.2 Determine a theme or central idea of a text and analyze in detail its development over the course of the text, including how it emerges and is shaped and refined by specific details; provide an objective summary of the text.
	RL.9-10.3 Analyze how complex characters (e.g., those with multiple or conflicting motivations) develop over the course of a text, interact with other characters, and advance the plot or develop the theme.
	RL.9-10.4 Determine the meaning of words and phrases as they are used in the text, including figurative and connotative meanings; analyze the cumulative impact of specific word choices on meaning and tone (e.g., how the language evokes a sense of time and place; how it sets a formal or informal tone).
	RL.9-10.6 Analyze a particular point of view or cultural experience reflected in a work of literature from outside the United States, drawing on a wide reading of world literature.
	RL.9-10.9 Analyze how an author draws on and transforms source material in a specific work (e.g., how Shakespeare treats a theme or topic from Ovid or the Bible or how a later author draws on a play by Shakespeare).

Common Core State Standards Alignment

Lesson	Common Core State Standards in ELA/Literacy
Lesson 6, *continued*	W.9-10.4 Produce clear and coherent writing in which the development, organization, and style are appropriate to task, purpose, and audience.
	W.9-10.5 Develop and strengthen writing as needed by planning, revising, editing, rewriting, or trying a new approach, focusing on addressing what is most significant for a specific purpose and audience.
	SL.9-10.1 Initiate and participate effectively in a range of collaborative discussions (one-on-one, in groups, and teacher-led) with diverse partners on grades 9–10 topics, texts, and issues, building on others' ideas and expressing their own clearly and persuasively.
	SL.9-10.1c Propel conversations by posing and responding to questions that relate the current discussion to broader themes or larger ideas; actively incorporate others into the discussion; and clarify, verify, or challenge ideas and conclusions.
	SL.9-10.1d Respond thoughtfully to diverse perspectives, summarize points of agreement and disagreement, and, when warranted, qualify or justify their own views and understanding and make new connections in light of the evidence and reasoning presented.
	SL.9-10.4 Present information, findings, and supporting evidence clearly, concisely, and logically such that listeners can follow the line of reasoning and the organization, development, substance, and style are appropriate to purpose, audience, and task.
Lesson 7	RI.9-10.7 Analyze various accounts of a subject told in different mediums (e.g., a person's life story in both print and multimedia), determining which details are emphasized in each account.
	W.9-10.4 Produce clear and coherent writing in which the development, organization, and style are appropriate to task, purpose, and audience.
	W.9-10.5 Develop and strengthen writing as needed by planning, revising, editing, rewriting, or trying a new approach, focusing on addressing what is most significant for a specific purpose and audience.
	SL.8.2 Analyze the purpose of information presented in diverse media and formats (e.g., visually, quantitatively, orally) and evaluate the motives (e.g., social, commercial, political) behind its presentation.
	SL.9-10.1 Initiate and participate effectively in a range of collaborative discussions (one-on-one, in groups, and teacher-led) with diverse partners on grades 9–10 topics, texts, and issues, building on others' ideas and expressing their own clearly and persuasively.

Lesson	Common Core State Standards in ELA/Literacy
Lesson 7, *continued*	SL.9-10.1c Propel conversations by posing and responding to questions that relate the current discussion to broader themes or larger ideas; actively incorporate others into the discussion; and clarify, verify, or challenge ideas and conclusions.
	SL.9-10.1d Respond thoughtfully to diverse perspectives, summarize points of agreement and disagreement, and, when warranted, qualify or justify their own views and understanding and make new connections in light of the evidence and reasoning presented.
	SL.9-10.4 Present information, findings, and supporting evidence clearly, concisely, and logically such that listeners can follow the line of reasoning and the organization, development, substance, and style are appropriate to purpose, audience, and task.
Lesson 8	RL.9-10.1 Cite strong and thorough textual evidence to support analysis of what the text says explicitly as well as inferences drawn from the text.
	RL.9-10.2 Determine a theme or central idea of a text and analyze in detail its development over the course of the text, including how it emerges and is shaped and refined by specific details; provide an objective summary of the text.
	RL.9-10.4 Determine the meaning of words and phrases as they are used in the text, including figurative and connotative meanings; analyze the cumulative impact of specific word choices on meaning and tone (e.g., how the language evokes a sense of time and place; how it sets a formal or informal tone).
	RL.9-10.5 Analyze how an author's choices concerning how to structure a text, order events within it (e.g., parallel plots), and manipulate time (e.g., pacing, flashbacks) create such effects as mystery, tension, or surprise.
	RL.9-10.6 Analyze a particular point of view or cultural experience reflected in a work of literature from outside the United States, drawing on a wide reading of world literature.
	W.9-10.4 Produce clear and coherent writing in which the development, organization, and style are appropriate to task, purpose, and audience.
	SL.9-10.1 Initiate and participate effectively in a range of collaborative discussions (one-on-one, in groups, and teacher-led) with diverse partners on grades 9–10 topics, texts, and issues, building on others' ideas and expressing their own clearly and persuasively.
	SL.9-10.1c Propel conversations by posing and responding to questions that relate the current discussion to broader themes or larger ideas; actively incorporate others into the discussion; and clarify, verify, or challenge ideas and conclusions.

Common Core State Standards Alignment

Lesson	Common Core State Standards in ELA/Literacy
Lesson 8, *continued*	SL.9-10.1d Respond thoughtfully to diverse perspectives, summarize points of agreement and disagreement, and, when warranted, qualify or justify their own views and understanding and make new connections in light of the evidence and reasoning presented.
	SL.9-10.4 Present information, findings, and supporting evidence clearly, concisely, and logically such that listeners can follow the line of reasoning and the organization, development, substance, and style are appropriate to purpose, audience, and task.
Lesson 9	RI.9-10.1 Cite strong and thorough textual evidence to support analysis of what the text says explicitly as well as inferences drawn from the text.
	RI.9-10.2 Determine a central idea of a text and analyze its development over the course of the text, including how it emerges and is shaped and refined by specific details; provide an objective summary of the text.
	RI.9-10.3 Analyze how the author unfolds an analysis or series of ideas or events, including the order in which the points are made, how they are introduced and developed, and the connections that are drawn between them.
	RI.9-10.4 Determine the meaning of words and phrases as they are used in a text, including figurative, connotative, and technical meanings; analyze the cumulative impact of specific word choices on meaning and tone (e.g., how the language of a court opinion differs from that of a newspaper).
	RI.9-10.5 Analyze in detail how an author's ideas or claims are developed and refined by particular sentences, paragraphs, or larger portions of a text (e.g., a section or chapter).
	RI.9-10.6 Determine an author's point of view or purpose in a text and analyze how an author uses rhetoric to advance that point of view or purpose.
	RI.9-10.9 Analyze seminal U.S. documents of historical and literary significance (e.g., Washington's Farewell Address, the Gettysburg Address, Roosevelt's Four Freedoms speech, King's "Letter from Birmingham Jail"), including how they address related themes and concepts.
	W.9-10.4 Produce clear and coherent writing in which the development, organization, and style are appropriate to task, purpose, and audience.
	W.9-10.5 Develop and strengthen writing as needed by planning, revising, editing, rewriting, or trying a new approach, focusing on addressing what is most significant for a specific purpose and audience.

Lesson	Common Core State Standards in ELA/Literacy
Lesson 9, *continued*	SL.9-10.1 Initiate and participate effectively in a range of collaborative discussions (one-on-one, in groups, and teacher-led) with diverse partners on grades 9–10 topics, texts, and issues, building on others' ideas and expressing their own clearly and persuasively.
	SL.9-10.1c Propel conversations by posing and responding to questions that relate the current discussion to broader themes or larger ideas; actively incorporate others into the discussion; and clarify, verify, or challenge ideas and conclusions.
	SL.9-10.1d Respond thoughtfully to diverse perspectives, summarize points of agreement and disagreement, and, when warranted, qualify or justify their own views and understanding and make new connections in light of the evidence and reasoning presented.
	SL.9-10.4 Present information, findings, and supporting evidence clearly, concisely, and logically such that listeners can follow the line of reasoning and the organization, development, substance, and style are appropriate to purpose, audience, and task.
	RH.9-10.1 Cite specific textual evidence to support analysis of primary and secondary sources, attending to such features as the date and origin of the information.
	RH.9-10.2 Determine the central ideas or information of a primary or secondary source; provide an accurate summary of how key events or ideas develop over the course of the text.
	RH.9-10.4 Determine the meaning of words and phrases as they are used in a text, including vocabulary describing political, social, or economic aspects of history/social science.
	RH.9-10.5 Analyze how a text uses structure to emphasize key points or advance an explanation or analysis. RH.9-10.8 Assess the extent to which the reasoning and evidence in a text support the author's claims.
Lesson 10	RI.9-10.1 Cite strong and thorough textual evidence to support analysis of what the text says explicitly as well as inferences drawn from the text.
	RI.9-10.2 Determine a central idea of a text and analyze its development over the course of the text, including how it emerges and is shaped and refined by specific details; provide an objective summary of the text.
	RI.9-10.3 Analyze how the author unfolds an analysis or series of ideas or events, including the order in which the points are made, how they are introduced and developed, and the connections that are drawn between them.

Common Core State Standards Alignment

Lesson	Common Core State Standards in ELA/Literacy
Lesson 10, continued	RI.9-10.4 Determine the meaning of words and phrases as they are used in a text, including figurative, connotative, and technical meanings; analyze the cumulative impact of specific word choices on meaning and tone (e.g., how the language of a court opinion differs from that of a newspaper).
	RI.9-10.5 Analyze in detail how an author's ideas or claims are developed and refined by particular sentences, paragraphs, or larger portions of a text (e.g., a section or chapter).
	RI.9-10.6 Determine an author's point of view or purpose in a text and analyze how an author uses rhetoric to advance that point of view or purpose.
	RI.9-10.9 Analyze seminal U.S. documents of historical and literary significance (e.g., Washington's Farewell Address, the Gettysburg Address, Roosevelt's Four Freedoms speech, King's "Letter from Birmingham Jail"), including how they address related themes and concepts.
	W.9-10.4 Produce clear and coherent writing in which the development, organization, and style are appropriate to task, purpose, and audience.
	W.9-10.5 Develop and strengthen writing as needed by planning, revising, editing, rewriting, or trying a new approach, focusing on addressing what is most significant for a specific purpose and audience.
	SL.9-10.1 Initiate and participate effectively in a range of collaborative discussions (one-on-one, in groups, and teacher-led) with diverse partners on grades 9–10 topics, texts, and issues, building on others' ideas and expressing their own clearly and persuasively.
	SL.9-10.1c Propel conversations by posing and responding to questions that relate the current discussion to broader themes or larger ideas; actively incorporate others into the discussion; and clarify, verify, or challenge ideas and conclusions.
	SL.9-10.1d Respond thoughtfully to diverse perspectives, summarize points of agreement and disagreement, and, when warranted, qualify or justify their own views and understanding and make new connections in light of the evidence and reasoning presented.
	SL.9-10.4 Present information, findings, and supporting evidence clearly, concisely, and logically such that listeners can follow the line of reasoning and the organization, development, substance, and style are appropriate to purpose, audience, and task.
	RH.9-10.1 Cite specific textual evidence to support analysis of primary and secondary sources, attending to such features as the date and origin of the information.

Lesson	Common Core State Standards in ELA/Literacy
Lesson 10, *continued*	RH.9-10.2 Determine the central ideas or information of a primary or secondary source; provide an accurate summary of how key events or ideas develop over the course of the text.
	RH.9-10.4 Determine the meaning of words and phrases as they are used in a text, including vocabulary describing political, social, or economic aspects of history/social science.
	RH.9-10.5 Analyze how a text uses structure to emphasize key points or advance an explanation or analysis.
	RH.9-10.8 Assess the extent to which the reasoning and evidence in a text support the author's claims.
Lesson 11	RL.9-10.1 Cite strong and thorough textual evidence to support analysis of what the text says explicitly as well as inferences drawn from the text.
	RL.9-10.2 Determine a theme or central idea of a text and analyze in detail its development over the course of the text, including how it emerges and is shaped and refined by specific details; provide an objective summary of the text.
	W.9-10.4 Produce clear and coherent writing in which the development, organization, and style are appropriate to task, purpose, and audience.
	RL.9-10.5 Analyze how an author's choices concerning how to structure a text, order events within it (e.g., parallel plots), and manipulate time (e.g., pacing, flashbacks) create such effects as mystery, tension, or surprise.
	RL.9-10.4 Determine the meaning of words and phrases as they are used in the text, including figurative and connotative meanings; analyze the cumulative impact of specific word choices on meaning and tone (e.g., how the language evokes a sense of time and place; how it sets a formal or informal tone).
	SL.9-10.1 Initiate and participate effectively in a range of collaborative discussions (one-on-one, in groups, and teacher-led) with diverse partners on grades 9–10 topics, texts, and issues, building on others' ideas and expressing their own clearly and persuasively.
	SL.9-10.1c Propel conversations by posing and responding to questions that relate the current discussion to broader themes or larger ideas; actively incorporate others into the discussion; and clarify, verify, or challenge ideas and conclusions.
	SL.9-10.1d Respond thoughtfully to diverse perspectives, summarize points of agreement and disagreement, and, when warranted, qualify or justify their own views and understanding and make new connections in light of the evidence and reasoning presented.

Common Core State Standards Alignment

Lesson	Common Core State Standards in ELA/Literacy
Lesson 11, *continued*	SL.9-10.4 Present information, findings, and supporting evidence clearly, concisely, and logically such that listeners can follow the line of reasoning and the organization, development, substance, and style are appropriate to purpose, audience, and task.
Lesson 12	Varies based on product choice